For more on this book, visit:
www.HeavyweightMarketingBook.com

★ ★ ★

For more about the author, visit:
www.NikolasAllen.com

SPARRING PARTNERS

"I have been working with Nikolas Allen for many years and have never been disappointed! He continues to exceed my expectations in both his level of professionalism and commitment to his work. He is exuberant, high-energy and straight-forward. His marketing strategies are cutting edge and easy-to-follow, making them a valuable and user-friendly tool anyone can use to start or grow their business."
—**Lauri Sturdivant**, *Former Executive Director, Siskiyou Arts Museum and Gallery*

"Nikolas Allen has a knack for presenting marketing how-to in a crisp and easy-to-understand fashion, and is the brains behind some of the best marketing programs currently earning money for local business owners in Northern California's Siskiyou County."
—**Arthur Cronos**, *Voltos Business Systems*

"Nikolas Allen could make reading the phone book interesting and entertaining. His presentation style is outstanding because he combines wit, intelligence, creativity and real-world ideas and applications for the serious entrepreneur."
—**Stephanie Hoffman**, *Founder, Workshop Training Institute*

"Nikolas Allen is so good at getting businesses to think about and focus on what sets them apart from the competition, what makes THEM unique, what THEIR niche is. This really is his gift. We always struggled with these questions at New England Multimedia, especially because we offer so many different services. His advice really hit home and changed the way we present ourselves on our website, and that changed everything. The emails and contacts started coming in on a regular basis. I'm so glad to have Nikolas in my network."
—**Michelle Quillin**, *New England Multimedia*

"Nikolas impressed me with his ability to break away from conventional molds and really make my business stand out. I saw Nikolas give a 'Branding for Small Business' presentation and immediately I had new ideas to improve my advertising."
—**Atara Melo**, *Owner of A Melo Place*

"Nikolas is awesome! I heard him speak at a JEDI business meeting last year and at a Women in Business in meeting in Mt. Shasta this year. He is fun, upbeat, and right on! He is passionate about helping you and your business be successful. I booked him to help me work on my website, and he makes complicated software seem easy. Whatever level you are at with your business, Nikolas is there to help!"
—**Alison Willis**, *Scott Valley Bikes*

"Thank you, Nikolas, for all of your help and direction on getting our website up and running. We are excited to work on it more and use it to promote our store and our local artisans. I want you to know how much I have appreciated your professionalism in meeting deadlines, calling as promised and generally doing what you said you would do."
—**Debra and Carlee Punt**, *Alpine Originals*

"Thank you Nikolas for making such a GREAT presentation at Women In Business Network! Your energy totally filled the room! The concepts were presented in such a fresh, entertaining way that you inspired many of us to take a deeper look at how we represent ourselves. I loved it!"
—**Marguerite Lorimer**, *EarthAlive Communications*

"Working with Nikolas Allen for the past two years has been productive and fun. Most importantly, I believe through following his lead in our marketing, we stepped our game up."
—**Kim Presley**, *Executive Director, Liberty Arts Gallery*

HEAVYWEIGHT MARKETING

KNOCKOUT STRATEGIES FOR BUILDING CHAMPION BRANDS

★ ★ ★ ★

NIKOLAS ALLEN

Copyright © 2015 Nikolas Allen
All rights reserved.

ISBN-10: 1502931826
ISBN-13: 978-1502931825

Author Photo by **Brenda Woods**.

Cover Design, Interior Layout and Section Graphics
by **Nikolas Allen**.

BIG THANKS TO THESE CHAMPIONS:

Brenda Woods, my partner, bestie and creative copilot on this most excellent journey.

Jessie Zapffe, for bringing me into this world and imparting much love, support and wisdom through the ages.

The Fam: Cam, Chris, Zander, Coleman, Otto, Ric, Cindy and an extended posse too numerous to mention but loved and appreciated all the same.

Arthur Cronos, for sharing his passion and experience in business, tech and all things marketing.

Nate Dorward, for his mad editing skills and downright gentlemanly nature. So glad he's in my corner.

Each and every one of my former clients who helped make my business, and this book, possible. Many are mentioned within—some as examples of what not to do—but I speak of them all with the utmost respect and I admire each of them.

Heavyweight Marketing is dedicated to the brave entrepreneurs and business owners who pursue their passions and chase their dreams in an effort to share their vision, ideas and talents with the world. Wishing you all the success you deserve!

TABLE OF CONTENTS

Sparring Partners iii
Acknowledgements xi
Intro: Shadowboxing 1

Round 1: Build Marketing Muscle 5
1. The Law of Effective Frequency 9
2. Three Primal Rules of Marketing 13
3. Six Imperative Attributes of Successful Entrepreneurs 19
4. What Do You REALLY Do for a Living? 23
5. Why Meaningful Messages Trump Empty Hype 27
6. Stop Sending Mixed Messages 31
7. Speak the Language of Results 35
8. Online Marketing vs. Traditional: Which Is "Better?" 39
9. The Motivational Value of Stiff Competition 41
10. Gain Marketing Mileage From Business Milestones 45
11. Thirteen Ways to Go Big on Small Business Saturday
    and Beyond 51
12. Hook Seasonal Customers Year-Round With
    Marketing Trident 59
13. The Triple Benefit of Strategic Partnerships 67
14. In Business, Communicating Is Caring 73
15. Why Fear-Based Marketing Strategies Don't Work 77
16. Marketing Your Business Is Like Joining a Gym 81
17. Case Study: Building Maximum Buzz 85

Round 2: Tackle Your Tools 93
18. Seventy-Six Tactics and Tools to Promote Your Business 97
19. Dissecting the Formula for Effective Print Ads 103
20. Email Marketing: Still Not Dead 111
21. Eight Insider Tips for Cracking the QR Code 119
22. Five Things You Need to Know About Text
    (SMS) Marketing 125
23. To Blog or Not to Blog, That Is the Question 131
24. Were Social Media Ever Intended for Business? 135

xiii

Table of Contents

25. Twelve Tips for Tweeting Like a Champ 141
26. Stop Trying So Hard to Make Your #StupidHashtags
    Happen 149
27. Pinterest Is Hot, but Can It Benefit Your Business? 155
28. Is Google+ a Social Network or Data-Mining Experiment? 163
29. Dispelling the Myth of YouTube 173
30. An Instagram Is Worth a Thousand Words 179
31. Interview With the #InstagramGal 191
32. Facebook Is Dead, Long Live Facebook 199

Round 3: Buff Your Brand 211
33. Why Branding Matters for Small Business 215
34. What's in a Brand Name? Everything 223
35. Successful Marketing Starts With Strategic Positioning 233
36. Getting Your Employees on the Brandwagon 239
37. Your Business Needs to Tell a Better Brand Story 245
38. Does Your Brand Suffer From Multiple
    Personality Disorder? 259
39. How to Create a True Brand Experience 265
40. Resisting the Seduction of Low Price 273
41. Do You Innovate or Imitate? 283
42. Fourteen Ways to Position Yourself as an Expert 295
43. Communicate Your Value Before AND After the Sale 309
44. Being Irreplaceable Means Being Different 317
45. Why "Jack of All Trades" Is a Poor Branding Strategy 323

Round 4: TKO 331
46. Interview With a Marketing Man: A Dozen Questions for
    Nikolas Allen 335

Become a *Heavyweight Marketing* Brand Ambassador 343
Marketing Resources 345
Notes 351
Index 355
About the Author 361
Also by Nikolas Allen 363

"Marketing is the devil."
—Billy Bob Thornton

INTRO: SHADOWBOXING

St. Louis Park, Minnesota, June 1990—I sprawled on a tattered couch staring at a second-hand TV in a low-rent townhouse after another exhausting day at the car wash. At 22 years old, I wasn't much for introspection, but I was pretty fed up with the circumstances of my life, and so I was taking stock. Here is what I knew to be true: the shabby couch wasn't even mine. Nor was the welfare-district townhouse, which I was sharing with an engaged couple who would soon kick me out when they got hitched, sending me back to the dank confines of my dad's moldy basement.

I was working at the aforementioned car wash—a deluxe, full-service behemoth near the corporate office parks of Bloomington. Day after day, I wiped down the endless procession of cars emerging from the elaborately mechanized washing apparatus. Clearly, this was not a growth-job. In fact, the most profound lesson I learned there was that Corvettes are notorious for having brake problems. Note to self: when your band finally does make it big, don't buy a Corvette.

Ah, my band. I had graduated high school four years prior and while all my friends, peers and classmates scattered about the country in pursuit of higher education, I chose to eschew college and pursue music. And by "pursue music," I mean spend the next four years playing smoky bars and venues of ill repute for the liquored-up dregs of society. Well, them and anyone else we could convince to drive to a strip club in St. Paul on a Tuesday night in the middle of winter to watch us play a half-hour opening set. Eventually, things did get better for the band, but that was later. Right now things were looking pretty dismal.

Plan B from Outer Space

Then it happened. Like a universal transmission from God himself, a random commercial on the TV beamed straight into my brain and snapped me from my introspective stupor.

"Are you creative? Do you like to draw?" inquired a chipper announcer over images of happy people effortlessly mocking up logos and cartoons on drafting tables. "There could be a career for you in advertising!"

I leapt from the couch, grabbed a phone and was on the line with the school before the announcer finished repeating the number in triplicate. Although I *was* creative, and I *did* like to draw, my visceral response to the ad was more instinct than intellect. It seemed my life purpose was subconsciously galvanized by the new avenue presented in this commercial. When fall quarter came around, I was student-loaned up and enrolled in the Advertising Design program at Brown Institute.

Two swift years later, Associate of Applied Science degree in hand, I was on the horn with every print shop, graphics studio and ad agency in the Twin Cities looking for work. I got hired at one place, then another and another, and my career was underway. From graphic designer to art director to freelance creative, I enjoyed a wonderful 15-year run before getting fed up with the arctic winters of Minnesota.

My mom was living in northern California and I hadn't seen her much over the years, so I headed west in 2008, just as the economy was crumbling. Upon arriving in Siskiyou County, I noticed the small business landscape was fragile. On the one hand, there were a lot of brave entrepreneurial souls attempting to pursue their dreams in every business category. On the other, many of those businesses were barely scraping by and way too many storefronts stood empty: victims of a crumbling economy, a small and frugal local population, and shrinking tourist traffic.

Stepping in the Ring

Since employment opps were scarce, I decided to launch my own company, and BAM! Small Biz Consulting was born in 2010. The acronym stood for Branding And Marketing, and I set out to help business owners define their unique brand value, create meaningful marketing messages, and determine the best tools to reach their ideal audience with. The aggressive name perfectly encapsulated the bold brand I wanted to present. Clients immediately understood that I was not just another laid-back denizen of this sleepy little hamlet, but a mercenary marketing madman hell-bent on helping my fellow entrepreneurs ignite their passion for effective marketing.

BAM! enjoyed solid growth for three years. Every client presented new and unique opportunities to assess, diagnose and produce effective marketing solutions. The more clients I worked with, the more I learned about what was working—for both my clients and myself—and what was not. I started writing notes, articles, case studies and blog posts based on specific scenarios, successes and frustrations from my day-to-day dealings with prospects and clients.

Around year three, business slowed a bit and I started getting antsy for new growth opportunities. It came in the form of a job offer from a renewable energy company that was locally based, fiscally strong, and employee-owned. I accepted a position as director of marketing, and slowly brought BAM! to a close by the first quarter of 2014. As I was wrapping up my client projects, I

★ **HEAVYWEIGHT MARKETING** ★

came upon my writings and decided to tweak, update and expand them to turn them into the book you are holding in your hands.

A Manual for the Modern Marketer

The book consists of three main sections: Build Marketing Muscle, Tackle Your Tools and Buff Your Brand. I've had a few people question why the Branding section is at the end. No special reason. Truth is, that's just the way I laid the book out. You can start there if that feels more appropriate for you. You can read the book from beginning to end, or you can jump around to sections and chapters that rouse your interest. Either way, there's tons of info here and you may consume and assimilate it in whatever way feels comfortable for you.

You will notice that, with a few exceptions, most of the chapters are pretty short. So are the paragraphs. That's because people's attention spans are short. I wanted to create a book that modern readers (myself included—hey, I gotta read this too, ya know) would find enjoyable and not laborious.

Since I'm not currently offering consulting services, you won't find any sales pitches within. What you will find is a slew of stories, stats, opinions, ideas, insights and examples with a single purpose in mind: to help you turn your small business into a champion brand.

As it is, the subject of marketing can be pretty dry. I've worked very hard to make *Heavyweight Marketing* fun to read while still packing a powerhouse punch of practical information that will truly benefit those who commit to taking action. Does that sound like you? Good, then step in the ring and let's get ready to rumble!

"Advertising is only evil when it advertises evil things."
—David Ogilvy

Round 1: Build Marketing Muscle

★ 1 ★
THE LAW OF EFFECTIVE FREQUENCY

The modern advertising landscape is a clamorous one. Seemingly every available space, surface and screen is imploring us to Try This, Buy That, Shop in Our Store, Visit Us Online, Like, Friend, Follow, Consume, Spend, Splurge, all while Save, Save, Saving! The public has become quite adept at tuning out the multitudinous marketing messages they are bombarded with on a continuous basis. Therefore, in order for consumers to notice, assimilate, understand and act upon your marketing message, two things need to happen. First, the message has to be meaningful and relevant to their lives. Second, they have to see the ad enough to really notice it, instead of viewing it peripherally as worthless marketing graffiti coloring the walls of their daily existence.

Effective frequency is the number of times a person must be exposed to an advertising message before a response is made and before further exposure is considered wasteful. So, how frequently must an ad be seen to be effective? That's still debatable. Marketers like to talk about "The Rule of Seven," or the idea that people need to see your marketing message seven times before they take action. Actually, research has shown that the number ranges from five to twelve, but seven is a good rule of thumb.[1]

Throughout this book, we talk about the importance of consistency. As a business owner, it's common to get bored with your own ad campaign, marketing message or brand identity because you live with it every day. Instead, you need to consider your audience, for which every day may be the first time they experience your company and the branding signals it sends.

The 129-Year-Old Manifesto That's Still Valid Today

Way back in 1885, an astute ad man named Thomas Smith wrote a guide called *Successful Advertising*, and the manifesto he created is still popular today. As mentioned above, the current number of impressions required before taking action has dropped from his day, when it took 20. Either way, the message is clear: successful advertising takes time. Here is the process, according to Mr. Smith 129 years ago:

> **The first time** people look at any given ad, they don't even see it.
>
> **The second time**, they don't notice it.
>
> **The third time**, they are aware that it is there.
>
> **The fourth time**, they have a fleeting sense that they've seen it somewhere before.
>
> **The fifth time**, they actually read the ad.
>
> **The sixth time**, they thumb their nose at it.
>
> **The seventh time**, they start to get a little irritated with it.
>
> **The eighth time**, they start to think, "Here's that confounded ad again."
>
> **The ninth time**, they start to wonder if they're missing out on something.

Round 1: Build Marketing Muscle

The tenth time, they ask their friends and neighbors if they've tried it.

The eleventh time, they wonder how the company is paying for all these ads.

The twelfth time, they start to think that it must be a good product.

The thirteenth time, they start to feel the product has value.

The fourteenth time, they start to remember wanting a product exactly like this for a long time.

The fifteenth time, they start to yearn for it because they can't afford to buy it.

The sixteenth time, they accept the fact that they will buy it sometime in the future.

The seventeenth time, they make a note to buy the product.

The eighteenth time, they curse their poverty for not allowing them to buy this terrific product.

The nineteenth time, they count their money very carefully.

The twentieth time prospects see the ad, they buy what is being offered.[2]

Whew, makes you wonder how merchants sold anything back in the 1800s without going broke in the process. Even if this enduring manifesto has morphed into advertising folklore, it's very interesting to see similar truths still in place today.

★ HEAVYWEIGHT MARKETING ★

The challenge is to be patient with your marketing. Don't feel tempted to reinvent the wheel every other month. Spend time crafting meaningful messages, potent campaigns, and solid strategies. Then, stick with them—not until you're bored with them, but until their effectiveness has truly run its course.

★ 2 ★

THREE PRIMAL RULES OF MARKETING

In the Golden Age of Advertising, the popular maxim was to "sell the sizzle, not the steak." Well, the Golden Age is long dead and these days, it's all about the steak. In today's crowded marketplace, consumers are seeking real solutions, convenience and value. They are seeking authentic brands from companies built on integrity and transparency. As fewer large corporations are truly able to deliver on these promises, the playing field is opened up for creative entrepreneurs and agile small businesses to engage, connect and build relationships with consumers who are fed up, disillusioned or wary of Big Business and its impersonal, profit-over-everything methods of operation. Sure, some big companies have managed to keep their souls even as they have grown, but they are few and far between.

The following trifecta of rules is by no means comprehensive; you will find many rules along the way—discussed in this book and discovered throughout the life of your business—that you may choose to break or abide by. Consider these pointers a warm-up to get you thinking about the optimal relationship between you and your audience, and about the current and future tools with which you plan to reach them.

Rule #1) It's Not About You, It's About Them—This is the single most important rule that I have learned in my 20 years in advertising. Most of us spend so much time touting the features and benefits of our products and services, we often ignore the true value that our offering provides for our customers. This is a mistake.

★ HEAVYWEIGHT MARKETING ★

Marketing is about identifying the customer's problem (values, needs, desires) and solving it with your solution (product, service, offering). When you know the values of your customers, you can speak to them in a way that aligns your offering with their values, and craft your solution in a way that directly solves their problem.

This is even more effective if your offering has a strong point of difference (that which sets you apart from your competition). So make sure every marketing message you send answers the fundamental question on the mind of your prospects and customers at all times: "What's in it for ME?"

Rule #2) Authenticity Is Key—When you boil it down, marketing is about building relationships. John Jantsch, owner of Duct Tape Marketing, defines marketing as "getting people who have a specific need or problem to know, like and trust you."

The key word here is trust. Building business relationships is similar to building personal relationships in that honesty is the best policy. You have to keep it real. Some people think that "being authentic" gives them license to put all their messy human foibles on display. They think "keeping it real" means they can act like an ass because, hey, they're only human, right? Wrong. That might work for a select few personalities such as Simon Cowell, Kanye West and Gordon Ramsay. It might have even worked for the brilliant yet brutal Steve Jobs, but it certainly doesn't apply to everybody. In fact, marketing kingpin Seth Godin defines authenticity as "doing what you promise," rather than simply "being who you are."

In this technologically advanced age, there is no room for error when it comes to saying what you mean and meaning what you say. Any slip-up, lie, half-truth or scandal will be exposed in an instant for all to see. This happens to bigger brands quite often. Chobani yogurt markets its product as all-natural, yet it uses milk from cows fed with GMO animal feed.[1] When this news broke, influential grocer Whole Foods pulled Chobani from their shelves, and consumers continue to challenge and berate Chobani across their social media channels. A similar—and more costly—incident happened with Naked Juice, a brand owned by PepsiCo, when its "all natural" juices were found to contain GMO soy. The company faced a class action lawsuit for its misleading claims, resulting in a $9 million payout to Naked Juice drinkers who were duped by the company's fictitious marketing spin.[2]

> "The 'all natural' claim on our label described the fruits and vegetables in the bottle—not the vitamin boosts added to some Naked beverages. Naked juice and smoothies will continue to be labeled 'non-GMO,' and until there is more detailed regulatory guidance around the word 'natural,' we've chosen not to use 'All Natural' on our packaging."
> —Naked Juice Spokesman

Way to worm around the truth there, guys. No wonder Billy Bob Thornton thinks marketing is the devil. Consumers are smart enough to understand that the entire supply chain matters, even if marketers would prefer to lawyer-speak their way around the truth while treating their audience like a herd of deaf, dumb and blind sheep.

Generally, people would far prefer to do business with people they know than with strangers. This is one area where small business has the advantage over big business. When customers have greater access to you and your staff, they can build a rapport with the people behind the company and create relationships that engender trust. The larger corporations have to work extra hard at putting a human element into their business marketing (and, quite frankly, it usually feels forced, phony and inauthentic). The larger a company becomes, the more faceless they become, and when they become faceless, their authenticity diminishes and consumers' trust levels plunge.

When solving your customer's problems, make sure you're being honest, and not just telling them what they want to hear. Because, in this digital age, word-of-mouth travels at the speed of light and hell hath no fury like a consumer scorned. History is littered with the carcasses of failed brands who underestimated the intelligence of their audience. If you approach your business relationships and marketing with authenticity, your company can avoid that fate.

Rule #3) Explore New Channels—If you always do what you've always done, you'll always get what you've always gotten. As economies fluctuate, buying trends change and technology advances, it's important for you to adapt and adjust. There is massive hype surrounding social media and other digital platforms, which seem to proliferate on a monthly basis. This hype can make business owners feel pressured to adopt every new platform that comes along. A big question on many people's minds right now is, "Should I be using these platforms for my business?"

The answer, in a word, is yes. That's not to say you have to jump on all of the social media platforms. Some of them are simply not going to be relevant to your customer base, no matter how much hype you are hearing. A little research will help you understand what platforms your customers and prospects are using, which will dictate where your company needs to establish its presence. You will always find several justifiable excuses why NOT to add a social media element to your marketing (large time investment, little return, the difficulty of gauging effectiveness), but this is not just a fad that will go away if you ignore it.

Round 1: Build Marketing Muscle

If you don't jump in now, while the social media landscape is still being developed, the learning curve will only get steeper. However, there is a certain etiquette required in using these platforms for business (which we'll explore more deeply in Round 2). Simply treating these new marketing tools (interactive, engaging, personal, dialogic) as updated versions of the old ones (impersonal, static, monologic) will be as effective as using a feather duster when you need a hammer.

Keep Rule #1 in mind when using social media to make sure you are sharing WITH your audience instead of talking AT them. Use your tweets and profile updates to educate, enlighten and entertain. Share knowledge, tips, tricks, tutorials, links and items of interest to establish your brand as an important source of trustworthy and desirable information.

Social networking offers new avenues to connect with your audience, but don't expect your sales or profits to increase overnight. Exploring these new channels should be viewed as a long-term strategy in building relationships with your customers, which will only enhance the opportunity for success from your future marketing efforts.

There are many essential rules when it comes to marketing best practices, many of which we'll explore throughout this book. These three starter tips will engage your marketing mind as we delve deeper into your training en route to heavyweight status.

★ 3 ★

SIX IMPERATIVE ATTRIBUTES OF SUCCESSFUL ENTREPRENEURS

A local Small Business Development Center produced a Youth Entrepreneur Program in which young entrepreneurs pitched business ideas and competed for cash prizes that would help them launch their own startup. I was invited to be on an Entrepreneur Panel of speakers who attempted to inspire these youngsters with stories and ideas of what they could expect on the road to self-employment. Since the audience consisted of eager and enterprising students who were wet behind the ears, I crafted a presentation around a half-dozen personal traits that would serve them well as entrepreneurs.

There are myriad types of people starting and running their own businesses, and while each entrepreneur is unique, they share a handful of common traits that are necessary for entrepreneurial success. Unfortunately, these traits are not written on stone tablets carried down the mountain by Moses, nor are they printed on the inside of a box as if they were Scrabble rules. Rather, they are personal characteristics that get targeted, challenged and developed every day throughout the course of running a business.

Are there only six? No, there are numerous attributes that will be tested along the way. But the following six personal qualities are imperative when traveling the bumpy, thrilling, unpredictable road of self-employment:

★ HEAVYWEIGHT MARKETING ★

Strength—It takes a strong person to break away from the pack and pursue their own dreams despite heavy expectations from family and society. It's often easier to take the safe route towards employment as opposed to self-employment. When you are the captain of your own ship, strength of character is the rudder that will guide you towards success or destruction. Business owners are a lot like Atlas: responsible for holding their own little worlds aloft as they spin overhead. As their worlds grow, entrepreneurs need to be strong enough not to collapse under the pressure and weight of their own creations.

Confidence—If you lack confidence in yourself and your business concept, you will never make it as a business owner. You can only succeed if you believe it to be possible. There will be plenty of people around you who are doubting your choices, ideas and actions. Therefore, you must possess enough confidence for everybody until the success of your actions turns doubters into believers. As your team grows, people will look to you as their leader, and your confidence will inspire them to work together towards a shared purpose. This doesn't mean every one of your decisions has to be successful. Even the best leaders experience occasional failures, but they mustn't let those setbacks erode their confidence.

Passion—This is the fuel that stokes the fire in your belly that burns brightest when you're chasing your dreams. It's easy to feel passionate in the beginning of your journey, but sustained passion is necessary to go the distance. Eventually, things get difficult. The work is no longer fun, or the reality turns out differently than the dream. When that realization kicks in, the fire in your belly still needs enough oxygen to keep burning brightly so you can continue to move towards your entrepreneurial goals.

Motivation—What's your motivation for starting your own business? Freedom? Money? Leadership? Desire to share your offering with the world? Define your motivation and embrace it. Make certain it's strong enough to propel you from your bed to face each day no matter how difficult, tedious or uncertain it may be. Motivation is the coruscating beacon of light on the horizon leading you through choppy waters towards the destination of your dreams.

Willingness—There are plenty of enjoyable aspects to running your own business. However, there are equal amounts of wearisome activities. Entrepreneurs are the Chief Cook and Bottle Washer of their own enterprise. They must be willing to carry out all necessary tasks—no matter how menial or challenging—until they are able to delegate. Great leaders would never ask their staff to do things they would not be willing to do themselves. Therefore, entrepreneurs must lead by example and be willing to do whatever it takes to succeed with integrity.

Resilience—In business, mistakes will happen and failures will inevitably occur. However, true failure is not simply falling down; it's staying down. Therefore, leaders must possess the ability to bounce back from difficult situations so failure does not defeat them. Great lessons can be learned from bloopers, blunders and fiascos. Resilient business owners absorb these lessons, learn from their mistakes and come back stronger, wiser and more determined than before.

> *"If rejection slows you down, entrepreneurship isn't for you."* —Nathan Blecharczyk, co-founder, Airbnb

When reading the above list, make sure you're not simply seeing these attributes as words on a page. Try to imagine specific examples in your own life where each attribute has come into

★ HEAVYWEIGHT MARKETING ★

play. While running a business, you will continually discover new things about yourself. You will find there are certain things you enjoy doing, and other things that will test your skills, your patience and your character. When this happens, you can either face these challenges in an effort to improve, learn and grow, or you can build a well-rounded team consisting of people with complementary skillsets, attributes and personalities.

Whatever route you take, understand that the above six attributes—as well as many others you will discover along the way—are imperative for entrepreneurs to acknowledge. While they may become evident at any stage of their business, they will prove especially helpful in the beginning stages when optimism is highest, the rose-colored glasses are on and the starry-eyed visions are plentiful.

★ 4 ★

WHAT DO YOU REALLY DO FOR A LIVING?

Whenever you attend a business mixer, community networking event, or social occasion, the most common question you will hear is this: "So, what do you do?" Most people answer by simply stating their job title, which doesn't always say much and rarely answers the question. Even worse is when people drone on about their job description or start listing their responsibilities. Congrats, you've just embarked on a slow trip to Yawnsville. Now, instead of listening with interest, the person who asked the question is busy plotting her escape. Don't put your listeners through the same verbal torture. Instead, ditch the typical, snooze-worthy reply and formulate a response that will snap the querist to attention and have her begging for more info.

Here's the trick: don't think about what you DO; think about the benefits people enjoy from what you do, the specific market you serve, and the unique problems you solve. Then, craft a concise reply that touches on each point briefly. Some people call this an elevator pitch, but I prefer to call it your purpose statement. You are distilling the purpose of "what you do" into a compact statement that your audience can easily comprehend.

How to Formulate Your Answer:

"I (action verb) (target market) (problem you solve)"

Using my marketing consulting business as an example, here are some examples of how I might have answered this question:

★ HEAVYWEIGHT MARKETING ★

"I turn small business owners into heavyweight marketing champions."

"I help small business owners attract more loyal customers."

"I teach entrepreneurs how to improve their brand in order to grow their business."

See the pattern? These answers are far more intriguing than, "I'm a marketing consultant."

Instead of merely stating what you do, you're stating the purpose of your company, and articulating the single greatest benefit of doing business with you. The more you can tap into the emotions, needs and desires of your audience, the more powerful your answer will be. Keep in mind, sometimes this question will simply be rhetorical. After all, not everybody is going to be a qualified prospect. The person inquiring might just be making small talk or being polite. No problem. Your concise response will help you avoid wasting time blathering on to someone whose not really interested. However, you'll know your answer is powerful when it initiates the follow-up question, "Really? How do you do that?" or, "Oh yeah? Tell me more."

At that point, you can elaborate slightly on the unique way your solutions solve problems, fulfill desires or meet the needs of your customers. Be careful not to give away too much! For starters, it may be a tad crass to try to close a sale at your kid's soccer game. Additionally, if they seem interested and have the makings of a potential customer, it may be more appropriate to invite them to schedule an appointment, sign up for a demo, or purchase your product or service to experience this amazing benefit for themselves.

Prepare Your Purpose Statement With These Action Steps:

1) Write down as many action verbs as you can that apply to what you're doing (e.g., help, teach, build, invest, produce).
2) Define your target market—get as specific as possible.
3) List all the problems, frustrations, wants or needs that are solved by your unique benefit—go beyond the obvious and dig deep!
4) Try different combinations of your statement to see which ones feel both natural and powerful.

If your audience inquires further:

5) Craft a concise follow-up answer that further details the results your product or service provides.
6) Practice closing the sale (or scheduling an appointment or follow-up) in a way that feels like a natural transition.

As an entrepreneur, you never know where your next customer will come from. So why not turn a typically sleepy response to a frequently asked question into a powerful marketing message worth remembering? After all, even when out networking, you should take every opportunity available to turn strangers into prospects and prospects into customers.

So, what do YOU do?

★ 5 ★

WHY MEANINGFUL MESSAGES TRUMP EMPTY HYPE

There's an independent bank in Northern California that had exterior signage and banners on display that contained a marketing message I found to be worth discussing. Unfortunately, it's for all the wrong reasons. The following case study provides a great example of what NOT do when creating your core marketing messages.

A large banner hung on the exterior of the bank proclaiming: "The Buzz is all good about us!" Unfortunately, that statement is vague, meaningless hype and here's why: consumers have become expert researchers. Armed with the internet, search engines and social review features on Yelp, Foursquare, Google+, Facebook and others, any prospect or customer has the ability to compare and contrast products, services and companies before they decide to invest their money, loyalty and trust.

Modern consumers are not afraid to take their time before making any purchase, especially major ones. While they are considering their options, consumers can (and will) find all the buzz—and the dirt—on your company. Therefore, telling people that the buzz is all good is a wasted opportunity. Instead, the bank should be stating WHY the buzz is good.

In this case, the bank could let people know what has people buzzing about their products or service. For example, they could be shouting about any of the following:

★ HEAVYWEIGHT MARKETING ★

- Free Donuts Every Friday!
- Unparalleled Customer Service!
- Best Interest Rates in the Business!
- Hassle-Free Loan Services!

See the difference? Every marketing tactic and tool you employ needs to tout the meaningful difference of your company. Your messages should inform your audience how their lives are going to be better—however incrementally—if they choose your product or service.

Instead of just ridiculing this bank's lack of marketing savvy, I decided to dig a little deeper to see if I was missing something about this vapid message. I stopped in to see the bank manager and asked her what the message on the banners meant. Unfortunately, she didn't offer much clarity. She mumbled some evasive response before suggesting I visit the website, where it allegedly elaborated on reasons why "the buzz was all good."

"Yes, but, the banner doesn't direct people to the website," I pointed out gently. "How are we to know that all these buzz-worthy benefits are waiting there to be discovered?"

She bristled, clearly annoyed, and attempted to change the subject. I suddenly felt like the Michael Moore of marketing, and I smiled to myself as I watched her fumble to regain her managerial composure.

At that point, she handed me some printed collateral from a different campaign that was touting a "heritage" message, and launched into her History of Our Bank spiel. My ears perked up immediately when she informed me that this bank is the oldest independent bank in Northern California. BAM! That's the message they should be touting! In an era of ginormous corporate banking institutions, securities fraud, government bailouts and exorbitant bank fees, staking their claim to a message of independence, longevity and heritage would be a far stronger message to tout than "The buzz is all good about us!"

The lesson here is to dig deep and determine what your company does best, what you did first, or what you're doing that nobody else can claim. Discover what is important and meaningful to your customer and align your company's unique value with the unique needs, interests and desires of your audience.

Doing this will allow you to craft a meaningful marketing message that will truly connect with your audience, instead of striking out with a meaningless message based on empty hype.

★ 6 ★

STOP SENDING MIXED MESSAGES

Whoever is responsible for this remarkable lack of marketing savvy needs to be…educated. Possibly flogged, but definitely educated.

First off, we've got a sign promoting the motel's "New Pillowtop Beds," which is placed, get this—on top of—a sign touting their AAA-approved status. Now, individually, both of these benefits could be strong messages to send. They each offer a value-added benefit to the lodging experience that could justify a higher nightly rate for a room: soft, new beds, plus a stamp of approval from AAA, which extends a discount to card-carrying members.

★ HEAVYWEIGHT MARKETING ★

Sounds like just the winning combination that could convince road-weary travelers to pull in for the night. However, by carelessly slapping the New Beds sign right over the AAA sign, this proprietor has created a confusing mess that doesn't allow either one of the messages to shine. Not to mention it shows blatant disregard for aesthetics of any sort. And if I were a AAA rep and I saw this flagrant violation, I would strip the motel of their credentials faster than the sheets off a new Pillowtop bed! Okay, maybe not, but you better believe I would not go easy on 'em when re-certification time rolled around, no siree.

While this particular example pertains to the outdoor signage medium, the mixed marketing message concept also applies when it comes to other forms of advertising. A quick glance through any printed periodical reveals that many business owners try to cram as many messages, features and benefits into their tiny ad as possible. Again, this results in mental overload and confusion. Instead of absorbing your intended message, the reader ends up taking nothing away from the ad.

Before sending any marketing message, regardless of the medium, ask yourself the following question: what one thing do I want the audience to take away from this?

Is it a specific call to action? Then make sure the action you want the audience to take is crystal clear and the phone number, website, email or physical address is prominent.

Is it about brand awareness? Then make sure you tout the most unique and meaningful benefit that your brand delivers.

Is it an urgent, time-sensitive event? Make sure you convey a strong sense of urgency, what the audience needs to do, and how they can avoid missing out.

Round 1: Build Marketing Muscle

Is it about your company's amazing point of difference? Then shout it loud and proud and stick to that—and only that—message.

The bottom line is that you should resist the temptation to tout all of your products, all of your services, all of your features and benefits in your marketing pieces. Determine your core message first and stick to it. If any other message does make its way in, be sure it supports your chosen primary message. This will allow you to send a focused, powerful, meaningful marketing message that your desired audience will read, remember, and act upon.

And whatever you do, for the love of Pete, do not stack two signs on top of each other!

★ 7 ★

SPEAK THE LANGUAGE OF RESULTS

One of the most effective ways to improve your marketing message is by articulating the end results customers derive from your offering. Humans make decisions based on emotions, then use their rational mind to justify decisions. In the battle of the heart vs. the mind, the heart often wins. Therefore, in order to earn the attention of your prospects, you need to hook them emotionally.

Your marketing materials need to paint a beautiful picture of how much better your customers' lives are going to be after purchasing your offering. This is similar to touting the benefits of your product or service, but in our hyper-connected, instant-gratification society, consumers want more than benefits, they want results—and they want 'em now!

Emotional engagement is still a novel idea to business owners who comfortably tout product features, so it may take some time before it feels authentic. That's why it's important to build relationships with your customers, so you know what their points of frustration, obstacles, and objections are. When you have a comfortable rapport with your audience, you can ask them important questions such as:

- Why they patronize you
- How their lives are better because of it
- What benefits they would highlight when referring your business to friends.

★ HEAVYWEIGHT MARKETING ★

This information is golden when it comes time to write copy for marketing collateral such as your website, brochures, advertisements, direct mail pieces and radio spots. You can use it in your sales calls and networking, and even tout the results of your offering when managing your social media platforms.

Case Study—Three Real-World Examples:

#1—The Joy of Home Ownership: There was a real estate team trying to break into a crowded, upscale market outside their normal area of operations. The entirety of their message was focused on the combined experience between them, and they wondered why they weren't making much headway.

This reminds me of a saying that goes, "People don't CARE how much you KNOW, until they KNOW how much you CARE." Sure, experience is important, but there are many more priorities, details, hopes and frustrations involved in the challenging process of buying and selling your home. By focusing only on experience, these realtors were leaving it up to their clients to decipher exactly what that meant. They weren't articulating how the clients could benefit from this experience in the midst of a stressful, life-changing event that could get delayed or fall apart at any time.

Instead, we tweaked their message to speak to the alleviation of headaches, obstacles, delays and red tape that first-time home buyers often face, and the joy, excitement and thrill of finally getting the keys to your first home. Buying and selling a home can be a long, arduous process. By communicating the successful end results, clients were more willing to choose these realtors to accompany them on their journey.

#2—The Freedom of Fitness: A health club was showcasing their wide selection of machines and amenities in their marketing materials. The photos didn't even include people *using* these machines, instead they just stood at attention like robotic sentries awaiting orders. While the photos looked nice and the variety of machines was impressive, people don't make emotional connections with workout equipment.

The emotional charge comes from losing weight, being able to fit into your favorite clothing, building muscle, increasing strength and stamina, improving flexibility, and all the great feelings of pride and accomplishment that go along with this. Different people of all age groups go to the gym for myriad reasons. Therefore, we created several customer profiles so we knew who we were speaking to in each case. We were able craft marketing messages that targeted various age groups, while still putting the focus on the thrill of experiencing results and an improved quality of life enjoyed by people who are committed to fitness.

#3—The Power of Simplicity: While consulting with an insurance agent, we decided to avoid the fear-based concepts and policy-jargon that plagues most insurance advertising. Instead, this agent felt strongly that her main point of difference was in her simple, easy-to-understand policies. The next step was to ask, "What are the results people experience by simplifying something that's typically arduous and confusing?"

Let's think about it. Perhaps simplicity means less stress, which is good for optimal health. Maybe there's a fun connection that equates simple policies with less stress, which means better health, which means lower premiums or deductibles. Or maybe simple policies means customers have more time to do things they really enjoy. Rather than leave it at that, we could then go deeper into specific activities enjoyed by target audience members: playing at the beach with their grandkids, hiking with their spouse and the dog, or spending the day at the park with a picnic basket and a good book.

★ HEAVYWEIGHT MARKETING ★

Once you start riffing on these questions and concepts, you begin to chip away at obvious, surface-level scenarios in order to mine the meaningful, results-driven solutions that will forge emotional connections with your audience. As for my client's project, we managed to inject a little fun into her brand with a memorable marketing message that felt unique in the typically humdrum category of insurance.

Touting your company's experience, equipment and policies may be enough to satisfy the logical mind, but that's not enough to break through the cluttered advertising landscape of today. Speaking the language of results will allow you to create a meaningful marketing message that bypasses the logic center of the brain and plants itself in the soft, squishy landscape of the heart, which is where relationships blossom between consumers and the small business brands that matter to them.

★ 8 ★

ONLINE MARKETING VS. TRADITIONAL: WHICH IS "BETTER"?

I was at a business networking meeting where a debate ensued regarding the merits of traditional marketing versus online marketing. One party was partial to print advertising and praised its time-honored effectiveness, while another extolled the virtues of the online marketing realm. The debate seemed to boil down to this single question: which medium is better?

Just as I did at the meeting, I will chime in here and say: that is the wrong question to be asking. After all, traditional media (printed collateral, billboards, radio, television, etc.) and new media (websites, blogs, search engines, video, social media, etc.) are merely different tools in the same marketing toolbox.

Sometimes you need a screwdriver and sometimes you need a monkey wrench, but it all depends on the task at hand. Instead of asking which is better, here are several questions that are even more important to ask yourself before deciding which tools to utilize in your marketing efforts:

What is our message? One of my favorite and most frequent questions is, What's the story? This is an easy conversation-starter that helps excavate the message, which should be the first step in any campaign. What result do you want from your marketing? How do you want to position your company? What is your competitive advantage and how will you tout it? How does your message align with your company's brand promise?

★ HEAVYWEIGHT MARKETING ★

How will your offer benefit the reader? What action do you want the reader to take? Scrutinize your ideas until there are no more questions left to ask. The strongest ideas will be the ones that hold up to the interrogation.

Who is our audience? Once you determine what you're saying, you need to determine who you're speaking to. When defining your ideal audience, it pays to get specific. After all, if you are marketing to everybody, you are marketing to nobody. Keep your sights focused on the people who will get the most benefit from your offering.

Where is our audience? Once you know who your audience is, you need to determine the best way to reach them with your meaningful message. Are they using Google search or flipping through the Yellow Pages? Do they read newspapers or blogs? Do they listen to music on the radio or stream it on the web through services like Spotify, Pandora, or iTunes? Do they gossip with friends at the hair salon or on Facebook?

Once you answer all these questions, you'll have a very good idea of the right tools to use to hit the right people with the right message. In some cases, you will use a mix of several tools, or you may find you only need the tried-and-true favorites. You may find you need to dip your toe in the water and experiment with new tools in order to reach your desired audience. Just make sure that whatever tactics and tools you decide to use, you keep track of the results. This can be as simple as asking people where they heard about you, or as complicated as having different phone numbers, codes, coupons or web pages for different promotions.

Once you have explored and answered all the questions above, then—and only then—will you discover the answer to our original query: which media are better? The ones that work!

★ 9 ★

THE MOTIVATIONAL VALUE OF STIFF COMPETITION

While driving through a quiet suburb of Minneapolis a few years back, I saw a funky little independent coffee house called Joe's Coffee Shack on the corner of an intersection. On the opposite corner was a Starbucks. Of course, this is a common sight in large, urban areas where there's a coffee shop on every block, but this was a small retail pocket in a sleepy backstreet neighborhood.

I remember thinking how upset Joe must have been when the Big Green Behemoth moved in on his turf. Then I realized that there are "Starbucks people" and there are "shop-local, anti-corporate, support-the-little-guy people." Besides, with so many coffee drinkers, I'm pretty certain both stores had their fair share of business.

Competition is often thought of as a bad thing, but it is actually a good thing. When other businesses are offering products and services that are similar to yours, it indicates that there is a large enough market to support your business concept. If nobody else is offering what you're offering, you are either a supreme innovator who's way ahead of the curve, or an unfortunate dreamer who might realize the hard way that there is no demand for your supply.

However, competition is only beneficial if it motivates you to differentiate your offering in a way that sets you apart from the pack. If you allow competitors to crop up around your business and you fail to define and articulate your company's unique value, your brand will be reduced to a commodity. When shopping for commodities, people base their purchasing decisions on price, location and convenience, and these are all difficult areas in which to compete.

Remember, perception is reality. Your objective is to create the perception that there is no other product or service on the market quite like yours. In order to maintain your competitive edge, you must regularly study your competition.

Ask these questions about your competitors:
1. What are my competitors doing right?
2. What are they doing wrong?
3. What seems to be selling well for them?
4. What price range do they occupy?
5. Do we share a similar customer base, or is there more of a niche market that we can hone in on?
6. What are they not doing that we could be taking advantage of?

Answering these questions will help you discover the strengths and weaknesses of your competitors. You will know the areas in which you can afford to challenge them, and where you should concede. This knowledge will allow you to position your company as distinctive in your business category. One client hired me to help clarify their brand. First, I created a questionnaire and worked with management to flesh out answers to some essential questions. But our job wasn't done. Next, we made copies of the same questionnaire to hand out at all four of the company's locations, and offered customers an incentive for filling it out. Why? Because business owners, management and employees don't always have all the answers. Shocking, I know.

When you want real insights from people who see your company from a totally different perspective from those on the inside, you should seek direct feedback from those whose opinions matter most: the paying customers.

Exploring the questions below as they apply to your business will illuminate your areas of strength, weakness, and focus as you attempt build a heavyweight brand that can hold its own against your strongest competitors.

Ask these questions about your own company:
1. What are the three greatest strengths of our brand?
2. Where is there room for improvement?
3. What are the three greatest strengths of our competitors?
4. How is our offering different than theirs?
5. How do we express that difference in words, images and actions?
6. What value do we bring to our audience?
7. How does our offering improve people's lives?
8. What emotions are attached to our offering?
9. What makes customers buy from us the first time?
10. What keeps them coming back?

Think about Joe from my opening story for a moment. While he faced a monumental challenge, his task in the situation was clear: Joe's Coffee Shack needed to offer a coffee experience that was completely different than the Starbucks experience.

Judging by the tiki-bar vibe of its grass-thatched awning covering a patio full of mismatched furniture, I'd say Joe was on the right track. With a little effort and imagination, I believe your company can take its position on that track as well.

Round 1: Build Marketing Muscle

★ 10 ★

GAIN MARKETING MILEAGE FROM BUSINESS MILESTONES

In 2012, Oreo celebrated their 100th anniversary, and to commemorate the event, they created the "Oreo Daily Twist." These daily images featured Oreo cookies that had been customized or modified in relation to current events happening around the world. For 100 days in a row, Oreo posted these images online to their website, Pinterest, Tumblr, and Facebook platforms. Many of the resulting images were quite brilliant, and their efforts earned Oreo an astounding amount of buzz, PR and

Some of the notable events honored in Oreo's Daily Twist campaign

social media activity—the highest level of brand engagement ever to be realized by a cookie. They even incurred some backlash by choosing to kick off the campaign with a polarizing image of a cookie with rainbow-colored filling in support of gay rights.[1]

Oreo's "Daily Twist" took on the Mars Rover landing, Talk Like a Pirate Day, Elvis Week, and every other pop culture event that took place during their three-month digital media blitz. This promotional juggernaut did more than improve brand awareness; it altered the public perception of Oreo. This campaign turned Oreo from a cookie that's always been around into an important brand with a strong voice that is relevant to our times.

"Consumption of media has shifted quite a bit to digital, social and mobile," explained the brand's marketing director Cindy Chen. "To be on pace with that is really important for the brand to continue to grow; that's why the Daily Twist program was born."

Campbell's Perfects "The Art of Soup"

More recently, Campbell's soup launched "The Art of Soup," marking the fiftieth anniversary of Andy Warhol's iconic artwork, *32 Campbell's Soup Cans*, in which he immortalized the product in silk-screen paintings. In honor of the event, Campbell's deviated from their rigid red, white and gold color scheme and printed a limited-edition run of soup can labels in a plethora of pop palettes that would have made Andy proud.

The back of the can featured the story of the promotion along with a photo of Warhol, his signature and one of his many pithy quotes, such as "In the future everybody will be world famous for 15 minutes." The clever part is this: Campbell's then turned Warhol's quote into a call to action to follow the brand on Facebook (e.g., "Use the 'Pop Art Portrait' app on our Facebook

Round 1: Build Marketing Muscle

Campbell's celebrates a Pop-tastic business milestone with "The Art of Soup"

page to begin your 15 minutes.") and to visit The Art of Soup website. This one essential addition is what encouraged passive bystanders to become active brand ambassadors.

The campaign resulted in:

Increased Awareness—Art fans like myself were more than happy to provide a brief history lesson to our pop-culture-challenged brethren who thought Campbell's was simply sprucing up their cans with "pretty colors" for soup season.

Social Engagement—The company built a custom, limited-run website dedicated to the campaign, but they didn't expect their audience to simply come to them. They also went where their audience was, encouraging people to connect on Facebook to learn more about The Art of Soup. Campbell's even created a "Pop Art Portrait" app for Facebook that allowed visitors to upload their own pictures and get the Warholian Pop treatment.

★ HEAVYWEIGHT MARKETING ★

Massive Word of Mouth—People were actually talking about Campbell's soup again for the first time since, well, 1962, when Warhol's prints were created! I've been hearing lots of buzz about this promotion from media outlets, from my extended social circle, and—as a Pop Art fanatic—I've even been doing my own part to engage with and post about this milestone.

Increased Sales—From the soup fans who simply enjoy the colorful cans, to the Warhol fans who make a pilgrimage to their local Target stores (my girlfriend drove an hour both ways to buy me a stash as a gift), Campbell's has surely moved additional units by capitalizing on this important milestone in their brand's history.

So, how does all this apply to your business? By illustrating that you can use business milestones as a theme for a creative promotional campaign that will benefit you in the ways mentioned above. Don't bother trotting out the excuse that you don't have a Campbell's-size marketing budget. Get creative, think outside the box, go beyond a simple sale and do something special that will build awareness, drive traffic, increase sales and be newsworthy enough to earn PR—even if you have to write the press release and submit it yourself.

Food for Thought

- Are you approaching 10,000 customers?
- How about 1,000?
- Has your business just passed its five- or ten-year mark?
- Have you won an award lately?
- Are you launching a new product?
- Have you landed a new client or partner?
- Did you make a new hire recently?

- Have you extended your hours, rebranded your company, or launched a new website?
- Heck, maybe you even had to fire one of your biggest clients!

Take a good look at your company, your calendar and your history. With a little effort and ingenuity, I'm certain you can unearth several potential business milestones around which to create a clever newsworthy event, offer, campaign or promotion that will intrigue and excite your audience and earn your company some major marketing mileage.

★ 11 ★

THIRTEEN WAYS TO GO BIG ON SMALL BUSINESS SATURDAY AND BEYOND

Business owners often look forward to the holiday shopping season because it gives them an opportunity to end the year on a financial high note. While the fourth quarter in general provides a welcome bump in shopping activity, I'm specifically referring to the Black Friday/Small Business Saturday/Cyber Monday trifecta that takes place just after Thanksgiving.

Now, unless you're a big-box superstore, don't even bother competing for attention on Black Friday. Heck, with its crazed consumer chaos, mad-mob mentality, and annual death-by-trampling tendencies, I prefer to stick my head in the sand and pretend it doesn't exist at all. Small Business Saturday, on the other hand, is a far more civil and enjoyable affair in which consumers are encouraged to "shop small" on the first Saturday after Thanksgiving. With a little planning and effort, small business owners can take advantage of this day to generate stellar sales and increase their customer base by forging new business relationships that will extend well beyond the holidays.

Small Business Saturday was started by American Express in 2010. It followed the long-standing Black Friday, which has become known as the busiest shopping day of the year, and the more recent Cyber Monday, which was started by Shop.org in 2005 after consumer studies showed the Monday following Thanksgiving to typically be the biggest online shopping day of the year. Is it a wee bit ironic that Small Business Saturday was started by a $15 billion multinational financial services corporation? Yes, but the hefty promotional muscle American Express has put behind the SBS initiative cannot be denied—even if the underlying motive is to get people to use their AmEx cards. Small Business Saturday has recently spurred over 100 million shoppers to support small businesses throughout the country, and a 2013 study found that "customers who were aware of Small Business Saturday spent $5.7 billion with independent merchants." This was an increase of 3.6% from a strong $5.5 billion in 2012.[1]

For many consumers, the approach of holiday season means they automatically start planning their yearly trips to the overcrowded malls, superstores and big-box retailers. While it may be difficult to completely alter the holiday-consumer paradigm that has become entrenched in our culture over the past sixty years, small businesses can do their part to offer a shopping alternative. The idea is to build a strong connection with customers over the course of the year, so when it comes time to shop—whether for holiday gifts, special events, or whenever they have a need or desire for your offering—they think of *your* business.

Take note of the following ways in which your company can go big on Small Business Saturday and beyond:

Instore Promotions

Educate Your Customers—Promote Small Business Saturday instore and online by utilizing free resources from American Express. You can download free Small Business Saturday promotional materials from American Express such as web banners and logos, instore posters and even email and social media templates. You can also get these free items by "liking" Small Business Saturday on Facebook *(see Resources section for* *links)*. This is also a prime opportunity to educate your customers why shopping small is important. Let them know how keeping their dollars local benefits your community.

Play Upon the Local—There's a growing segment of consumers that appreciates small-batch, hand-crafted products. If you carry products that are locally crafted, point them out and promote them as such. People love sampling local crafts and cuisine because it is something special and unique to the area, so offering these types of products provides a great shopping incentive for people who care about quality.

Highlight Gift Items—Think of which products would truly make great gifts, and promote the gift concept like crazy. Arrange special "gift displays." Create custom branded signage to showcase gift-y items or special promotional items related to the occasion. Make sure your gifts are original and not things people could find anywhere online.

Make a Day of It—This is the chance to celebrate your business for all that it is. Put up some balloons, offer coffee, snacks and goodies—make it a party! Hire a solo musician, small band or DJ to perform live music. In Minneapolis, many of the record stores and cool-kid clothing stores frequently have DJs spinning instore on Saturdays—sometimes right in their window displays. It adds an extra-special energy and hip ambiance to the store's atmosphere that really draws people in and makes 'em hang out longer while shopping.

Grow Your Mailing List—On Small Business Saturday, ask visitors to sign up for your mailing list so you can notify them of future special offers and events. Remember, give people a reason to join, perhaps even an incentive. You can even treat it as an "Enter to Win" and give away a gift basket, gift certificate, membership or specialty item. Continuing to engage your customers will make sure you aren't forgotten once Small Business Saturday comes to a close. Just make sure that somewhere in the fine print of your mailing list sign-up, you indicate people are giving consent to receive periodical communication from your store.

Online Promotions

Rally the Troops—In order to maximize your reach, be sure to employ all your online platforms, including email, website, blog and social media. Use the free email and social media templates and graphics available from American Express and create specific Small Business Saturday messages. Emphasize the benefits of Small Business Saturday for your customers as well as its impact on small businesses in America.

Present a Great Offer—Don't just expect consumers to visit your business on Small Business Saturday out of the goodness of their hearts. Give them a great reason to make your store a must-visit location. Compelling offers could be free gift wrapping, stocking stuffers with purchase, or a percentage off future purchases after spending a certain amount. If you decide on a desirable giveaway incentive for joining your mailing list, you can promote that in your marketing as well.

Use Trending Hashtags—If you use Twitter and other social media, include the hashtag #ShopSmall in your tweets and posts. Identify other trending hashtags around Small Business Saturday and employ those as well. This will make your tweets, posts and pins visible to anyone searching for SBS info. It will also contextualize your content and express your solidarity and support for the small business sector. This will help you attract followers and encourage conversation with consumers and fellow entrepreneurs who support "shopping small."

Get Visible—In the days leading up to your event, be sure to revamp your website with SBS messages, graphics, images and blog posts. Post photos of your best (local, unique) gift items to your Facebook, Instagram or Pinterest accounts. Don't forget Google+ if you want to rank for SBS search terms *(see Chapter 28 for more on Google+)*. Be sure to include short stories or descriptions along with your #ShopSmall marketing message.

Post Your Party—When Small Business Saturday rolls around, take photos throughout the day of your guests, employees, musicians and instore crowds and post them to your photo-sharing social platforms. You do need permission to post photos of people, so be sure to ask if it's okay. Then, let guests and visitors know where you'll be posting the pictures so they can view and tag themselves later. This will create online activity around your brand after the day is done, helping you to make more connections and earn more followers and fans.

Engage Your Audience—Conversation is a key part of a successful social media strategy. To encourage engagement, be sure to ask questions, and invite feedback, stories and opinions from your audience. You want your content to prompt likes, shares and retweets organically. Beware of asking directly (e.g., Share this post! Like if you agree! Please RT!), which is cheesy and in poor taste. People do it all the time, but even the bigwigs at Facebook, Twitter and Google are starting to discourage users from being so blatant about it.

Become a Movie Star—Post videos on YouTube about what makes your store special. Make it fun and personal, or add a human, emotional element by sharing how pursuing your entrepreneurial dream has impacted your life. During your event, you can interview customers on camera, asking fun questions like: What's the best/worst gift you've ever received? Who are you shopping for today? Or, What are you hoping to find under your tree this year?

★ HEAVYWEIGHT MARKETING ★

Blast Off—Send email blasts to your mailing list that give plenty of advance notice about Small Business Saturday. I get so many emails within two or three days of an event and that is never enough time to work it into my plans. People are busy, so respect their schedules and don't expect them to be spontaneous just because you didn't have time to send your email out early enough. A couple days prior IS a good time frame to send a reminder, however.

Remember to give your audience a compelling reason by using the stories and talking points we've been discussing. Tout it as a fun, can't-miss party that will be made even better by their presence. Then, after the fact, be sure to send a follow-up "Thank You" email to show appreciation for their support.

In the run-up to Small Business Saturday, your goal should be to educate your audience, make them aware, and associate your store with this big shopping day at as many customer touchpoints as possible. Think of a creative way to draw your customers in, make sure they have a fantastic shopping experience, then ask permission to maintain the connection via email or social media.

So, should you only be implementing the above strategies one day out of the year? Absolutely not! However, if you're not already doing everything listed above, it may be overwhelming to think of adding all those activities to your everyday marketing efforts. That should be the long-term goal, though. For now, with a little planning, you can ramp up your efforts for the big holiday shopping weekend, then expand those efforts as they become more familiar.

Round 1: Build Marketing Muscle

In fact, not long after the holidays, you have another opportunity to scale your efforts to a full week! That's right, every May, the U.S. Small Business Association promotes National Small Business Week.

> *"Every year since 1963, the President of the United States has issued a proclamation announcing National Small Business Week, which recognizes the critical contributions of America's entrepreneurs and small business owners."*
> —Small Business Association

1963?! That's crazy, because I only became aware of Small Business Week in 2014, while I've known about Small Business Saturday since its inception in 2010. The reason? SBW is promoted by the government, while SBS is promoted by American Express. Who do you think has a bigger marketing budget? At any rate, your goal should eventually be to utilize every tool, tactic and strategy in this chapter on a regular basis. Start where you are, and grow from there. By capitalizing on Small Business Saturday, but also thinking beyond that one day, small businesses have an opportunity to develop meaningful long-term relationships with their customers.

★ 12 ★

HOOK SEASONAL CUSTOMERS YEAR-ROUND WITH MARKETING TRIDENT

Every summer, the small, mountain community of Mt. Shasta is inundated with tourists, travelers and visitors who come to experience the bounty of the picturesque region. Winters can also be a big draw for the sporty folks who enjoy coming to play on the mountain, but inconsistent weather patterns have put a damper on our winter tourist season for the past couple years. In fact, the ski park didn't even open for business during the 2013–14 season. Ouch.

In order to alleviate strict dependency on tourist traffic as the sole lifeblood of your business, it is especially important for companies operating in tourist destinations to build business relationships with the local community. The challenge in our area is that locals are generally interested in practical, basic-needs items and the tourists are interested in New Age tchotchkes, trinkets, artifacts, and anything containing a picture of the mountain. In fact, there's a standing joke in our community about there being 18 shops that sell crystals, and none selling socks and underwear.

Some seasonal businesses solve the feast/famine cycle by only opening during high season. In Section 2, we talk with the owner of the Cape Cod boutique SueB.Do, who operates on such a schedule. But what about businesses that do operate year-round? How can they even out the typical high/low volume of seasonal traffic? The ideal solution includes a three-pronged marketing plan that allows you to continue engaging your audience after they've come and gone.

The Three Prongs of Your Marketing Trident:
- E-commerce Website
- Email Marketing
- Social Media Marketing

We discussed a couple of these tools in the previous chapter about Small Business Saturday. Of course it would be a shame if you did all the work we mentioned just for one day of the year! No, the trick is that you must use all these tools together in a consistent and strategic way every week of every month of every year that you're in business. And I'm sorry to say, but simply creating a Facebook page doesn't quite qualify as a "social media strategy."

Let's look at each of the tools and how they work together.

1) E-commerce Website—If your customers have to physically be in your store to make a purchase, you are severely limiting your sales opportunities. Allowing customers to shop your products online opens up an entire new stream of revenue that doesn't exist otherwise.

While e-commerce works best with retail establishments that can ship product across the country, this still applies if you're running a bed and breakfast, a mountain guide service or a fly fishing tour business. In that case, you'll want an online presence that allows prospects and customers to book rooms and tours online. You could also get creative and include the option to purchase customized souvenirs, memorabilia, branded gift items or maps of the area from your website.

Round 1: Build Marketing Muscle

E-commerce websites require more investment than a typical website, but it will pay off over time as your audience becomes aware of your online shopping capabilities *(see Resources section for several e-commerce options)*. Once you do offer online shopping, it is your responsibility to let people know it's there. Your e-commerce site should be considered your online hub and every other marketing tool utilized should actively drive your audience back to your site. That's where the next two tools come in.

2) Email Marketing—With a continuous slew of fresh and exciting social platforms like Snapchat, Instagram, and Pinterest coming along and jockeying for the spotlight, it may be tempting to dismiss stalwart tools like email marketing despite their proven track record. That would be a mistake.

> *"I've been hearing email pronounced dead every year for the last 20 years, but every year its performance stays strong. Email will continue to thrive so long as marketers strive for integration with other channels and a better understanding of the data points. They can effectively message the consumer with the things they care about in the manner and time they expect to be messaged."*
> —Ed Kats, President, MediaWhiz

Using a robust, user-friendly email marketing solution—not just firing off plain text emails from your Yahoo! account—is still a great way to communicate with your audience and drive them to your site. As a seasonal business, you need to focus on growing your list while the traffic is high so you can keep in contact during the off-season. Continue to send timely, relevant promotions and communications over the course of the year so you are top of mind when your customer is ready to buy. Be sure to include a strong call to action in your newsletters and announcements that will drive readers back to your site. The more time customers spend on your site, the more likely they are to make a purchase. We dedicate an entire chapter to email marketing in Section 2, so I won't yammer on about it here. Just keep in mind that email is a key prong in your marketing trident, so don't discount it as old hat.

3) Social Media—Your social strategy could include maintaining an active presence on any of the multiple platforms available. We discuss several individual platforms in depth in Section 2, but in case you've been living under a rock for the past six years, I'll briefly outline the networks that currently matter:

Facebook—The granddaddy of social media. Best for communicating with friends and family. Organic reach has plummeted for business pages, so to effectively use Facebook for marketing, you had better plan on dedicating a budget for Promoted Posts and Facebook Ads.

Twitter—The confusing one. Best for brief, witty observations, newsjacking, breaking news, bridging the communication gap between commoners and A-listers, sharing interesting links and driving traffic to your blog posts. Currently experiencing major identity crisis and campaigning hard for mainstream acceptance. Its recent makeover looks more like Facebook than ever.

Pinterest—The pretty, smart one. Best for bonding with your audience over beautiful photos, driving e-commerce traffic, business categories that lend themselves to visual storytelling. Pinterest has evolved and improved nicely in its short lifespan and has emerged as strong traffic-driving source for online retailers.

Instagram—The pretty, dumb one. Limited capabilities reduce Instagram to a passive consumption platform with lots and lots of pretty pictures. No easy way to share other users' photos, no outbound links, and more hashtag abuse than anyone should have to endure. Oh, and don't get me started on the ungodly number of #selfies. This mobile app was made for narcissism. A recent upgrade introduced 10 new photo manipulation features, which offers users more creative control of their images. Some companies are finding innovative uses for the platform, so Instagram's future is still being written. Best for building brand awareness through creative visuals, images and short videos.

Google+—The misunderstood one. Best for SEO purposes, since your posts come up in Google searches. Hailed as the "Facebook Killer" when launched in 2009, only to have its reputation downgraded to "Ghost Town." This divisive platform has some vocal proponents but its overall value is dubious at best.

LinkedIn—The exclusive one. Best for job-seeking, networking, ladder-climbing and connecting with movers and shakers of the business world. The only social network where discussing business is actually encouraged. LinkedIn has finally realized its own value and has been moving more and more features into its premium (i.e., paid) version. These days, free accounts are pretty sparse and almost every action prompts an "Upgrade to Premium" message.

YouTube—The deep one. Best for hosting all your business videos, interviews, testimonials, behind-the-scenes tours, and in-store shenanigans, which you can then share to all your other media platforms. Wanna watch an obscure commercial from the 70s? How 'bout a buzzed-about clip from Jimmy Fallon's *Tonight Show* that you missed? Perhaps a vintage performance by Elvis on the Ed Sullivan show? YouTube's got it all. And, because it's owned by Google, the search capabilities are phenomenal.

Yelp—The vocal one. Best for helping tourists, visitors and travelers find your business when they are exploring a new area.

★ HEAVYWEIGHT MARKETING ★

This social review site is the first place consumers go when they want to rave about, or rage against, a business. Versatile platform allows check-ins, reviews, photo sharing and search. Managed to outlast Foursquare, which backslid into irrelevance when the whole "check-in" fad fizzled.

Snapchat—The troubled one. Best for marketers with "shiny-object syndrome" who want to appear cutting-edge by adopting whatever's getting the most hype. The concept is simple: Snapchat allows you to send photos that disappear 10 seconds after being opened. An awesome tool for sexting but for marketing? Not so much. Plus, the app has already been hacked, compromising over 4.5 million user accounts. It was also discovered that the photos don't really "disappear," but still exist on a server—which prompted an investigation and slap on the wrist from the FTC.[1] Oh, and, the CEO is a cocky, arrogant pretty boy—which would be slightly more sufferable if his product was amazing enough to live up to the hype. But it ain't, so his cocky, arrogant prettiness is that much more irritating.

There are way more platforms than you will have time to manage, so choose the ones your audience is already spending time on, rather than the one that's just getting the most hype at the moment.

> *"Social media is not a fad. It is a powerful, global communication revolution that requires new approaches for all businesses."* —Robert Safian, Editor, FastCompany

Everyone says that social media is free, which is not quite true. While there's no cost to set up profiles on the various networks, you still need to spend time building relationships and engaging your audience on whatever platforms you are using. As an entrepreneur, your time is valuable. Therefore it's important to have some sort of strategy so you're not simply getting stuck in the time-sucking vortex of inane posts that can exist on any platform.

Sticking to our theme of engaging your seasonal visitors, you want to post a balanced mixture of promotional posts—new products, contests, sales, or exclusive deals—that will drive traffic to your website, and personalized posts that allow your audience to glimpse the human element that exists behind the brand.

The most frequent complaint I heard while consulting was that, with so many tools, tactics and techniques, business owners were easily overwhelmed by the very prospect of marketing. It's okay to be selective. Utilizing a few proven, effective and familiar platforms such as the three-pronged marketing trident outlined above will help you build and maintain ongoing relationships with your audience during every season. Then, should your visitors return to your area in the future, they will surely make it a point to visit your business again and again.

★ 13 ★

THE TRIPLE BENEFIT OF STRATEGIC PARTNERSHIPS

One of my clients ran an art gallery that held opening receptions every six weeks. The receptions were only two hours long, and the gallery is located a half hour away from a large portion of its customer base. We found that people were not willing to drive an hour in total for a two-hour event, so our challenge was to create a destination event that people would not want to miss.

There was a restaurant next door to the gallery that was experiencing a mid-life slump. Its initial "new restaurant" buzz had tapered off and instead of implementing any active marketing, they were sitting back and hoping that positive word-of-mouth would carry them along. It wasn't.

In a burst of inspiration, the gallery approached the restaurant with the idea to partner up for opening night. We discussed the pros and cons, the expectations and limitations and came up with a plan that made everybody happy.

Here's how it worked. The restaurant promoted the gallery's art show on their event calendar and Facebook page, and displayed postcards on every table throughout the month prior to the event. The gallery mentioned the "After Party" at the restaurant in its press releases, email blasts and on its website. Normally, the restaurant closed at 4pm, but on nights the gallery opened a new exhibit, it stayed open until 10pm. Of course the gallery served

★ HEAVYWEIGHT MARKETING ★

wine and finger foods during the reception to tide people over, then the crowd of gallery employees, artists and guests would migrate across the street throughout the evening. The restaurant served a limited-selection dinner menu, including beer and wine, and booked a band or DJ to provide music for dancing.

This partnership did wonders for the town, which usually rolled up its sidewalks at 5pm and had no night life to speak of. Even though the event took place every six weeks, it was regular enough that people anticipated and looked forward to it. Both the restaurant and the gallery benefited from the cross-promotional efforts, and the patrons and customers had a fun event destination for the evening that was worth driving an hour for. Win-Win-Win. Triple benefit.

When you hear the term "strategic partnerships" you may think of mounds of legal paperwork, contracts and detailed agreements. Depending on the size of your company and complexity of your agreement, some partnerships may indeed require this, but not always. When Taco Bell came up with the idea for Doritos Locos Tacos, the two companies moved forward on a handshake deal. The fact that they share parent company PepsiCo may have helped, but they are still set up as two separate companies operating independently. Only after Taco Bell had perfected the Doritos-flavored shell, tested the product and realized it was going to be a success did Taco Bell make a more formal deal with Doritos.

For small businesses, it may be helpful to think of the strategy I'm referring to more as a business alliance than a legal partnership. In my mind, the best marketing methods are not only effective, but simple as well. Let's examine a few simple partnership strategies that will benefit your business, your partner's business, and your combined customer base.

Reduce Costs Through Shared Expenses

One of the main reasons for partnering is to save money or reduce expenses. A common example of this is seen in the hair salon business. One stylist opens her own shop and rents out the stations to other stylists, colorists and mani-pedi specialists. This keeps the overhead manageable for the owner, offers a simple and low-commitment situation for the renters, and creates a one-stop beauty destination for the customer.

The partners can also double up their marketing muscle by pooling their resources to promote the whole shop as opposed to being responsible for individually marketing themselves (which they may choose to do as well).

Diversify Your Offering

Another good reason for partnering is to diversify your offering. There's a technology company in town that shares its space with an office supply store. In this case, the two complementary businesses can share their expertise and resources with a wider customer base than if they each maintained two separate storefronts. According to the owner of the tech company, a large percentage of walk-ins to the office supply store have become clients of his, and vice-versa.

Diversifying your offering through partnerships is also popular with web designers, marketers, media producers and business consultants. If a client wanted to implement a new e-commerce website with a blog, a social media presence including YouTube video channel, plus email marketing and PR services, it might be too much for any single business-provider to design and implement on its own.

However, by creating a virtual team and tapping your partnership network of web designers, writers and video producers, you could work together to create the deliverables for your client. The caveat here is that the client's budget needs to be proportionate to the cost of the team. If not, you'll need to scale down the deliverables and focus on the most effective solution to meet the client's objective.

Maintain Inventory

There's a local glass company that gets its inventory from Oregon and each shipment requires a minimum order amount. My friend went in to get a large piece of plexiglass, and they were out of stock. Unfortunately, the glass company hasn't been selling enough plexi to justify a full order, so my friend had to wait… and wait…and wait until they had enough demand to restock the supply. This type of anti-customer-centric behavior drives me nuts! This company is practically begging consumers to go spend their money elsewhere.

What if the glass company partnered with several other window companies, frame shops, or hardware stores in Northern California, combined their orders to meet the minimum and guaranteed each store carried stock? Sure, this requires extra work, but it makes more sense to me than sending customers away angry and empty-handed.

Referral and Affiliate Programs

Referral programs are another popular form of partnerships. In this case you are essentially partnering with your clients, turning them into sales generators and rewarding them for new business you get from them. There are tons of massage therapists and body workers in my area and most of them have programs that earn their clients discounts if they refer people who become paying customers.

There's a real estate agent who understands that many people are involved in the process of selling a house. Therefore, every time she sells a property, she gives out flowers, gifts and cash rewards to everyone who was involved in the sale. While her gifting is an "unofficial" rewards program, she has certainly earned a positive reputation in the community and built an eager team of people willing to lend a helping hand when she needs it. Perhaps that is one of the reasons she has maintained consistent sales even in a sluggish market.

Anyone who does internet marketing is familiar with affiliate programs. This is when you help sell someone else's product and get a cut of the sales. This is a popular concept with authors and content producers who build a network of people to help them sell e-books and digital products that can be delivered quickly and easily over the internet. Since the overhead for digital content distribution is negligible, some affiliates make up to 50% of the product's cost with every sale. Affiliate programs are even used by web hosting companies, email marketing platforms and stock photography websites.

When I was building websites, I joined an affiliate program offered by HostMonster that paid me $65 every time I purchased a hosting plan for a new client's site. They say you can't buy loyalty, but I beg to differ: guess which hosting company was my go-to choice for every website I built? Of course, it helped that I was totally happy with their service and used them to host several of my own websites. I wouldn't recommend garbage no matter how much kickback I was offered.

Another form of affiliate program is the one used by multilevel companies such as Amway, Orenda, NuSkin and many others. Company representatives enlist people to become distributors of their products, who then get discounts and commissions when they make sales. In most cases, these distributors don't just sell products, they're also expected to enlist other distributors, and so on and so on. Eventually the network grows like a multilevel pyramid with cash trickling down from the top to each successive level. This business structure has a pretty unsavory reputation that causes most people to run the opposite direction at high speeds. However, I've known several multilevel marketers who have been very successful with it, so for the right type of person, it can be a desirable and profitable business option.

As you can see, strategic business partnerships can exist in many forms: between you and your colleagues, your customers, your suppliers, even your competition. People love to save money and they love to make money. Anytime you can help fellow entrepreneurs, clients, or even your competitors do this, they will be happy to spread positive word-of-mouth on your behalf, effectively becoming your marketing ally. And, in most cases, the partnership's sum is greater than its individual parts. So, get creative and think about who you can partner with in order to deliver savings, profits and value to everyone involved.

★ 14 ★

IN BUSINESS, COMMUNICATING IS CARING

It's not easy for me to find a good hair stylist. While most guys aren't too picky about who cuts their hair, I demand a super-hip, razor-shag, rock star cut. That's just the way I roll. Now, in a big city, I could walk into any salon and find a stylist who gives good rock star, but I'm in a small town where salons and mad hipster steelo are mutually exclusive.

When my initial stylist moved away from the area, I was on the hunt for a replacement. Eventually, I did manage to find a stylist who knew her way around a razor and, while her cuts were inconsistent, they were more than acceptable.

Unfortunately, her salon was three towns away from mine about 35 miles due north. Add to the equation her three-day work week and it started to get a bit difficult to make my scheduled appointments. In fact, over a period of twelve months, I probably missed three appointments. What really chaps my hide is that in the two years I patronized her, she never called me. Zero. Zed. Nada.

Not once did she call with a reminder about an upcoming appointment, which is not salon law by any means but is typically de rigueur in any appointment-based business. She never called a half-hour past our scheduled time to say, "Hey, Bucko, you're late. Time is money!" Never did she call the following day to inform me that I'm a flaky, inconsiderate fool who doesn't respect her time, before attempting to reschedule our aborted appointment.

★ HEAVYWEIGHT MARKETING ★

In fact, every time I made a new appointment, she asked me for my phone number. After two years, you would think that she had migrated it to a database somewhere. And why did she bother asking for my number if she never planned on using it?

So, how did this make me feel as a customer? Unimportant.

Her lack of communication was a clear indication that my business was not important to her, which was a real drag considering the unruly mop that took up residence on my melon between cuts. I wrestled with whether I should have kept putting up with the same ol' same ol' or cut my losses, tried someone new and risked a run-of-the-mill dude-cut from a recent graduate of Scissors-R-Us.

Allow me to share a tale from the other end of the spectrum:

My partner and I are obsessed with vintage typewriters and we scour antique stores every chance we get. We found a great little shop in nearby Dunsmuir, CA, called Lennan's Junktion that had a sweet 70s model, which we promptly bought. We asked the proprietor if he ever got older models in, and he said they occasionally did. He promised us that if we gave him a cell phone number he would text us a photo of any old models that arrived. Now, my better half is a consignment store junkie, so she's heard that pitch a few times before. Problem is, after doling out her digits, she never hears a peep.

This time was different: the shop owner texted a shot of a lovely vintage beauty within a month. We didn't end up buying that one, so he sent a pic of a different model a few weeks later. In fact, he reached out to us three times with three different typewriters and it brought us into his store every time until we found another great model to buy. Ever since, we have made this store a must-visit destination every time we've been in the area, and usually end up making some type of purchase.

Round 1: Build Marketing Muscle

A Royal vintage lovely from my antique typewriter collection

This is a business owner who gets it. His communication has indicated that he listens to the needs of his customers, he cares about providing value, and he delivers on his promise. My partner and I are looking to buy a house in the near future, and you better believe when it comes time to decorate it with unique conversation pieces, we'll be paying Lennan's Junktion a visit or three.

As for my incommunicado hair stylist, I gave her the boot. I found another salon that is even further away than she was, but it's worth the drive because I get a great haircut, and they have a text-message system in place. It only took one appointment for the new salon to get me in the database and start sending me confirmation and reminder texts well before my scheduled appointment. And, because I've worked with the owner's husband, they even give me a Friends and Family discount. Now that's communication—and caring.

★ HEAVYWEIGHT MARKETING ★

Communication is not simply a vehicle for sharing ideas, thoughts and information; it's an expression of gratitude, of solidarity, and a cornerstone of sound relationships. Whether communicating with customers, vendors, employees, prospects, browsers, competitors, journalists, critics or complainers, it's important to reach out with honesty, integrity and authenticity.

And when you reach out, make sure you're not spewing mindless marketing twaddle with purely self-serving intentions. Instead, make your communiqué relevant to your audience and try to provide at least an inkling of value. Your recipients will feel acknowledged and appreciated, and little things like this will go a long way towards establishing enduring relationships, building a reputable brand and setting yourself apart in the world of business.

★ 15 ★

WHY FEAR-BASED MARKETING STRATEGIES DON'T WORK

About a year into my consulting business, I started hitting a nice stride of consistent incoming business. I chalked it up to a combination of active PR, event marketing, direct contact and follow-up, social media marketing and word-of-mouth referrals. I no longer had to constantly scramble to go out and find new clients; instead, they started finding me. It was a thrill to receive phone calls from numbers I didn't recognize. Unlike in previous years when those usually turned out to be telemarketers or debt collectors, these were hot, new prospects on the line.

As I met with more and more prospects, submitted more proposals, and worked with more clients, I started noticing a common and pervasive emotion among business owners: fear.

In the name of honesty, I suppose some of it belonged to me as well. After all, having to go out and sell your services has a tendency to activate that little voice that tries to protect you from rejection and failure. But, while my fear was tempered by excitement and enthusiasm, many prospects were burdened by the fear of an uncertain business climate.

They knew they needed to do SOMETHING in order to meet their business objectives (most of which shared the common theme of getting more clients/sales/profits), but they were afraid to spend the money to make it happen. So, instead of making an uncomfortable investment in marketing initiatives that would

★ **HEAVYWEIGHT MARKETING** ★

move them toward their objectives, they kept on doing what they had been doing: a whole lot of nothing.

> "The best time to plant a tree was 20 years ago. The second best time is right now." —Chinese Proverb

In some cases, several of them were actually making some effort, but it was either too little or too inconsistent to achieve the desired results…which is about the same as doing nothing.

Please understand that my intention is not to mock cautious business owners, nor to complain that they weren't willing to spend money on my services to help them achieve their objectives. After all, financial fear is a universal feeling that many of us have been experiencing throughout the dismal economic climate and slow recovery of the past several years. While I do understand this, I also understand that in order to be effective, marketing needs to be a consistent endeavor that is worked into the structure of the company, rather than an optional, dreaded expense that is doled out on an as-needed basis—which is usually too little, too late.

Entrepreneurs are gamblers. We know at the outset that starting a business is a calculated risk. Therefore, I would like to encourage you, Dear Readers, to work through your fear and try to make bold choices where your business is concerned. Just because those black and red chips are starting to look pretty thin on that green felt table does not mean it's time to freeze up and paralyze your marketing efforts. It means that it's time to improve your strategy.

> "If you're not a risk taker, you should get the hell out of business." —Ray Kroc, Founder, McDonald's

Round 1: Build Marketing Muscle

Making bold choices is not the same as making stupid choices. It doesn't mean throwing your money away because you hear a slick sales pitch. It means knowing the difference between a (non-fixed) expense and an investment, and having the courage to make the occasional difficult choice between them in order to improve the condition of your business.

Where marketing is concerned, more than ever before, you must be absolutely clear on what your company stands for, which benefits are most meaningful to your customers, and how to articulate that in your marketing message. You need to determine exactly what your marketing objectives are, who your ideal audience is, where they are and how you can best reach them.

The unfortunate thing was that many of the prospects I was meeting with were NOT clear on the imperative elements mentioned above. They knew they needed help defining and articulating these things (which was the service that I was offering them), they knew their efforts were not achieving their desired results, yet they often still opted for the Fear-Based Marketing Strategy of inaction. Taking a "let's wait until things improve" approach is a passive strategy that will ultimately weaken the foundation of the business you have worked so hard to build. Plus, it simply prompts the question, "when are things REALLY going to improve?"

And, once things finally do improve is no time to be playing catch-up on your marketing strategy. That's the time to be laser-focused on innovating your offering, improving your customer service and generally knocking the socks off your customers who are finally loosening their grip on their wallets. You may have heard the saying, "If you always do what you've always done, you'll always get what you've always gotten." Therefore, if you want the results to be different, the actions need to be different.

★ HEAVYWEIGHT MARKETING ★

There's no better time than right now to work through the fear, to improve your strategy, to make bold, calculated decisions about what truly is the most effective way to grow your business. Then, once you've made those decisions, look fear in the eye and laugh as you take audacious action. Your actions may turn out to be right and they may end up being wrong, but you'll never know until you try.

Round 1: Build Marketing Muscle

★ 16 ★

MARKETING YOUR BUSINESS IS LIKE JOINING A GYM

I was a chubby kid. In fact, all the way into my early teens, I was overweight. Eventually I slimmed down, but those early years instilled me with an awareness of health and diet that has stuck with me throughout my life. In the 80s, I bought my first gym membership and I loved it. Over the years, I've belonged to several gyms and, while I've been more diligent some years than I have others, I've always enjoyed the physical and mental benefits of a consistent fitness routine.

Recently, a friend of mine joined the gym I belong to and I was super excited to encourage him on his awesome journey to improved health. I probably sounded like an irritating know-it-all as I grilled him about his goals and explained which routines, weights and machines he should try, but I truly wanted to inspire him with knowledge and experience that I've gleaned over the years. My passion for working out is equivalent to my enthusiasm for the world of marketing. So, as I was chatting my friend's ear off about the best ways to achieve his workout goals, I started to notice similarities between the advice I was sharing with him, and the advice I've shared with my marketing clients.

Four Correlations Between Marketing and Working Out

It Pays to Have a Plan

You can always spot the newbies at the gym: they're the ones doing the No-Plan Shuffle. They ping-pong from machine to machine without rhyme or reason hoping they don't look too out of place. Their reps lack form, their sets are inconsistent and it seems they're making up their routine as they go. After an indeterminate amount of time—usually when they run out of things to do—they pack it in and head on home.

Business owners do the No-Plan Shuffle with their marketing. They ping-pong between tools and tactics without clearly defining their objectives. They do just enough to feel like they're covering the bases, yet they neglect to adequately track outcomes or measure results. It's no surprise that this is ineffective. It's not that they are planning to fail, it's just that they are failing to plan.

Determining your objectives, knowing your goals, understanding your audience, planning your strategy and choosing the appropriate messaging and tools of delivery will require extra thought and effort up front, but will pay off in the long run. Do you create detailed marketing plans for your business, or do you make them up as you go?

It's Better With a Buddy

Luckily, my girlfriend enjoys working out as much as I do, so we keep each other inspired and motivated. We have standing workout dates three times a week, to which we hold each other accountable. If I know she's coming to pick me up for a workout, it's a lot harder to slack off than if I were simply planning on heading to the gym myself. During the workout, the presence of a buddy drives you to push a bit harder and longer than if you were there on your own. It's also fun to have a workout buddy so you can compare notes on technique and form, share new routines, and encourage each other as you progress.

While I don't have a lot of buddies who are as interested in marketing as I am, I do have a couple, which keeps me from operating in a vacuum. Getting together with peers, fellow entrepreneurs and other marketers allows business owners to share ideas and experiences, commiserate, learn about new tools and technologies, troubleshoot problems and discuss industry news. This pushes action and innovation, and may even inspire a little healthy competition, which ensures that everyone's business continues to evolve.

It's Frustrating Not to See Results

It takes time to lose weight and it takes time to build muscle. When people join a gym, they're hoping to see results. Immediate results, preferably. When they don't see results, they get frustrated and lose their momentum. They start to lose faith in the idea of getting in shape, and eventually they quit. Before long, they're back on the couch in their pajamas binge-watching *Downton Abbey* and licking Cheetos dust from their fingers.

The same thing happens to those business owners doing the No-Plan Shuffle. They try a few marketing methods hoping for a quick fix, an immediate boost in customers, or a spike in revenue. When they don't see the results they hoped for (which were not clearly defined to begin with), they get frustrated and adopt a negative opinion about marketing. They say things like, "Marketing doesn't work," or "We don't need to advertise."

It is frustrating not to see results, but business owners need to approach marketing as a marathon rather than a sprint. Define short-term and long-term goals and acknowledge that achieving them will take time. Track response to your efforts, fine-tune your regimen as needed, and celebrate the victories along the way. Oh, and stay away from the Cheetos.

Consistency Is Key

The only way to achieve those elusive results is through consistency. If you pop into the gym at random intervals, work out only when you feel like it, or slack off until just before swimsuit

★ HEAVYWEIGHT MARKETING ★

weather hits, you will have a hard time reaching your goals. Only through regular, consistent, ongoing dedication will your efforts pay off. When you see the physique you've been striving for start to emerge over time, it's exciting! It motivates you to stay the course, and helps you to understand that optimal fitness is not a New Year's resolution, but rather a lifetime commitment.

Marketing is also a commitment to be implemented throughout the life of your business. Give your chosen tools and tactics enough time to work, then determine whether or not they are successful and focus your efforts on the ones that are. That could mean placing regular ads, promoting frequent sales and events, keeping your website fresh, actively engaging your social media following, and keeping up with new consumer trends or technologies that you may wish to try. Whether building a buff brand or a buff bod, consistency will get you there.

Time will tell if my friend sticks with his new workout routine. However, as long as he develops a plan, stays consistent, works through his frustrating plateaus, and connects with others who share his passions, he will do just fine. And the same goes for business owners hoping to achieve success with their marketing.

★ 17 ★

CASE STUDY: BUILDING MAXIMUM BUZZ

Speaking to an engaged crowd at a Women In Business meeting

A local chapter of the Women In Business Network invited me in to deliver a speaking presentation at one of their monthly meetings. Since I'm a marketer who wants to lead by example, I set out to build maximum buzz for the event by launching an integrated, multi-media marketing juggernaut.

I knew the Women In Business Network featured guest speakers at their monthly meetings, so I contacted them in early October with a speaking proposal. They accepted my proposal and scheduled me to speak at their December meeting, which gave me over two months to promote the event. My contact told me that the monthly meetings usually draw between 15 and 20 members. My goal was to double that number and aim for 40 attendees. This may not seem like a huge number, but any chance you get to speak directly with a roomful of highly-qualified prospects who all have a direct need for your offering is a golden opportunity.

When all was said and done, the event drew a full-capacity crowd, received no less than eight mentions in the press, earned me two immediate new clients, several hot prospects, and a dozen new names on the mailing list. Not to mention that it spread brand awareness to a whole new section of our business community. The best part is, I didn't spend a dime on advertising, and only had to make a small investment of time and effort.

In order to inspire you with ideas of how you can build maximum marketing buzz for your own business events, I decided to detail the steps I used to market and promote this successful event. Of course, the outlets and tools you employ may be different than the ones listed below, but my account should at least offer plenty of ideas and motivation for finding similar outlets and promotional opportunities in your area.

Before the Event

Step 1: Utilize the Power of Video
My first marketing step was to round up my WIB contacts and shoot a promotional video of us talking about the event. While we were creating the video, we also took a couple promotional stills (photographs) to submit along with all the PR materials.

I posted the promo video in the following places:

- My company website
- The Women In Business website
- My personal Facebook page

- The WIB Facebook page
- A Facebook event page I created to promote the event

Step 2: Write Press Release

In order to get the attention of the press, I had to write a compelling "story" about the event that would pique the interest of the public. In this case, since the meeting was open to members and non-members of Women In Business, I chose an informational angle in an effort to spark interest among the business community.

In order to encourage local business owners to attend, I mentioned the particulars of the meeting, gave a brief summary of how my presentation would benefit attendees, and included a boilerplate blurb about Women In Business. I created two versions of the press release: a long version for newspapers and websites, and a short version for calendar-style listings and email promotions. Of course, I included the promotional photo with every submission.

Step 3: Submit, Submit, Submit

I made a list of the local media outlets I could hit with the promotion. My list included the following:

- *Mt. Shasta Herald* newspaper
- *Mt. Shasta Herald* calendar of events
- *Mt. Shasta Magazine* email list—a local, subscription-based community email list
- Mt. Shasta Connect—a local, online community calendar
- JEDI email list—Jefferson Economic Development Institute helped promote the event
- My BAM! mailing list—included in my monthly email newsletter
- Plus, the BAM! and WIB websites and Facebook pages mentioned earlier.

★ **HEAVYWEIGHT MARKETING** ★

All of the above outlets ran the promotion, and in the case of the *Mt. Shasta Herald* (weekly) newspaper, they mentioned it three weeks in a row leading up to the event, in both the Area News section and the Calendar of Events section. Plus, they ran a full follow-up article online and in print after the event.

As the event drew nearer and the marketing machine was in motion, I also used word-of-mouth and Twitter to promote the event. As for Twitter, since my target audience was local, it most likely did not directly affect the attendance like the other platforms did. However, it earned me some new #WomenInBusiness followers and helped promote my community activity and thought leadership.

Step 4: Practice Makes…Pretty Darn Good
All the buzz in the world is worthless if I get up in front of a crowd and bomb. Therefore, once I had the final edit of my speech, I ran through it continually. On the bus, on the street, in my living room, in the shower, whenever I had an extra 20 minutes, I was working the speech.

I even went to the venue two days before the event and videotaped myself giving a speech to the empty room. This helped a couple things: it got me comfortable with the room, and it allowed me to watch and see what last-minute improvements or changes I needed to make. Some people do pretty well winging their speeches, but I prefer the confidence instilled by over-preparedness. There's just too many things bouncing around in your brain when you're staring at a roomful of faces to expect you'll be able to form cohesive thoughts on the fly.

During the Event

The multi-channel marketing strategy worked! We drew a full-house, standing-room-only crowd of close to fifty female business leaders…and three men. Actually, men are welcome to attend meetings, but cannot become WIB members. This is "Women" In Business after all. Getting people to the event is only half the battle. The other half is making sure you deliver on your promise once they are there.

Step 5: Know Your Objectives
Speaking engagements are excellent marketing platforms because they allow you to reach a large segment of your target audience at once. However, it must be clear (to you, the organizers, and everyone in the room) that your primary goal is to provide valuable, applicable information or education to your audience. As long as that comes first, then your secondary goal can be to rustle up some new clients. Therefore, you need to have a lead-capture system in place to grow your list of contacts and hot prospects.

I placed a BAM! Mailing List Signup Sheet at the front desk, plus business cards and postcards for people to take. I also placed a small box for people to leave their business cards in if they didn't want to take the time to fill out the mailing list.

Step 6: Be Awesome!
As I mingled with attendees before my presentation, I heard several comments like, "whoever promoted this did a great job!" Other people said they "heard about this event all over the place," and I even got some light-hearted teasing from a business owner who said, "you better live up to the hype!"

Thanks to good ol' Murphy's Law, the P.A. system I lined up had a faulty mic, so I had to project in full theatre mode to keep those in the back engaged. Despite the busted mic, the speech went great, the audience was rapt, and I made sure to involve them, humor them and educate them with a fun, fresh and dynamic performance.

★ HEAVYWEIGHT MARKETING ★

After the presentation, there was positive feedback, rave reviews, great press, an increased mailing list, several hot prospects, two immediate new clients, and a new business partner with whom I worked during the following year—indicating that things went pretty awesome indeed.

Step 7: Capture Your Media

In the heat of the moment, it's easy to forget about capturing the event with various forms of media, but for promotional purposes, it's essential to do so. Since you are going to be too busy and otherwise preoccupied to think about producing media, it's best to hire a media assistant or producer to do so. This can be someone from inside your organization or it can be a professional person or team you bring in for each event. The latter option could get quite spendy, so make sure you measure your financial risk/reward ratio before hiring Michael Bay to film your PowerPoint presentation.

My philosophy is, "Shoot first, ask questions later." That means you record your EVERY event with either audio, photography, video, or all of the above, then figure out how you're going to use the content later. Some options could be podcasts, training programs, photos and videos for your website, social media channels, and follow-up press releases and other promotional vehicles.

Step 8: Work the Room

I like to network and mingle before the event, so I can connect with people who will make up the audience. It's always nice to have familiar, friendly faces out in the crowd and, if you can work the names, stories or comments of people you know into your speech, it adds a personal touch. It's also essential to mingle after the event, because that's when the hot prospects emerge. Be sure you're ready to engage them, determine their needs and desires, and schedule an appropriate time to follow up with them.

After the Event

The work is not over just because your event is. Now is the time to maximize the longevity of your message, act on your new contacts and implement your new media.

Step 9: Follow Up

If members of the press were there, contact them to express gratitude for their presence, and offer to answer any questions or clarify any points. If the press wasn't there, write and submit a follow-up press release, including images from your event (see Step 7). If you spoke with any new prospects, follow up to see how you can help them with their needs (i.e., move them into the sales cycle). As for your new mailing list contacts, start sending them valuable content, communications, and occasional special offers or sales messages on a regular basis with your email marketing program of choice.

Step 10: Keep Your Message Alive on the Web

I immediately posted a photo of the crowd on Facebook and Twitter and got tons of engagement from people who commented, offered feedback and testimonials, and tagged themselves and their friends. I posted a four-minute "highlight" video on Facebook, the BAM! website and YouTube channel, and submitted a written recap of my speech to the Women In Business website.

Be sure that you or someone from your company is monitoring and replying to the feedback, comments, mentions and shares so you can keep your audience engagement alive for as long as possible. Don't force it. Once the energy surrounding your event fades, let it die naturally and move your focus to whatever is next.

★ HEAVYWEIGHT MARKETING ★

Whew! Okay, maybe it does take more than the "small" investment of time and effort that I mentioned earlier. But the sad truth is, too many business owners simply send out a press release announcing their event and call it a day. Then they wonder why their promotions aren't successful. It takes more effort than that to build a maximum marketing buzz for your small business, but it IS very possible to achieve.

A couple weeks after my WIB presentation, I received a comment confirming that all my efforts had not been in vain. It came from my mom, no less, who said, "Nikolas, I'm getting sick and tired of seeing you in the paper every week." To which I replied, "Maximum marketing mission accomplished!"

ROUND 2

TACKLE YOUR TOOLS

"Marketing is too important to be left to the marketing department."
—David Packard

★ 18 ★

SEVENTY-SIX TACTICS AND TOOLS TO PROMOTE YOUR BUSINESS

After working with enough business owners, it becomes clear that many are dealing with the same marketing problems, and have similar complaints. At one point, I started to hear several clients making the bold proclamation that "Newspaper advertising doesn't work for us." These business owners may have made legitimate efforts and discovered that their ideal audience truly can't be reached via that medium. However, there could also have been many other factors at play that hampered the effectiveness of their advertisements.

Perhaps their messages simply weren't compelling enough. Maybe their ads lacked a clear call to action. They may not have had any tracking system in place to gauge how the ad was performing. Or, it's possible that they just weren't consistent enough with their print buys. In this case, the particulars don't really matter. If a business owner has made up her mind about something not working, it's far more prudent to explore other options rather than trying to sway her opinion.

Finding the right marketing mix requires testing different vehicles to determine which ones work and which ones don't. This helps you ascertain where you should be investing time and money. You may have a poor experience with more than one medium, but that shouldn't sour you on the overall marketing process.

And it is a process! If you are inconsistently dabbling with various messages sprinkled through various media, the chances

★ HEAVYWEIGHT MARKETING ★

of your efforts being successful are pretty slim. However, if you are sending a strong, consistent message to a clearly defined audience using a strategic mix of marketing vehicles, your efforts WILL yield results.

Lest you find yourself wondering what options are available, I have compiled a list that will get you started in the right direction. The objective is to pick and choose the ones that feel feasible and relevant to your business, and try them out.

There is a common dictum in the marketing world known as the "Advertising Rule of Seven," which states that it can take up to seven impressions for your prospects to even notice your marketing. Actually, research has shown that the number ranges from five to twelve, but seven is a good rule of thumb. So employ your marketing tools for at least six months to a year before declaring them a success or a failure.

Seventy-Six Marketing Tactics and Tools

Essentials:
1. Company Logo
2. Signage
3. Business Card
4. Letterhead
5. Envelopes
6. Website
7. Email Signatures
8. On-Hold Messages
9. Word of Mouth

Traditional Marketing:
10. Postcards
11. Brochures
12. Direct Mail
13. Cold/Warm Calling

Round 2 - Tackle Your Tools

14. Newsletters
15. Coupon Books
16. Yellow Pages Ads
17. Local Magazine Ads
18. Radio Ads
19. Posters
20. Sales Letters
21. Promotional Items

New Media Marketing:
22. Google Maps
23. Google AdWords
24. Google+
25. Facebook Ads
26. Facebook Pages
27. Twitter
28. Promoted Tweets
29. LinkedIn
30. YouTube Channel
31. YouTube Ads
32. Pinterest
33. Instagram
34. Snapchat
35. Vine
36. Tumblr
37. SEO (Search Engine Optimization)
38. Mobile Advertising
39. Text Marketing
40. QR Codes
41. Online Directories
42. Online Review Sites

Content Marketing:
43. E-newsletter
44. Email Blasts

★ HEAVYWEIGHT MARKETING ★

45. Blog
46. Podcasts
47. Articles
48. eBooks
49. Books
50. Videos
51. Tip Sheets
52. Sales Sheets/Info Sheets
53. Portfolio
54. Bio/Resume

Event Marketing:
55. Speaking Engagements
56. Workshops
57. Open Houses
58. Trade Shows
59. Business Expos
60. Educational Seminars
61. Daily Deals
62. Flash Sales
63. Pop-Up Locations
64. Contests

Partnership Marketing:
65. Networking Groups
66. Business Associations
67. Chambers of Commerce
68. Referral Programs
69. Strategic Alliances
70. Sponsorships

Public Relations:
71. Media Pitches (Bloggers, Television, Radio)
72. Press Releases
73. Thank You Gifts/Cards

Round 2 - Tackle Your Tools

74. Customer Appreciation
75. Loyalty Programs
76. Free Consultations

Seeing all of these marketing options can be overwhelming, but remember that you're not trying to incorporate all of them. Instead, pick a quantity that feels right and start there. Some of these are essential, some are recommended, and others are optional. Many are free, some require a minor investment, and others require a large, dedicated budget. In addition to the first group of "Essentials," I suggest testing 3-6 other tactics on the low side, 8-10 on the high side, and 12 or more if you've got the resources.

Once you choose your tools and plan your strategy, be sure to keep track of expenses and measure results so you can better determine your ROI. Then, if you find that some are not working for you, as my clients did with their newspaper ads, try something else. After several months of consistent advertising, you will have a good idea of which vehicles are most effective for your business. Once you have determined that, continue to use what works and drop the rest.

★ 19 ★

DISSECTING THE FORMULA FOR EFFECTIVE PRINT ADS

Despite the rapid growth and popularity of internet marketing techniques, print advertising is still a popular and effective medium for many small businesses. Compared to some marketing tools, which only require an investment of time and effort, print advertising can be quite expensive, so you need to make sure your have a dedicated marketing budget. The multitude of available options includes newspapers, weekly periodicals, local magazines, directories, catalogs, and various other forms of consumer-targeted printed matter.

When I travel, one of my hobbies is collecting a variety of regional print media from wherever I happen to be. I enjoy perusing these rags to investigate the local business sector, and to see what small business owners are doing right—and wrong—when it comes to marketing their companies with printed advertisements.

I often visit Ashland, Oregon, which is home of the world-famous Shakespeare Theater Festival. During one visit, I collected several local rags and mags with the intention of crafting a case study on the good, the bad, and the ugly ways companies were utilizing print ads. Glancing through these papers, it seems that most business owners think a quarter-page print ad is a chance to finally write that novel they've been pondering since college!

★ HEAVYWEIGHT MARKETING ★

In paper after paper, tiny ads are jam-packed with more information than the reader could possibly digest in the split second their eye scans the page. From multiple bullet-point product lists to overly-detailed service descriptions, these advertisers presume the only way to make an impression is to over-inform. One restaurant printed their ENTIRE MENU in 6pt. type! Many business owners have yet to realize that, when it comes to print advertisements, especially small ones, less truly is more.

Below, we take a look at a few examples, both good and bad, and dissect the formula for an effective print ad.

Bad Apples

Round 2 - Tackle Your Tools

The Problem: Too Many Elements

You need some pretty strong brain muscles to lift all the elements packed into this fitness center advertisement. With its Fall Special promotion, oddly-cropped photo of an unidentified muscle man, mini mission statement, checklist of features, testimonial, employee quote, plus logo and contact info, there are way too many messages competing for attention. In cases like this, the reader ends up taking nothing from the ad.

The Solution: Focus on One Main Message

Let the ad be about the Fall Fitness Special. Keep the info related to the special, and let that take up most of the room. Keep the descriptive text that's in the green oval (just the text, ditch that amateur oval graphic), because it speaks to the company's point of difference. Create a strong call to action to drive readers into the facility to sign up, and play up the expiration date in order to create urgency. Obviously, keep the contact info.

Move everything else to the website. If the reader is not ready to come into the facility to sign up, they will visit the website, where they can discover the company features, quotes, testimonials, and quite possibly the identity of that mysterious muscle man.

• •

★ **HEAVYWEIGHT MARKETING** ★

The Problem: Not Enough Info

While the fitness ad suffered from too much information, this ad for Munchies has the opposite problem. It doesn't answer the most important question at the forefront of every consumer's mind, "What's in it for me?" Readers need to know why they should care, how they're going to benefit, and what's unique about your company's offering.

This ad answers none of those questions, and assumes that people will be interested in meeting at Munchies for the sole reason that they presumably serve food. Well, so do a million other restaurants, and at least the rest of them have the decency to tell us what type of food they specialize in. Heck, this ad doesn't even bother to include a city in their address, nor do they list a website.

The Solution: Give Us a Reason to Meet You at Munchies

One of the more effective restaurant ads I saw touted themselves as "Ashland's meat-centric restaurant." Another one specialized in "Casual, contemporary Italian cuisine." Create a unique tagline that lets people know what your specialty is, and why they should try your offering over everybody else's. Also, include your city in all of your marketing materials because you never know where they may end up. And, it's 2015 for goodness' sake, get a freakin' website!

Good Eggs

Peppered amongst the glut of overly-informative, poorly-designed ads, I did manage to find some that were eye-catching, compelling and effective. The following are a couple examples:

Agency-Quality Eye Care

This ad has a quintessential "agency" feel to it. I was an Art Director in Minneapolis for many years, and this was the type of work being created by my colleagues and me. Snappy headline, related image, concise body copy, logo, contact info and lots of white space. Truthfully, that's all you need.

Of course, clients always wanted less white space and bigger logos, but the eye appreciates a little breathing room. As for logos, they should be used like a signature on a work of art, not a main focal point.

· ·

★ **HEAVYWEIGHT MARKETING** ★

Fun, Flirty Fashion

Here's another good one that manages to include all the right elements. The main focal point is an attractive, fun lifestyle photo that speaks to their target audience, with a vivid color scheme (when it's not printed in black and white) that begs to be noticed.

I also like the three-adjective headline. When consulting with clients in an effort to help them define their brand, I often have them choose three adjectives that describe their company. This results in three power-words they can use in various places throughout their marketing. In this case, Deja Vu has chosen to use their three adjectives as a headline, followed up with a catchy tagline. They tout their "Best Of" credentials, include their logo, contact and Facebook address, and that's it. Nothing else needed. Well played Deja Vu, well played.

Sure, it's tempting to cram everything you can into your ad in a desperate, one-shot attempt to capture the attention of your audience. But, that causes the opposite of your desired effect when it short-circuits the viewer's brain with TMI.

As you can see from this case study, the secret to effective advertising is to achieve the following simple objectives:

1) Catch their attention
2) Describe your offering
3) Pique their interest
4) Drive them to action

Anything else is simply extraneous information that will muddle your main message and create more obstacles on the road towards gaining a customer.

★ 20 ★

EMAIL MARKETING: STILL NOT DEAD

One of the most potent and cost-effective marketing tools available for small business is email marketing. I'm not talking about the random, plain-text emails you shoot out from your Yahoo! account two days before your upcoming sale (you know who you are—stop it!). I'm talking about well-designed, branded, trackable, HTML email blasts such as newsletters, announcements, invites and coupons that provide information, value and engagement to your audience. Sure, lots of business owners are using email. I know because I'm on tons of email lists. But some of the promotions I get from local businesses are so dreadfully lackluster, I wonder why they bother at all. There's a difference between using something and using it well.

As with any marketing tool, there are some best practice tips, rules and techniques to keep in mind, which will ensure greater success with your email campaigns.

Choose Your Platform

Constant Contact

One of the front-runners in the email marketing industry is Constant Contact. I've had accounts with them off and on over the years and have been pleased with almost everything about my experience. Their pricing plans start at $15 per month, go up to $150, and are based on the number of contacts you have and how much storage capacity you need. They offer great customer support and send out informative monthly e-newsletters that I always looked forward to reading.

★ HEAVYWEIGHT MARKETING ★

With over 400 templates to choose from, it's pretty easy to find ones that will represent your brand. Plus, the templates are easily customizable, so you can start with one you like, and turn it into one you love. Social media integration was Constant Contact's main weakness for some time, but with their acquisition of NutshellMail, they proved their desire to step their game up in that department. They continue to tweak, upgrade and improve, which shows a dedication to staying in the game.

My biggest complaint with Constant Contact is that their signup boxes bite the big one. Which is kind of a big problem considering that their entire company is built on the concept of capturing leads. Their little "Join Our Mailing List" graphics haven't been updated for decades, making them very outdated visually. Many of the signup boxes are not dynamic enough to capture information right on the web page, forcing subscribers off your site to enter their information on a different web page.

Any email marketer knows that when someone is ready to give up their contact info, you gotta make it as easy and seamless as possible. There's an option to build your own signup box, which leads you through several steps before providing a snippet of code that you drop into your website page or sidebar widget. I've tried this several times and every time the code has been faulty, forcing me to abandon it. That's the type of email fail that has sent me scurrying to Mail Chimp. Constant Contact does offer a generous free trial period, so I recommend testing it out to see if it's right for you.

Mail Chimp
People love Mail Chimp because it offers a free option that allows up to 2,000 contacts. They do offer paid versions as well that extend the available features, which are pretty robust. Mail Chimp is definitely a more modern product, especially since their recent redesign that completely overhauled the interface,

optimizing its ease-of-use on all platforms. That they did this in response to how prevalent mobile phones and tablets were becoming proves their dedication to relevance.

The current name of the game for Mail Chimp is simplicity. They have stripped the user interface down to its bare essentials yet still offer hearty features like detailed list segmentation, tracking analytics, social media integration, and easy scheduling. Mail Chimp doesn't offer as many pre-designed templates as Constant Contact, and those available are pretty basic, but very customizable. There are also options for advanced users to code their own templates or upload their own designs.

As for their signup boxes, they also allow you to code your own HTML to create your lead capture system, and unlike my experience with Constant Contact, Mail Chimp's code actually works! They also offer plugins for websites and mobile signup apps for capturing leads on the go. I love Mail Chimp, and though I may stray, I always come back for their user-friendly, feature-rich platform that just keeps getting better.

AWeber
Another player that is very popular with content marketers is AWeber. They excel at automated communication, but prefer to keep it simple with text emails and templates with minimal graphics. The templates they do offer are pretty lame and hardly customizable. However, they do have the best signup forms! Oh, the irony. Overall, I find the AWeber platform to be a confusing mess that is neither intuitive nor design-savvy. I do still have an account with them, and I pay $29 a month ($19 if you have less than 500 subscribers) just so I can use their superior signup forms on my website. Then I manually add every new subscriber into my Mail Chimp account, and send my emails out through there. Not a super-efficient way to do it, but it allows me to utilize the best features of both platforms.

★ **HEAVYWEIGHT MARKETING** ★

There are other names in the email game such as Emma, iContact, Exact Target and Jango Mail. I haven't used any of these, so I can't vouch for them, but I do suggest that you examine your options before making a decision on which platform is right for your business.

Ask Before You Add

Once you've chosen your application, it's time to start building your list. The most important thing to remember is that ALL email marketing must be permission-based. You need to ask your prospects and customers if you can put them on your mailing list before you just start mining email addresses from your collection of business cards. Remember, marketing is about building relationships. If your customers think you are taking advantage of them by being sneaky, dishonest or careless with their contact information, they will revoke their trust in you and your business.

Besides, all of the platforms listed above are very serious about their anti-spam policies. If you get too many spam reports, it could result in your provider closing your account. So don't forget to ask before you add.

What's In It for Them?

When asking people to join your mailing list, you've got to let them know how it will benefit them. If you treat your email marketing simply as a selling tool, you're not going to win many fans. Instead, think of your email communications as opportunities to build relationships, engage your audience, educate them, entertain them and inform them. This is where your strategy comes into play. You need to decide what you want your audience to take away from your communications.

Round 2 - Tackle Your Tools

Questions to determine your strategy:

- What is our objective with email marketing?
- What kind of content are we going to produce?
- How does this reinforce our brand promise?
- How often will we send our communications?
- What can we do to provide value to our audience?
- How can we make it fun so our audience looks forward to our communications?

Once you've defined your strategy, you can craft your pitch to make it sound like joining your mailing list is a benefit instead of an obligation. For example, instead of, "Hey, can I put you on my mailing list?" it becomes, "I provide free weekly marketing tips that will help you grow your business. With your permission, I'd love to start sending them your way. Are you interested?"

Building Your List

Once you get into your "mailing-list mindset" it's important to take every opportunity available to acquire contact info from qualified prospects, leads or customers.

Here are a few ways to do so:

- Have a sign-up sheet available at your main point of contact (front desk, retail counter, trade show booth)
- Have visible opt-in boxes on several pages of your website that offer something of value
- Create a rewards program and let the participants know they will be receiving monthly communications
- Hold a monthly prize drawing and collect business cards to determine the winners (be sure the informational signage mentions that entrants will be added to your mailing list and notified via email of the results)

★ HEAVYWEIGHT MARKETING ★

When you're networking in person, always have plenty of business cards to exchange with qualified prospects. Express interest in signing up for other people's mailing lists as well. Don't just make it one-sided.

Getting Your Emails Opened

While we're on the topic of providing benefits, that same mindset is necessary when writing your email subject line. After all, having a hearty list is worthless if your contacts aren't opening your emails. When writing your subject lines, provide a little intrigue. Give recipients a taste of what awaits them if open the email. Give 'em a teaser that will pique their curiosity. Let them know how the enclosed information will improve their lives.

Does that sound overly dramatic? It should! Your audience is bombarded with so much information, you've got to prove to them immediately that the information your sending is going to be worth their time.

Give 'Em an Eyeful

One of the main advantages HTML emails have over plain text is that they look good! Be sure to maximize this advantage by adding images, logos and graphics that best represent your brand. If you're sending out e-newsletters, give your subscribers a glimpse behind the scenes of your company with photos of your staff, special events, new products and fun things around your office. If people post images of themselves with your product on your social platforms, create a Customer Corner section in your newsletter and feature photos, quotes or testimonials from your customers.

You want to showcase the personality of your company, while maintaining the objective of your strategy and protecting the integrity of your brand. The more you engage your audience, the more they feel like part of your community. This is key when building business relationships with qualified prospects who will eventually become loyal customers.

Track, Analyze and Adjust

All of the email platforms have in-depth tracking and analytics that allow you to see exactly who received your emails, when they opened them and what they clicked on. The platforms also make it easy for people to unsubscribe, automatically removing them from your list so you don't have to worry about managing your contacts.

You should get into the habit of studying the results of each email you send, even if it's a quick glance to see the percentage rate of opens and clicks. Of course the goal is to maintain a consistent rate of engagement. This can be challenging considering all the variables involved, which include the strength of your subject line, what day and time you send, and the sheer volume of promotional noise propagating rapidly in your customers' inboxes.

If you notice inconsistencies in your open and click-through rate, try adjusting your subject lines, your send dates, your offers and your call to action. Keep track of which ones generate results and which ones stink up the joint. Then, do more of the good stuff. Ha, how's that for awesomely obvious advice? It reminds me of an old Steve Martin joke: "Here's how to become a millionaire. First, get a million dollars…" However, it still rings true. Only by tracking, analyzing and adjusting will you be able to improve your communications and consistently send emails your audience is eager and excited to receive, read and react to.

★ HEAVYWEIGHT MARKETING ★

There's an old statistic floating around about the high rate of ROI on email marketing, that goes something like: "For every $1 you spend, you get $15 back!" There may be some truth to that, or it could simply be another urban legend swirling amidst the muskeg of ancient marketing lore. But if you're using email marketing as a revenue-generating device, you need to be certain you're creating compelling offers, including exclusive coupons or discounts, and utilizing effective calls to action to drive people to your store or your e-commerce website. Only then will you truly be able to measure the monetary effects of this proven instrument of marketing communications.

★ 21 ★

EIGHT INSIDER TIPS FOR CRACKING THE QR CODE

Whenever something reaches the point of ubiquity, a backlash is sure to ensue. This happened with Quick Response (QR) codes—those boxy graphic symbols marketers place on anything and everything with hopes of creating deeper brand engagement with their smartphone-toting audience.

The more articles and blog posts I read on the subject, the more disgruntled voices of frustration I hear railing against this technology. Marketing guru Scott Stratten even titled one of his books *QR Codes Kill Kittens*. However, upon further investigation, I've concluded that it's not the QR code itself that people find maddening, but rather the useless way that unsavvy marketers have employed them.

The offenses include simply sending people to a company's non-mobile-optimized website (gee, thanks), creating a non-user-friendly experience (fill out these 18 text fields on your phone to join our mailing list!) or putting them on highway billboards and semi trailers (do you really want people futzing with their phones when driving?). While marketers do seem to be going QR-crazy, their feeble attempts have mostly been lame.

If enough companies were using this technology in creative and innovative ways, it might balance out all the instances of clumsy deployment. Additionally, if enough consumers were utilizing the technology—rather than just the early adopters, who tend to be influencers—it would push QR code usage into the mainstream, which typically forces growth and innovation within any industry. Only then might all this early bungling be seen as growing pains instead of weighing so heavily against the overall perception of QR codes.

In order to experience the bounty that exists on the other side of a QR code, consumers have to take multiple steps:

- Download QR code reader to phone
- Unlock phone when they come upon QR code
- Open QR code reader
- Scan QR code with reader
- Curse you in frustration for wasting their precious time

Requiring a few cumbersome steps may not seem like you're asking too much of your audience, but in a hectic world of teeming busybodies with attention deficits, you want to keep the journey from A to B as easy and efficient as possible. And you darn well better make it worth their while once they get there.

I was a vocal proponent of QR codes when they first emerged, but seeing how poorly they've been implemented, my enthusiasm has waned. However, they're not quite dead yet, so I have still chosen to include them in this book, if only for some educational insight into a marketing tool you may, or may not, use.

To shed a little light on QR codes, I interviewed Arthur Cronos, author of *Get Endless New Clients: How to Build an Automatic Selling Machine to Ensure Business Growth and Cash Flow*. (Replies have been edited for clarity.)

Nikolas Allen: Many companies don't realize that QR codes necessitate having mobile websites, so let me ask you, how important is it to have a mobile website when implementing QR codes in your marketing?

Arthur Cronos: It's essential. Unfortunately, normal sites display very poorly on smartphones, so [it's best to] add a mobile site. People don't walk down the street carrying their desktop computer; however, every smartphone can become a scanner to visit the web through a QR code. As of right now, almost half of all the people in the world access the internet via smartphones instead of normal desktop or laptop computers. Why would you ignore half the market? *[Author's Note: According to the International Data Corporation, by 2015, more people in the U.S. will access the web through mobile devices than through PCs.]*[1]

NA: If you don't have a mobile site, can you still provide mobile-friendly content on your regular website?

AC: I don't know of any sensible way to do this. Because it's so easy to get a mobile website for your business it makes more sense to simply set up a site that works. Then program your regular site to send them to the mobile site automatically when they arrive riding on a cell phone.

NA: Do all QR Codes require downloading a special app or reader in order to work on smartphones?

AC: To the best of my knowledge, yes, but it's no problem. Just like getting the eBay app, or a Twitter app, it's free and takes about a minute.

NA: What are some of the benefits of implementing QR codes into your marketing materials?

★ **HEAVYWEIGHT MARKETING** ★

AC: QR codes are a recent evolution, similar to barcodes except that QR codes hold more information, and they're very forgiving about how they're oriented when you are scanning them. This makes them more useful than barcodes for the purposes of a marketer, or any small business.

Using a QR code is effectively the same thing as putting a link on your website, except that it's a link you can place in the physical universe. So just as your website can have a link to a free report, then so can a postcard you send have a "link" (a QR code) printed so that the person reading the postcard can immediately access that same free report. Effectively, QR codes can add the web to any object in the physical universe! *[Author's Note: The rules of creating Value and Engagement are important to keep in mind here. Don't just send people to your site; try to provide deeper, exclusive content, savings or offers to people who engage your brand via your QR codes.]*

NA: What common mistakes do you see people making when trying to implement QR codes in their marketing?

AC: The most common mistake with QR codes is the same mistake made with websites. Business people often advertise their website without giving the potential customer a reason to go there. Compare these two business cards, each with a web link:

John Jones
John's Hamburger Stand
www.johnshamburgers.com

VS.

John Jones
John's Hamburger Stand
Get the best burger in town…FREE ON US!
visit www.johnshamburgers.com/free-burger-offer

Round 2 - Tackle Your Tools

When using a QR code, do the smart thing: give them a reason to go to your website, and send them to the exact page that delivers on your promise.

NA: What Three Best Practice Tips would you suggest for business owners who want to implement QR codes?

AC: First, choose your best offer to get people to visit you, or sign up with your mailing list. Second, set up a mobile site, since people most often visit with smart phones and normal sites are unreadable or impossible to navigate on a phone. And third, get a QR code that points directly to the page on your mobile site that delivers on the promise you made.

NA: Where can business owners create custom QR codes of their own?

AC: A number of QR code generators are available on the web, so a search for "qr generator" will find those sites. Some are better than others, so be sure to test the QR code with your smart phone before implementing.

NA: Any key points you would like to add?

AC: Yes. In many cases, it is very wise to use a "redirect" when setting up your QR codes. That is where you set up one address that will redirect the visitor to another address.

If you were, for example, a real estate agent, and you were making signs that said, "Scan this code to see a video of the interior," you wouldn't want to reprint that sign with a new code every time you had a new house to sell. Instead you'd simply reprogram the redirect that's encoded in the QR code to point to the new video they can watch on their smart phone, while standing outside the house for sale.

★ HEAVYWEIGHT MARKETING ★

Or, suppose I want a QR code that takes people to my Amazon page to buy my book. Instead of coding my QR code to send them direct to Amazon, I'll code it to send them to the redirect. Down the road, Amazon could change the address where it shows my book, or I might come out with a new edition, which has a different address on Amazon.

If all my QR codes are out there in the physical universe, I can't change them. But I can change the redirect to point to the new Amazon address, so my QR codes will work year after year, even if the Amazon page address changes.

Any web professional should be able to help you with dozens of ways to employ QR codes in online-offline promotional campaigns that deliver a double-whammy to your advertising investment by turbo-charging your promotions, tempting your customers, and boosting your income. That's a good thing, right?

NA: It sure is, Arthur. Thank you for your time.

Arthur Cronos, marketer, therapist, and author of Get Endless New Clients, *offers a free, special report to business owners, "The 4 Proven Marketing Methods to Grow Your Business by 25% or More in the Next 12 Months," at* http://Voltos.com.

★ 22 ★

FIVE THINGS YOU NEED TO KNOW ABOUT TEXT (SMS) MARKETING

A rumpled man sat at the bar nursing a beer. His brow glistened from the pervasive heat, despite the best intentions of a squeaky fan whirling overhead. Gourmet burgers sizzled on the grill in the open kitchen to his left while a single chef darted about the kitchen, fluid as a ninja in houndstooth pants. The chimes above the door tinkled as a heavyset woman entered and planted herself just inside the door. She scanned the crowd before locking eyes with the bartender, who stared back, ever so curious. The woman brandished her cell phone towards the barkeep and bellowed, "You can't handle the truth!"

The rumpled man startled at the outburst, spilling several drops of his precious amber liquid. His head swiveled quickly towards the new patron as she cackled with laughter and approached the barkeep, who chortled along with her while drawing a fresh pint of microbrew from the tap. Just as Mr. Rumpled went back to minding his own business, a boisterous trio of baseball-capped college bros barged through the door. Pantomiming cell-phones-as-machine-guns, the posse barked in unison, "Say hello to my little friend," and proceeded to rat-a-tat-tat the restaurant to smithereens like a trio of coked-up Pacinos.

Bewildered, eyes wide as saucers, the rumpled man wondered what in Sam Hell was going on in this crazy place. Sensing his customer's anxiety, the proprietor, a kindly man

★ HEAVYWEIGHT MARKETING ★

with gentle eyes and an epic beard more hippie than hipster, approached the discombobulated drinker carefully.

"Welcome to Sunday Funday," he said in a soothing voice.

Sunday Funday was a text-message marketing program I concocted with a client who ran a brew pub restaurant. On designated Sundays, we sent out texts prompting customers to do crazy things in order to get a specialty microbrew for a mere 50 cents. In addition to shouting movie quotes upon entry, we also prompted customers to dance an Irish jig, sing lines from Broadway musicals, wear mismatched socks, and complete other absurd tasks in order to claim their booty. Only the people on the text marketing list would be in the know, so the other patrons would be wondering what the heck was going on. When they finally found out why these people were singing, dancing and shouting, you better believe they were eager to sign up!

Also referred to as SMS, which stands for Short Message Service, text marketing is just one facet of the red-hot mobile marketing category. I was real excited to add SMS to my list of services, as it offered many creative opportunities for my clients to connect with their audience. Since it was a relatively new player in the game as far as marketing tools go, not many clients were quite ready to buy into text marketing when I started introducing the service. However, those who did add it to their marketing mix quickly enjoyed notable results in their foot traffic and their bottom line. These clients were even having lots of fun with it, which is a big bonus in my opinion. After all, when business owners have fun with their marketing and are genuinely excited about it, they are more likely to be consistent with it.

Round 2 - Tackle Your Tools

If you're considering adding text messaging to your marketing mix, the following tips gleaned from first-hand experience may be helpful when making your decision:

1) It's Not Right for Every Business—I would be lying if I said that text marketing is a grand-slam solution for every small biz. In fact, just like any marketing tool you're considering, the very best reason to choose something is because it puts your business exactly where your audience is. In the case of text message marketing, this means your audience has to already be using text as a form of communication. Hard as it may be to believe, there are still some people who don't text! I know, OMG! right?

Text marketing works really well for restaurants, coffee shops, and general retail stores that can easily offer special promos, discounts and giveaways. It gets a little trickier as you get into upscale stores offering big-ticket items, service-based companies, or non-profit organizations. That doesn't mean it's impossible for these types of companies to effectively employ text marketing, but you do have to be a little more creative with how it is used.

2) You Have to Give in Order to Get—If you want your customers to give you permission to send them texts, each of your communications need to provide undeniable value for them. The campaigns that proved most successful for my clients were of the Weekly Deals variety, which drove recurring traffic into the business to take advantage of the featured specials. In order to build an audience of engaged, responsive consumers, you need to employ the following:

Carrot Offer—Building your text message list is similar to building your email marketing list in that you need to offer something valuable (i.e., dangle a carrot) to get people to opt in. Some examples are "Sign Up and Take $2 Off Today's

★ **HEAVYWEIGHT MARKETING** ★

Order," "Enter to Win $25 Gift Certificate," or "Join Today & Get Free Dessert." It needs to be special enough to get people to give you their cell phone number, without you losing your shirt in the process.

Exclusive Deals—Once people are on your list, you need to create text content to send them. However, you can't just send promotional texts of no value; they have to be unique, fun and special enough to make the recipient feel like they are part of a secret club getting an exclusive deal. Some of the deals that have worked well include buy-one-get-one-free offers, coupon-style discounts ("Show this text for $5 off your $25 purchase"), and flash-sale events such as "$1 lattes for the next hour only!"

As you can imagine, the deals that get the best response involve discounts. I'm not a fan of giving away the farm, but if done properly you will actually make money, even as you give discounts. If your company is allergic to discounts, refer back to Tip #1.

Freebies—Whether a free espresso drink, micro-brew, or small gift item, awarding a freebie to a random member of your list every week is a great way to surprise and delight your customers while building loyalty and generating positive word-of-mouth buzz. One of my clients used text message marketing as a customer rewards program and gave a $25 gift certificate to a random subscriber every week! Meanwhile, other clients chose not to give out weekly freebies at all, and instead focused on providing good weekly deals. The choice is yours, and whatever choice your company makes should feel comfortable. It should not be a cause of financial anxiety and stress.

One client signed up for the program, but resisted the idea of giving anything away. They also had a hard time coming up with special deals, and they didn't do much to promote the program.

It's no wonder that they limped along with tepid results for three months before bailing out on the service altogether. Like I said: not for every business.

3) You Need to Respect Your Audience—The same SPAM laws that apply to email apply to text marketing. Before people give you their cell phone number, they need to feel like they can trust you. If that trust is abused, you will lose customers and damage your hard-earned brand reputation as well. When crafting your deals, ask yourself, "Would this deal be awesome enough to get ME off the couch and into the store if I received it?" If not, keep crafting.

As for frequency, you can send weekly deals, bi-weekly deals, or monthly deals. Ultimately, you're trying to find the sweet spot between engaging your audience enough so they don't forget about you, but not so much that they get irritated and opt out.

4) Text Messages Are Personal and Fun—People have special connections with their cell phones, and they rarely go anywhere without them. One of my clients held a reception during an art walk and sent out a special limited-time offer via text. During the reception, I overheard a customer say she got the text while she was out hiking and got excited to come to the art walk later that evening. I can't think of any other marketing tool that would excite a customer by interrupting her while she was out enjoying nature.

5) Text Marketing Works—All the clients I worked with who used SMS marketing enjoyed noticeable results in a short amount of time. The patrons who enjoyed their 50-cent beers during the brewery's Sunday Fundays always bought additional beers and food at full price. The local gift shop was tracking 7–12 sales during their art walk events that were directly related to the text deals. A pizza parlor client tracked 15–30 customers

★ **HEAVYWEIGHT MARKETING** ★

redeeming their text deals with each offer. As for the coffee shack owner, her list swelled to 400 in no time and still continues to grow week after week. Do you think your business would benefit from placing secret, exclusive deals in the pockets of 400+ customers every week?

If I added up the text marketing lists from all my clients, we were collectively reaching close to 4,000 people with custom, value-oriented text messages. While this number may not seem staggering by big-city standards, we were pulling from a small NorCal mountain community of roughly 10,000 people, where the typical local business owner's marketing strategy consists of opening her doors and waiting for the tourists to stumble in. I am proud of these business owners for having the courage to step out of their comfort zones and give new marketing techniques a try. I suggest all business owners consider doing the same.

Round 2 - Tackle Your Tools

★ 23 ★

TO BLOG OR NOT TO BLOG, THAT IS THE QUESTION

During an introductory meeting with a small, non-profit arts organization, the client—we'll call her Zelda—asked me for a price quote to set up a blog for her company. Sure, no problemo, I said…until I started asking questions, at which time I detected mucho problemo.

"Do you read blogs?" I inquired.
"No," replied Zelda.
"Do you have an objective for the blog? What purpose would you like it to serve?"
"Um, I don't know. I just think we should have one."
"Have you ever maintained a blog, personal or otherwise?" I dug further.
"No," Zelda repeated.
"Are you aware of the commitment involved? Blogs require consistent, fresh content in order to maintain any type of relevance."
"Maybe we wouldn't have to be responsible for the content," countered Zelda.
"Oh, and who would create your content?" I probed, genuinely curious.
"Artists," she suggested.
"Really?" I pondered. "What would be in it for them? After all, none of the artists in our community are even writing their own blogs. Why would they interested in blogging for you? Furthermore, do you think it would be wise to enlist random

artists as the voice of your brand?"

"Hmm, I don't know. Actually, it's our Board of Directors who think we should have a blog," Zelda finally revealed.

"I see," I replied, knowing more answers were needed. "And do any of the board members maintain blogs?"

As you may guess, the answers didn't get any better. After more conversation, I summarized the following:

- Nobody in the organization was active in the blogosphere.
- They had no objective, vision, strategy, goals or ideas of how to represent their brand via that medium.
- They had neither staff nor budget to devote to the necessary long-term maintenance and content creation required.

"No," I told Zelda. "I'm sorry, but I will not give you a quote to set up a blog."

Instead, I suggested we meet with the Board of Directors to discuss some of these integral-yet-unanswered questions and try to decide if launching a blog is really the route they should go. Now, you may think I'm an idiot for turning the possibility of a quick payday into a stubborn stand-off with the Board of Directors. However, my goal has always been to sell effective marketing solutions to clients, not to bilk them of their hard-earned money by providing something they're not prepared for. After all, in the future, when my client's outdated, abandoned blog is floating static and worthless in cyberspace, I don't want any fingers pointing in my direction.

For the record, let me state that I'm a huge fan of blogging. When done properly, adding valuable content to your website on a regular basis can benefit your online presence and your organization in several ways:

Gets Google Juice—Search engines love active blogs because they indicate your website is a vital, relevant source of information, which is what search engine spiders are seeking when they index the web. Posting regular articles and using targeted keywords increases the chances of your web pages showing up in search results.

Drives Traffic—If your website is merely a static brochure floating in cyberspace, visitors might stop by once, but will have no reason to visit again. Posting new content gives people a reason to visit your website over and over, increasing your chances of converting prospects into customers. Plus, running a high-traffic site is another way to impress the all-knowing eye of Google, resulting in higher rankings.

Grows Mailing List—Providing your site has an email signup box and a compelling call to action, you can build your mailing list by capturing contact info from visitors who come to read your blog content. People will be far more inclined to join your mailing list if they know you're frequently posting new articles than if your website is merely a static online brochure.

Builds Brand—Creating a dynamic website with content that educates, informs or entertains your audience is a great way to establish your company as an expert in your field. People will support companies they know, like and trust, and blogging is a great vehicle for honing your brand voice and building trust among your audience. Your brand is expressed through more than words. Photos and videos, or rich media, are an essential part of blogging as well. Whether shooting your own or sourcing them elsewhere, make sure they align with your brand voice just as well as the text does.

★ HEAVYWEIGHT MARKETING ★

There's no doubt that blogging can be a significant tool for marketing, educating and communicating with an audience—providing business owners create a long-term plan. As you saw in my conversation with Zelda, there are certain essential questions to ask yourself that will help pull your plan together:

- Topic—what will we write about?
- Frequency—how often will we post?
- Execution—who will be writing these posts?
- Objective—what do we hope to achieve by churning out article after article?

Once you start inquiring, you may come up with several more questions that directly apply to your business. Great! Better to answer them up front than have them trip you up and stall your blogging efforts down the road.

Eventually, Zelda and I did meet with the Board of Directors. We agreed on a contract that had me producing blog content for the site, which I went on to do for over three years. We turned their visually horrific, static-brochure site into an attractive, interactive destination that helped grow our mailing list, attract national artists, build our online brand and keep our audience coming back month after month to enjoy rich-media posts showcasing the exhibits and events happening at the gallery.

Blogging is an ongoing commitment, so it's best if the person(s) responsible for maintaining your blog exhibits true passion, knowledge and excitement for writing, for the topics of choice and for building an active channel of communication with which to engage your audience. If these attributes are lacking, blogging will feel a lot more like slogging. And if it ain't fun, why bother?

★ 24 ★

WERE SOCIAL MEDIA EVER INTENDED FOR BUSINESS?

By definition, social media are tools used to socialize. These platforms allow people to connect, comment and share with friends, colleagues and acquaintances and interact online despite geographical boundaries. Quite frankly, the majority of the people who are using these social media platforms daily are not there for the purpose of discussing business (LinkedIn would be the exception to this rule but, c'mon, how much time does the general public really spend on LinkedIn?). Business owners must keep this in mind if they decide to implement these platforms in their marketing strategies. After all, you don't want to come off as the "suit" who's crashing the party.

In 2010, JCPenney and several other major retailers attempted to add shopping capabilities to their Facebook page, ringing in the short-lived era of F-commerce.[1] None of the stores took off and they all quietly reversed course and shut down within a year.

> "[Selling on social media] is like trying to sell stuff to people while they're hanging out with their friends at the bar." —Sucharita Mulpuru, Online Retail Analyst

There are different schools of thought on the "appropriate" use of social media for business. One school suggests using 'The 1/10th Rule', which means that one out of every ten tweets, posts or updates can be self-promotional, but no more. Then there are the new media purists who feel that business owners using social media should not do ANY selling or promoting, but rather treat these tools as a way to engage, interact and build relationships with their audience.

The supposed logic here is that an engaged audience will be happy to patronize companies who have earned their trust, but they don't want to be bothered by pushy sales messages. One thing that most of the experts in the field do agree upon is this: using social media as a purely self-promotional form of direct marketing is not cool.

I see people violating this maxim all the time. On Twitter, users have tweet streams consisting solely of links back to their own site or blog. I've seen event promoters whose updates stop abruptly for several months between events. Way to keep 'em engaged, buddy. Or how about the social media gurus who only have 198 followers and haven't tweeted since April, 2011? Apparently, these clowns fall into the "do as I say, not as I do" category. On Facebook, some business owners are so eager for engagement, their stream is clogged with low-value posts that beg and plead for likes and shares. You can practically smell the desperation wafting from the screen.

Another major irritant is people who join groups for the sole reason of bombarding said group with self-promotional poppycock. And don't get me started on those narcissistic fools who think Instagram was developed for the singular purpose of generating incessant selfies. When scrolling through their photo feed, I can't help feeling embarrassed for these self-absorbed souls.

So, how should you be using social media for your business? That depends on several things, all of which need to be determined and communicated to everyone in your organization.

Round 2 - Tackle Your Tools

Three Questions to Kickstart Your Social Strategy:

1) What is our audience using and how are they using it?

Ask your customers what their favorite social platforms are. Send a survey to your mailing list. Collect business cards and see if your customers are touting social media profiles. Follow and friend them to see what's important to them. Conducting this market research will help determine if it is worthwhile for your company to maintain an active social media presence. Let's face it, if your desired audience is NOT active in the social media sphere, there's no reason for you to be either. And, if they are, you need to meet them on their terms.

2) What is our objective?

It's not enough to jump on the social media bandwagon because everyone else is. You must determine HOW to represent your brand via that medium, WHAT messages you wish to send and WHY these tools should be used for your business. Whether your social media objective is to create greater brand awareness, offer real-time customer service, or share relevant news and advice with your audience, clarifying this before diving in will help keep you on track for the long-term commitment.

3) How will we measure success?

The primary question in the minds of most business owners is, "How will social media affect my bottom line?" They rightfully want to know what the return on investment (ROI) will be. Unfortunately, it's not as cut and dried as, say, a direct-mail postcard with a redeemable coupon that drives customers into your store, or a trackable Google AdWords campaign. There are analytics tools that measure how many people read your tweets, interact with your Facebook page, or view your videos on YouTube, but it's a little trickier to measure the exact conversion rate of those interactions. Therefore, your measurements for success may very well be defined by some of the things

★ HEAVYWEIGHT MARKETING ★

mentioned earlier, such as level of engagement, number of views and interactions (likes, shares, comments), improved customer service, increased awareness, and any other key performance indicators (KPIs) that you decide upon.

Six Top Tools for Social Media Management

Using more than one social media platform can become a time-consuming chore if you're not careful. There are many times that I log in to Facebook or Twitter to post something, only to get swept up in the rushing river of content. After pulling myself away and logging out a half-hour later, I realize I forgot to post what I came there to share. Even if you don't get lost in the vortex, having to log in, craft and post content manually on all your individual platforms can still be wearisome. That's where social media management platforms come in handy.

The half-dozen listed below are some of the bigger names in media management; some are free and some are premium. I've used the first two, but have only heard about the rest, so like any tool your are considering, you want to do a little research before going all in. You can find the corresponding URLs listed in the Resources section under Social Media Management.

Hootsuite—Currently the Heavyweight Champ of social management, this robust dashboard helps you manage and measure your social networks, schedule tweets and messages, track brand mentions, and analyze social media traffic.

Socialoomph—Easily schedule updates, find quality people to follow, and monitor social media activity on Twitter, Facebook (profiles, pages, and groups), LinkedIn (profiles, groups, and company pages), RSS feeds, blogs, Plurk, and App.net.

Socialflow—More than just a media-management platform, Socialflow acts as a smart distribution system using algorithms to send content to users when they are paying attention. Socialflow optimizes every post and releases messages that are relevant to users when they are online, consuming related content.

Buffer—Helps you manage multiple social media accounts at once. Users can quickly schedule content from anywhere on the web, collaborate with team members, and analyze rich statistics on how your posts perform.

Sendible—This social media monitoring platform allows users to engage with customers, measure results and monitor your brand across multiple social media channels at once.

Everypost—Currently available only as a mobile app, Everypost allows users to post multimedia content across multiple social platforms. Since each platform is a little different, you can customize your content per social network. After all, just because you can manage all platforms through one dashboard, doesn't mean your content should look automated. Instead, each post should contain the formatting nuances that are native to the platform being used.

Business is about building relationships between people who have needs, problems or desires (customers) and people who offer solutions (business owners). The benefit social media marketing offers versus traditional marketing is that it allows a direct connection via interactive channels of communication with the very people whose needs can be met by your solutions.

However, you must treat that connection with respect and use social media to offer value, accessibility and interactivity to your audience. You need to use your social platforms as tools

★ **HEAVYWEIGHT MARKETING** ★

for initiating dialogues instead of broadcasting monologues. If your audience feels like you are giving them a voice, they will sing your praises. If, however, they are on the receiving end of a continuous one-way sales promotion, they will tune you out. Then, no matter how great your marketing message is, it will be falling on deaf ears.

★ 25 ★

TWELVE TIPS FOR TWEETING LIKE A CHAMP

When it comes to determining which social platforms to use for business, Twitter is the one people seem to resist the most. Either they just don't get it (when you see someone's tweet stream for the first time, it does look a bit like hieroglyphics), or they question the validity of the medium. Many business owners who decide to employ Twitter for their marketing do so with the hopes of immediately increasing sales revenue. Unfortunately, that approach is guaranteed to disappoint.

Traditional thinking states that marketing tools should directly affect sales and produce measurable results. When it comes to social media marketing tools, that way of thinking—while certainly valid and legitimate—does not quite apply. Social analytics tools do exist (for detailed insights, check out "analytics.twitter.com" while signed in for a tweet-by-tweet analysis of activity surrounding your account), and there are digital agencies that specialize in tracking and measuring results, but for the everyday small business user, it's still difficult to accurately correlate social media activity with bottom line. Twitter can still be a valuable tool for connecting with your audience, and you can gauge its usefulness simply by tracking the number of quality followers you attract, their level of engagement and how many mentions and retweets your content generates.

Personally, I love Twitter. I don't own a TV, so it has become my go-to source for breaking news. The real-time nature of the platform means people are tweeting about hot topics long before

★ HEAVYWEIGHT MARKETING ★

they hit the airwaves of traditional media. It's also great for educational purposes. People in every industry are tweeting links to blog posts, articles, white papers, e-books, and everything else that will help you keep up with the latest happenings in your field of interest. And, of course, I use Twitter to share my own blog posts and activities, as well as links to articles, posts and videos that my audience might enjoy. This helps build my reputation as a thought leader in the field of marketing, which establishes credibility and attracts clients. You can do the same.

All of the same rules and principles we've discussed throughout the book (provide value to your audience, don't make it all about you, keep your activity consistent, etc.) apply to Twitter as well. After all, do your really want your tweet stream to look like this?

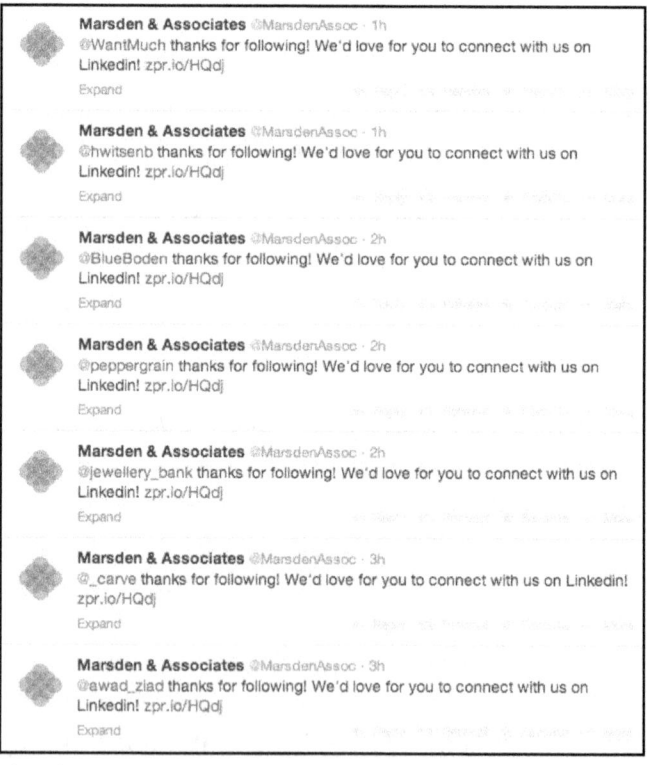

A perfect example of how NOT to use Twitter

Round 2 - Tackle Your Tools

If you decide you want to commit to using Twitter as a marketing tool, the following tips will help you get the most out of the platform:

Tweet Like a Champ With These 12 Tips:

1) Use Fab Photos—For most of its existence, Twitter didn't put much stock in photos. Instead, it was all about brevity via the simplicity of text. Profile pics were tiny and photos appeared in tweets as links, which would direct users to another page to view. That was fine when Twitter was a niche product, but these days the company is making a move towards mainstream adoption and it understands the power of visual storytelling. After its most recent makeover, Twitter looks more like Facebook than ever, with large profile pics, even larger header photos, and images that appear right in the post.

Take advantage of Twitter's newfound visual generosity by using big, bold, eye-catching photos that portray your brand. Your profile pic will still be small when shown in the tweet stream, so choose something bold and striking that will stand out. The header will be seen by everyone visiting your page, so use a brand-centric photo that looks good in a wide, horizontal format. Tweet photos from the workplace of staff, customers, products, office events, and fun, brand-specific visual imagery that showcases your unique brand voice. In all cases, opt for images of the real, live people behind your brand, and avoid relying on logos, storefronts, and cheesy stock photography from the "business" category to represent your company.

2) Secure Your @UserName—With so many people using social media, it can be difficult to find a user name that is not already taken. Ideally, your personal or business name is available across all platforms, so you can maintain brand consistency on the web. In that case, you want to secure @yourname or

★ **HEAVYWEIGHT MARKETING** ★

@yourbizname as your Twitter handle. If those aren't available, you can create a modified version by appending "store," "brand," or "biz" to your preferred handle. Either way, your Twitter name should be short, easy to read, and memorable—even if viewed as one word in all lower-case letters. A tall order, I realize, but aim for that and modify as necessary.

3) Don't Skimp on Profile Details—Every time I read a blog post from a social media maven on how to use a certain platform, they always include the tip: fill out your profile completely. My kneejerk response is always, "Gee, thanks for that awesome tip, Captain Obvious!" Then I'll surf around Twitter (and other platforms) and see exactly how many people skimp on their profiles: a lot. Touché. Your profile consists of your name or biz name, location, website and bio. You've only got 160 characters for your bio so make sure yours packs a punch by using your purpose statement that we discussed earlier.

4) Pick Your Palette—Unlike Facebook, where all brand pages conform to the same boring blue and white color scheme, Twitter allows you to customize your page's color palette to match your brand identity. You can choose a theme color, which is really an accent color that applies to your page's icons, notifications and links. You can also upload a background image, or adjust your background color, but those changes only affect your personal viewing experience within your account. The background of your main page will remain gray and any custom branding will be expressed through your combination of profile pic, header pic and aforementioned theme color.

5) Go on a Following Frenzy—In order to build your own follower count, you need to actively follow others. Everyone you follow receives a notification, which typically prompts them to check out your profile to see how interesting and relevant your content is to their lives. At that point, they may or may not follow

Round 2 - Tackle Your Tools

you back. Therefore, from a strategic perspective, you want to follow people and organizations that match your ideal customers. That way, if they do follow you back, you'll be communicating with a targeted audience.

From a user perspective, you also want to follow accounts that tweet content YOU find interesting. After all, if you're spending time on Twitter, you may as well enjoy yourself. Once you start tweeting, you'll start attracting more and more followers. Beware, many of them will be fake. Just like people check out your account to ascertain their level of interest, you should do the same thing with people who follow you. Don't simply follow everyone who follows you or your tweet stream will be clogged with irrelevant junk, noise and spam. Be selective, and remember that quality trumps quantity when it comes to followers.

6) Narrow Your Focus—The hardest part about starting a Twitter account is determining what the heck you're going to tweet about. It helps to create a plan beforehand by brainstorming content ideas. Remember, you want to position yourself as a specialist in your business category, so try to maintain a narrow focus with your tweet topics.

7) Get Personal—Wait! I'm not talking Anthony-Weiner-tweeting-pics-of-his-junk-personal; I'm talking about letting your own unique personality shine through in your posts. Occasionally injecting personal quips, thoughts, questions, or anecdotes will help to humanize your activity. Relatability is one of the main reasons consumers enjoy supporting small business, so keep that in mind as you're communicating with your audience. Even big brands are trying to "act small" on their social channels by allowing their social media managers to act as human representatives and not just faceless corporate mouthpieces. Of course, this has a tendency to backfire, so be sure you have clear social media policies in place before handing off the reins to your staffers, interns or contractors.

8) Drive Traffic—Tweet occasional links that drive traffic to your website, blog or other social channels—just be careful not to overdo it. Remember to use meaningful messaging and compelling calls to action. Don't just say "Visit our website," "Check out our latest blog post," or "Follow us on Facebook." Instead, let people know how doing any of those things will benefit them.

9) Don't Connect Twitter to Facebook—Both Twitter and Facebook have options allowing you to connect your accounts to each other. That means your tweets show up on your Facebook wall and your Facebook posts show up (in partial form) on your Twitter wall. The problem with this is that you are treating both platforms as the same, which they are not. You wouldn't run a radio ad as a TV spot, and you wouldn't run a print ad as a billboard. In each case, you would have to do some re-formatting to maximize the benefits of each medium. Same goes for social media.

While social platforms do share certain similarities, they each have their own unique attributes, nuances, strengths and limitations. In order to get the most from each platform, users need to create content that is native to the platform they're using. That means you should use each the way it was meant to be used. If you're using more than one platform and trying to save time, a better option is to use one of the social media management programs we discussed earlier. That way, you can tweak your message according to the optimal format of each platform.

10) Get #Hashtag Happy—Twitter is where hashtags originated, so it's only fitting to use them there. Hashtags have permeated mainstream culture to the point of saturation, so many people would prefer to deem them "over" and forget about them. But they do serve a purpose when it comes to social media, so it's best to put your bias aside—even if you're one of the people who feel hashtags have jumped the shark. We take a deeper look at hashtags in the next chapter, so I'll keep it brief here and say that hashtags can be useful for adding context to your tweets, helping your content to appear in targeted search results, adding a dash of humor, and injecting your content into trending topics via newsjacking. One thing I would suggest avoiding altogether is saying the word out loud in real-life conversations. It was pretty hilarious when Jimmy Fallon and Justin Timberlake did it in their video skit, but anybody else doing this is super #lame, and more than a bit #irritating.

11) Engage Your Followers—Engagement on Twitter can take several forms. Underneath each tweet is a little row of icons. The arrow allows you to reply to a tweet someone posted. The double arrow allow you to retweet (RT) posts that you like, which takes someone else's tweet and sends it through your stream. This is a compliment to share someone else's content with your audience. You can "favorite" a tweet by hitting the little star icon, which is Twitter's version of the like button. You can mention someone, or tweet to them by including their Twitter handle in your tweet. In order to notify the person you're tweeting to, you need to include the @ symbol before their name. Finally, you can send a direct message (DM) to anyone who is following you, which allows you to carry on a private conversation away from the public tweet stream.

12) Do Not Automate Your DMs—There are some third-party apps that let you set up auto DMs, or automatic direct messages that go out to everyone who follows you. The content of auto DMs vary, but the perpetrators are usually thanking you for following them and attempting to get you to connect elsewhere such as Facebook, LinkedIn, or a company website. In some cases, automation is a good thing, but this is definitely not one of those cases. People who use this feature think it's adding a personal touch, but it's doing the exact opposite—we

★ **HEAVYWEIGHT MARKETING** ★

know a robot sent your message! Auto DMs show a blatant disregard for their followers' intelligence and exhibit extremely poor social etiquette, yet tons of people still do it. Don't be one of them. If someone follows you, check out their profile. If you discover something in common, find their bio to be funny, or enjoy their content, go ahead and send them a manual DM. Do. Not. Automate.

By using Twitter, I have earned opportunities to write guest blog posts, been interviewed for people's websites, connected with fellow entrepreneurs, communicated with movers and shakers in the business world, and generally made some cool connections that may not have been possible otherwise. Twitter may not be right for everybody, but it can be incredibly useful and enjoyable for those who use it properly. The downsides are that Twitter can be a tremendous time-suck, there's a high noise-to-signal ratio, and it often takes a lot of effort for a little reward. If you do decide to implement Twitter as a marketing communications tool for your business, make sure you are disciplined with your time spent there, so the results you achieve are proportionate to the effort expended.

For your daily dose of #advertising #branding #marketing and #smallbiz news, follow Nikolas Allen on Twitter: @nikolas_allen.

★ 26 ★

STOP TRYING SO HARD TO MAKE YOUR #STUPIDHASHTAGS HAPPEN

In the movie *Mean Girls*, one of the characters is trying to get her new slang word, "fetch," to catch on among her peers as a replacement for "awesome." She fully commits to dropping her new term at every opportunity, until one of her friends finally snaps, "Stop trying to make 'fetch' happen! It's not going to happen!"

I'm reminded of this scene every time I read a magazine, watch TV, or view online videos and see the proliferation of hashtags that brands are trying to "make happen" in their advertisements. Never mind that you see hashtags all over social media, now they've infiltrated the world of mass media.

What Are #Hashtags?

Hashtags are words or phrases preceded by a pound sign (i.e., hash sign or number symbol), that people inject throughout their social media content for a variety of purposes (which we discuss below). They originated on Twitter before migrating to all the other social platforms, and eventually making the leap to all media including print, TV and movies.

> "I remember when we used to call it the pound sign."
> —Some Random Oldster lamenting days gone by

By using them, brands are hoping that consumers pick up on their hashtags and incorporate them into their social lexicon. After all, getting consumers to talk about your brand is an essential goal for every marketer. If the audience is using a brand's custom hashtag, that activity can be tracked and measured, which should be another goal of marketers. The problem is that very few hashtags seem like natural expressions that might be uttered by actual consumers of the brand or product. Most reek of Boardroom contrivance, and some are downright inexplicable.

Dannon offered a prime example: to promote their line of Greek yogurt, the company reunited the trio of male cast members from 80s TV show *Full House* for a Super Bowl® Halftime commercial. Their chosen hashtag, #FuelYourPleasure, was practically begging to be hijacked by rogue internet trolls hell-bent on creating headaches for Dannon's poor PR flacks. I imagined a firestorm of miscreant tweeters sending salacious suggestions of beyond-bromance status enjoyed by three grown men still living under the same roof. Fuel your pleasure indeed! Didn't happen. You know why? Because nobody cared enough to pick up on it. A search for #fuelyourpleasure today shows that the yogurt conversation—or more accurately, the "John Stamos is dreamy" conversation—stopped abruptly two days after the Big Game.

What Purpose Do They Serve?

Searchability—The primary purpose of hashtags is to improve searchability by acting as a category tag that filters content when you search for a certain hashtag.

Perhaps you wish pick up a few biz tips on Facebook. If you enter "#socialmediamarketing" into the Facebook search bar, all the posts that include that tag will come up. This allows you to narrow your reading focus while filtering out all the food porn, armchair activism and never-ending cat posts that populate the platform. Facebook actually came late to the hashtag party, so this example equally applies to Twitter, Google+, and especially Instagram.

Conversation—Social media best practices often suggest that you "join the conversation" which is another thing hashtags allow you to do.

Let's say you're watching an episode of *Project Runway* and you want to chime in on Twitter. Simply do a search for "#ProjectRunway" in the Twitter search bar and all the tweets containing that tag come up. Then you can send your own tweets and, as long as they also include the #ProjectRunway hashtag, they'll show up in the filtered stream. You can reply, talk trash, opine and generally geek out on this #SublimeRealityShow in real time with all the other viewers who are tweeting along.

Context—When you tweet, pin or post something on the web—especially if it's cryptic, dry humor, or deadpan irony—you can help readers determine the context by including hashtags. This usage was more common in the early days of Twitter when hashtags were still viewed as mysterious hieroglyphics. Since they have become more familiar to the masses, people are now using them more creatively.

Humor—Those with a quick wit use hashtags like comedians use punchlines. Capping off your comment with a funny hashtag—or three—is like the snap of a snare drum after a good joke. I've got a friend whose Facebook stream is chock full of humorous bon mots tossed off with the rat-tat-tat cadence of Rodney Dangerfield:

> *"Can we stop adding 'palooza' to the end of words yet? #itsamusicfestival #shutup #getoffmylawn"*

★ HEAVYWEIGHT MARKETING ★

Beware the Dark Side of Hashtags

Several brands have made the mistake of thinking they can control the conversation on social media. A company will promote a custom hashtag and encourage users to contribute their input, naively assuming that everyone will have the brand's best interest in mind. Then, when caught flat-footed in a maelstrom of scornful contempt, they wonder how it could have gone so horribly wrong.

Recent history is littered with cautionary tales of hashtag hijacking. These are a few of the notable ones:

#McDstories—McDonald's was one of the first victims of hashtag abuse in 2012 when an attempt to get customers tweeting about their #McDstories went horribly awry. The Twittersphere was inundated with tweets about fast-food horror stories discussing everything from projectile vomiting, diarrhea, obesity, pig meat, discovering wayward objects such as fingernails, bandaids and bugs in burgers, and every other radically off-brand message you could possibly think of.

#PaulasBestDishes—Southern fried chef Paula Deen found herself in a vat of hot oil when an employee blew the whistle on her for being an abusive, racist redneck. Before the scandal, tweets using the #PaulasBestDishes hashtag featured recipes for high-calorie comfort food. Post-scandal, tweeters employed the hashtag for a disturbing game of one-upmanship to see who could come up with the most racist names for popular food dishes. Nearly two years after the scandal, people were still tweeting racist food names with that hashtag, which begs the question: at what point does the villainizer become the villain?

#MyNYPD—More recently, some airhead manning the social media switchboard down at the NY cop shop came up with the brilliant idea to crowdsource photos of the public getting all chummy with New York police officers. Who on earth thought that would be a good idea? These are cops for cryin' out loud, not animals at the petting zoo. Well, before you could say "Rodney King," photos of police beatdowns, brutality and excessive force were inundating the tweet stream. Welcome to Twitter, NYPD! Uh, you may wanna rethink your strategy though.

An Unofficial Investigation

While reading an edition of *GQ Magazine* (what, you think I was born with mad style?) I found myself quite curious about some of the phrases brands were trying to make happen via their print ads. I launched an unofficial investigation and performed Twitter searches for each of the hashtags used in the ads (which are listed below followed by their brand parent). I made some very interesting discoveries about exactly WHO was using these hashtags in the social sphere. Let's take a look:

#PhilipLimforTarget—Target
- People associated with Target
- Models used in the Target campaign
- Photographers used in the Target campaign
- Fashion editors who love Target and probably pronounce it "Tarjhay"

#onlyonestar—Macy's
- People who work at Macy's
- Film critics who reviewed *John Carter*

#liveinit—Paige Denim
- The 16 people who wear Paige Denim
- A muscle-head bragging about how often he's at the gym
- Inspirational guru tweeting about "the present moment"

★ HEAVYWEIGHT MARKETING ★

#LexusIS—Lexus
- Social Media Managers who work for Lexus
- The 27 rich people who use Twitter

#backtoblue—GAP
- Employees of GAP
- Models in GAP campaigns
- Magazines that rely on GAP to buy advertising

#makeourmark—Levi's
- I couldn't quite figure out what the hell this was all about
- Actually, I got bored trying to

Whether you love 'em, hate 'em, or are simply confounded by them, hashtags have become a full-on phenomenon that have wormed their way into our public consciousness. But unlike, say, QR codes, which never quite took off, hashtags are here to stay. If you're still a #hashtagvirgin, go ahead and try them out in the context that we have discussed. Just be careful that you're not trying too hard.

★ 27 ★

PINTEREST IS HOT, BUT CAN IT BENEFIT YOUR BUSINESS?

Photo-sharing social platform Pinterest has officially evolved from a promising contender into a key player in the social media stratosphere. In the fast-moving world of social media, Pinterest may not be the red-hot social darling du jour it was in 2012, but is certainly holding its own in the wake of newer platforms such as Instagram, Vine and Snapchat. And, unlike many formerly-hot platforms such as Foursquare, Groupon and Flickr, Pinterest has actually improved over time rather than backsliding into irrelevance.

In its own words, Pinterest is an "online pinboard to organize and share things you love." The online equivalent of a swipe file or inspiration board, this social image bookmarking site allows users to create "boards" on which to "pin" items of interest. Users can Follow other users, Like, Share and Comment on content, as well as Repin other people's content to their own boards.

Pinterest launched in March 2010, and by June 2011 had a respectable 275,000 visitors. Then, just past the site's year-and-a-half mark, traffic skyrocketed by 4,000% with 11 million visits during the week ending December 17, 2011. In an effort to determine who this new audience was, competitive intelligence website Hitwise launched a study and found that over 10% of these visitors were web-savvy baby boomers and young adults who typically spent time on house and garden, sports and fitness, and family-oriented websites.

★ **HEAVYWEIGHT MARKETING** ★

Within months the blogosphere had exploded with post after post about this hot new social photo site. As is the case with many new tech tools, there was the implication that all businesses should be flocking to Pinterest. Marketing-guru authors raced each other to press and at least three separate "Pinterest for Business" books were hastily published in an opportunistic—and way premature—bid to capitalize on the site's newfound popularity.

I'm always dubious when anything is heralded as a one-size-fits-all solution (which seems to happen every time a new social platform is introduced). And, while Pinterest certainly showed promise when it first emerged, I was hesitant to become yet another parrot hyping its awesomeness to every business owner I met. Kevin Roose, writer with *NYMag.com*, wrote about Pinterest in its early stages and summed it up nicely when he called the platform "a nifty if ultimately unpromising attempt to bring the offline cult of scrapbooking online." So Pinterest had its fair share of sceptics when it launched, but nothing turns sceptics into believers like a little success.

In its four years of existence, Pinterest has shown impressive growth and stability and has even addressed some of the problem areas that plagued its early stages. As of this writing, the site boasts more than 70 million users, of which 80% are female. In an effort to lure the business sector, Pinterest introduced business accounts in October 2012 and currently hosts over 500 thousand business accounts.[1]

Pinterest Strengths

Building Buzz—When Pinterest first launched, the site was invitation only. In order to join, you had to request an invite. After the traffic explosion of 2011, there was a month-long waiting list to join, which generated a frantic desire among active social media users to be included in this elite new group. This was the online equivalent of a technique nightclubs have been using for decades: keeping an eager line of people waiting out front even when the club is half empty. Eventually Pinterest ditched the invitations and opened membership up to the public, at which time the ravenous social vultures circling the gate were finally admitted to the party. A hand well-played.

SEO Power—Search engine optimization is the practice of injecting your online content with relevant keywords and phrases that will help you get found by people searching the web. Whether trying to become more visible for general searches or in-platform searches, it's important to know what terms you want attached to your business.

"You can increase your content's visibility in SERPs (search engine results pages) by adding keywords within the title of a Pinterest board, the board's description, and you even have up to 500 characters to describe an individual pin so you'll want to include keywords there as well," says Danielle Cormier, Social Media Community Manager for Constant Contact. "Additionally, you can customize the pin's link and point people back to your website or blog—further increasing the opportunity for your content to rank higher in a SERP."

Driving Traffic—As mentioned above, all the posted images contain backlinks to their original site, which is an excellent source of referral traffic. Stats show that a pin is repinned an average of 10 times,[2] increasing the amount of traffic-driving opportunities. This benefits you most if these links are leading back to YOUR e-commerce site. Otherwise, you're sending visitors off to explore other sites, which means you are...

Providing Value—Pinning photos that link to helpful sites providing recipes, how-to instructions, fitness tips or educational resources is a great way to provide value to your audience, which should be a primary objective for any business using social media. After all, if your boards were made up entirely of photos from your own website, your audience will be pretty limited.

Pinterest Weaknesses

Visual Medium—Placing a heavy focus on visuals is actually a great thing, but can be limiting for business categories that are not visually-oriented. Many of the Pinterest-pushing social media gurus emphatically suggest that "unsexy" business categories such as those existing in the B2B (Business-to-Business) realm can still create an awesome presence on Pinterest by posting "quotes, infographics and product shots." Sure, they can, but should they? After all, if you can't dance, sometimes it's best to stay off the dance floor no matter how many people are out there having fun.

In an effort to attract a wider swath of business users, Pinterest introduced Rich Pins, which allow users to post additional information in the following five categories: movies, recipes, articles, products, and places. To what extent that broadens the variety of business types effectively using Pinterest remains to be seen.

Search—When Pinterest first emerged on the scene, its search capabilities left much to be desired. Over the years, they have improved slowly. "Pinterest is more of a discovery engine than a search engine," states Danny Maloney, CEO and co-founder of Pinterest analytics firm Tailwind, "but I believe visual search could be a hidden gem of the Pinterest business model." As they've grown, Pinterest has been acquiring tech companies such as recipe site Punchfork, local recommendations app Livestar, and image recognition and visual search company VisualGraph.

Round 2 - Tackle Your Tools

These investments demonstrate Pinterest's commitment to future growth and innovation. "The acquisition of VisualGraph will help us build technology to better understand what people are Pinning," a spokesperson for Pinterest told Web Pro News. "By doing so, we hope to make it easier for people to find the things they love." So, while Pinterest continues to do its part to improve search functionality, users can improve their own chances of being found by using proper keyword tagging, categorizing and organization.

Questionable Connection Level—Many of the comments on people's pins are of the "Yum," "Cool," or "I want that!" variety. While eliciting engagement from followers is a good thing, I question the level of connection you are making with someone who posts "I'm hungry" on a picture of your Bacon Cheesy Bread.

Copyright Issues—In the smash-and-grab world of the internet, it seems copyright ownership has been reduced to a technicality. When Pinterest usage surged, there was controversy over the liberal publishing of copyrighted images, photos and artwork. Since then, Pinterest has changed its terms and conditions to make it easier for copyright holders to complain and have pictures taken down. The site has also introduced the "no-pin tag," providing those who want to stay off the site a simple way to let pinners know. "For the [Pinterest] user realistically, even if they're technically infringing on someone's copyright, it's probably not going to result in any kind of lawsuit or liability or damages," says Dallas intellectual property lawyer Casey Griffith.

Platform Overload—When Pinterest first emerged on the scene, business owners had finally gotten comfortable using Facebook for business and they were wrestling over whether or not to join Google Plus, which was enjoying its own moment of hype-fueled buzz. (As for Twitter, well, many business owners found it too confusing and didn't see its benefits, so they

★ HEAVYWEIGHT MARKETING ★

attempted to ignore it altogether.) Then, along comes Pinterest, and now they're supposed to bond with their customers over photographic inspiration boards, too? Since then, Tumblr has emerged as a hot property and Instagram, Vine and Snapchat have surfaced, and each has enjoyed its moment of social-darling status. Unfortunately, there are only so many hours in a day, and way more social platforms available than any company could possibly utilize. Therefore, business owners must be very diligent in selecting marketing tools that prove effective for them and not just popular with the masses.

Takeaways

Suggesting that every business should be using Pinterest is like saying that every individual should take up scrapbooking as a hobby. However, the platform has clearly evolved into an undeniable powerhouse for e-commerce referrals. The average order placed by Pinterest shoppers is $140–$180, compared to an average of $80 from Facebook and $60 from Twitter.[3] The most popular categories include home décor and furnishings, crafts, fashion and food, which are all categories that lend themselves well to strong visuals. If your business falls into these or similar categories—and especially if you have an e-commerce presence—then Pinterest should be a no-brainer for your company.

As with any social media endeavor, if you decide to get involved, you need to make a plan as to how you will use it to build your brand. I spoke with one business owner who has been using Pinterest since before the site's 2011 popularity explosion. While she was initially ahead of the curve, she admits to falling short in the strategy-planning department: "I know with Pinterest exploding that we need to have a laid-out game plan, but for now we are still just having fun with it."

Round 2 - Tackle Your Tools

Simply having fun with Pinterest is fine. In the site's early stages it mainly functioned as a portal for daydreamers to kill time window shopping. However, in its short lifespan, Pinterest has emerged as an essential source of retail referral and e-commerce traffic, while still maintaining its allure as a window-shoppers' paradise.

As for the question posed in the title of this chapter, two or three years ago my answer would have been "no." However, in light of the progress, upgrades and innovations Pinterest has demonstrated in that time, my opinion has been swayed. Pinterest is still hot, but can it benefit your business? Absolutely.

Round 2 - Tackle Your Tools

★ 28 ★

IS GOOGLE+ A SOCIAL NETWORK OR DATA-MINING EXPERIMENT?

Google entered the social media fray in 2011 with Google+ (Google Plus) and during the months following its launch, the hype machine was in full effect. In post after post, bloggers prognosticated the death of Facebook and Twitter at the hands of the mighty Plus. Early adopters jumped aboard, firing content into the gaping maw of cyberspace, hoping to hear an echo from their scant fellow frontiersmen. Social media experts and authors hastily rushed to press with books, missives and whitepapers leading the poor, uninitiated masses, bumbling brand managers and eager marketers through the finer, best-practice points of Google+ for Business. That's right! The pixels in the G+ logo were barely dry and already gurus were attempting to plant their flag of expertise in the virgin cyber-soil of this nascent network!

The platform debuted with some unique features including Circles, which was Google's answer to Facebook's Groups and Twitter's Lists. Circles allows you to put your friends and followers into different circles so you can share different items with different groups. Or not. To me, this always felt a bit like high school, where kids are divided into separate cliques and no matter how badly you wanted to join the popular crowd, you were relegated to hang with your own substandard ilk.

Hangouts is a video conference tool that allows up to 10 users to talk on screen, text, chat, and share YouTube videos simultaneously (Google owns YouTube). Hangouts made headlines early on for facilitating the world's first Google Plus-powered video press conference by the Tibetan advocacy group International Tibet Network. The group held an event featuring speakers in India, the United States, and the United Kingdom, who addressed China's oppression of Tibet. Using the Hangouts feature, they invited select journalists to join the press conference online and the resulting video was quickly rebroadcast via Twitter and YouTube.

The Instant Upload feature is great for people who make a habit of losing or breaking their phones. Any photo or video you take with your smartphone automatically uploads to a private album on Google+, where you can then share them with your friends.

A couple of the early features that were present for the debut were killed off as the platform matured. Sparks was similar to Google Alerts, only smarter. Users would indicate topics of interest and Sparks automatically sent related content from the Web to their stream, where they could watch, read and share at their convenience. It's too bad they killed this feature because Google Alerts blows. When I released my first book, I set up a few alerts so I can track any online mentions or reviews. So far, I've had to discover them all on my own via active search or by receiving an email notice from the reviewer. A better move for Google might have been to kill Google Alerts and supplant it with Sparks.

Huddle was a group chat feature that allowed several people in different locations to communicate via text. Instead of the typical one-on-one interaction of normal texting, everybody's comments could be seen by the whole group. While Huddle came in handy for indecisive teenagers trying to decide on a movie, or thirsty college kids attempting to agree on a bar, it was deemed redundant since Hangouts also had a group chat feature.

The feature was buried next to Reader, Wave, Buzz and a dozen other products currently residing in the Google Graveyard.

That Was Then, This Is Now

An interesting attitude developed over the next two years: despite all those earnest do-gooders attempting to lead the way towards massive adoption, Google+ developed a reputation for being a "ghost town." The *New York Times* used that very phrase in the opening salvo of a recent article that was quite critical of the social network and its parent company. To be fair, there are a lot of people who beg to differ. Any article you read about Google+ contains an active comment battle between two groups of people—G+ lovers and G+ haters. The former group claims to have successfully adopted the platform and uses it effectively to communicate with their network. The latter group is either opposed to the Big Brotherness of the Google empire, or they've tried Google+ and did not gain enough traction to view it as a completely worthwhile expenditure of their time.

> *"Declaring Google+ a ghost town doesn't make it so. We are a strong, vibrant community and proud that we are the 'un-Facebook.' G+ is an open platform and through my participation, I've met people from around the world with whom I communicate daily. Businesses savvy enough to jump on G+ now will see that investment pays off in ways not possible on Facebook. Smart social media/marketing/ PR managers will not overlook G+. Those who can't see beyond Facebook will be left behind. I think if Google weren't such a powerhouse on the Internet, articles about the lack of users on G+ wouldn't exist. It's ironic, really. If it is such a ghost town, why even discuss it?"* —Cyberkrinn, Washington D.C.

★ HEAVYWEIGHT MARKETING ★

> *"I recently posted a question on my Facebook page, 'who uses Google+, and what are your thoughts about it?'...can you hear the crickets from there? Even my tech savvy, social media guru friends aren't using it. I have to concur with the ghost town reference."* —KSL

Okay, so let's set aside the he said/she said opinions for a moment and look at the one metric that should put this back-and-forth argument to bed: the numbers. After all, numbers don't lie...or do they?

As of this writing, Google currently claims to have 540 million active monthly users—or people logging into any Google account—and 300 million people who are allegedly logging into Google+ and creating or engaging with content "in the stream."[1] Google likes to tout how many people have "created Google+ accounts," but here's the catch: every time you create a Gmail account, a Google+ account is automatically generated. Over the past couple years, I've set up at least five different Gmail accounts which goosed Google's user count number by five even though I was only actively using ONE of my five Google+ accounts.

> *"Their numbers are calculated by how many people use their Google account in the year. They claim Google+ is a 'layer' or 'portal' part of the site. So anytime you use: YouTube, Google search, Gmail, Calendar, heck any site/service that is part of the Google empire that you've logged into Google with, it counts as a 'use' of Google+. Oh, and for anyone who has signed up for a new Gmail account since Google+ launch? That counts as a Google+ login too even if you never set up a profile on Google+."*
> —Scott Stratten, UnMarketing

Round 2 - Tackle Your Tools

As Stratten mentions above, Google has many properties across the web, including Maps, Calendar, Gmail, AdWords, YouTube, Search, Picasa, etc. In order to consolidate all these products into one web experience, the company has created "One Account. All of Google." This means you sign in once and can access all the products Google offers which, of course, gives them better insight into your internet behavior.

> *"As a social network, Google+ is just a bunch of empty circles spinning in a barren wasteland. But Google could give a fuck if consumers prefer Facebook. What the $400 billion data vacuum really wanted, reports* The New York Times, *is to track everything you do online and sell that personal information to advertisers." —Nitasha Tiku, Valleywag.com*

The above quote is from an incendiary article titled, "Google Admits Google+ Was Just a Ploy to Track Your Behavior Online."[2] While this article may have been a pissed-off, paraphrased take on the info revealed in the *Times* article, it proved that nobody likes to feel like they've been used as a guinea pig in a "social experiment." In fact, the top brass at Google don't even refer to Google+ as a social network, but rather an "identity service," a "portal," and a "social layer" to their myriad products.

"Google+ is an important tool that helps the company identify and authenticate users across all its services," Bradley Horowitz, VP of product management at Google+, said in a 2013 press release. Google+ creates a social layer that provides a "coherent notion of a person" as they use other Google products. "The goal of Google+ is to make all Google services better, including ads," explained Horowitz. Remember, the core of Google's business is advertising sales (what, you think free search pays the bills?), so the more targeted data they can get on their audience, the more valuable it is.

★ HEAVYWEIGHT MARKETING ★

As far as being the Facebook-killer that so many predicted, a 2013 survey showed that 30% of smartphone users visited the G+ app or website "at least once a month."[3] Once a month? Facebook has more than 1.2 billion users with their eyeballs glued to their Newsfeeds at least once per minute!

Another metric that looks great to advertisers is page view count. On your Google+ profile page, there's a follower count, which shows how many people have you in their circles, and a page view count, which shows the reach of your content. However, the term "reach" is defined pretty loosely. In this case, any post that scrolls through a user's feed when they're mindlessly swiping their iPhone screen counts as a view.[4] Then, if one of your followers shares your content into their stream, all of their followers swiping through their feed count as views as well, regardless of whether anybody actually stops to engage with your content. As you may imagine, the page view number can swell to impressive numbers pretty quickly, giving users an inflated sense of accomplishment and advertisers a reason to salivate over how many eyeballs their content will "reach."

The young man below, who falls into the pro-Google+ camp, has been drinking the Page View Kool-Aid and is pretty stoked about it.

> *"If G+ is a ghost town how come I have 30,089 followers and have so far received 24,479,507 views? Don't believe me? Here's the link to my profile page. It's the most intellectual and engaging network I have ever had the pleasure of being part of." —Justin H.*

Round 2 - Tackle Your Tools

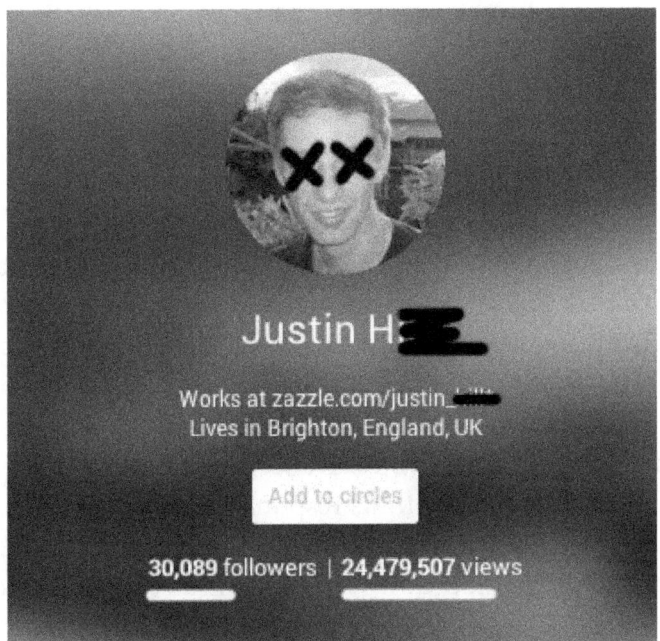

Even with over 30k followers, this G+ user has a negligible engagement rate

While young Mr. H. is proud of his number—and I'll admit, having 30k people put you in their circles is pretty impressive, assuming he didn't buy fake followers—a quick visit to his account shows that an average of 1 in 10 of his posts receives a comment. The comments are along the lines of "Thanks for the share," "Wonderful work," and "LEAVE THE SHARKS ALONE!!" Who knows, in the increasingly cynical, ruthless, rude, angry and opinionated world of internet commenting, perhaps that DOES pass for intellectual engagement.

As for receiving +1's (the Google+ equivalent to Facebook's "Like" button), he fares a little better, regularly earning between 1 and 16 clicks, depending on the post. I will happily give Mr. H. kudos for being active on this platform, for enjoying it, and for having a baker's dozen of his followers engaging with his content. However, if over 30,000 people are following you and only a dozen of them are making minimal effort to click a button or make a brief comment, then I would think twice about betting the farm on that platform as your primary small business marketing platform.

What Google+ IS Good For

Okay, enough negativity, let's talk about the strengths of Google+. First off, the mobile app is gorgeous. The way the content slides up into your stream from the lower left corner as you swipe your screen is not only a cool function aesthetically, it actually slows your scroll by "presenting" each piece of content. This slightly deters users from the endless finger-flick that sends content flying by so fast you can't see it. The desktop version is a little more confusing with its responsive masonry-style layout. The chronology of the posts is often unclear (unlike Twitter and Facebook with their top-down flow), and in an expanded browser, three uneven columns of content lack an obvious focal point. As a result, your eye careens around the page like a drunken pinball not quite knowing where to land.

Aesthetics aside, the number one benefit of using Google+ is that it will help you rank in Google search results. Doing a vanity search for my own name turned up not only my Google+ profile, but also any posts that I worked my name into. It also turned up videos I've posted to my YouTube channels. We've been hearing for a couple years that video is beneficial for ranking high in search results (which is due more to keywords found in video titles and descriptions than to media format). Since Google owns YouTube, as well as Google+, it doesn't hesitate to serve up search results located on its own web properties.

My vanity search also yielded hits from my author website, book reviews from bookseller and review sites, my Twitter profile, and other online properties bearing my name, so it's not like Google exclusively serves up content related to their own sites. However, it's clear that businesses wanting to show up in search results will benefit by using Google+ and working industry-related keywords into their posts.

Now that we've taken a deeper look at the pros and cons of Google+, let's directly address the question posed in the title of this chapter: is Google+ a social network or a data mining experiment? Yes and yes. By definition, Google+ is a social network. It's an online platform where people can post and share items of interest, and where they can hopefully connect and engage with a like-minded audience. Some users claim it's an active space that serves their purpose and meets their objectives, while others deride it as a dead zone, a ghost town and a waste of time. As for data mining experiment, Google has admitted to using Google+ as an "identity service"[5] that gives the company comprehensive and detailed insights into consumer behavior, which only benefits them when selling user data to advertisers.

I suppose the next logical question is: should you be using Google+ to market your business? That will depend on your own objectives. If you're looking for a vibrant community of friends, peers and prospects, you may do better by looking elsewhere. If you're a privacy fanatic, well, you probably shouldn't be on the web at all. If you run a business that would benefit from showing up in relevant searches for people seeking what you offer, then you should be actively posting to the platform in a strategic manner. By keeping a narrow focus, using specific keywords and hashtags in your posts, and including links back to your website, you can feed the voracious appetite of the internet, generate micro-content for the search engines to dish up, and provide value to your audience, which can build awareness and drive traffic to your website and business.

★ HEAVYWEIGHT MARKETING ★

You may have guessed from this chapter that I'm not an ardent advocate of Google+. Don't follow my advice blindly—or anybody else's for that matter. Take Google+ for a test drive and see for yourself if it meets your social needs and satisfies your business objectives. After all, when it comes to picking and choosing the most effective marketing tools for your business, the buck starts and stops with you.

★ 29 ★

DISPELLING THE MYTH OF YOUTUBE

I was talking with an acquaintance at my girlfriend's birthday party, and as is often the case with me, the conversation turned to business. This woman and her husband had recently become empty-nesters, and they were considering all sorts of small business options to pursue. One of the ideas lent itself well to video marketing in the form of "How-To" videos. My prospect seemed quite excited about the promise of YouTube. In fact, she actually said, "you can just upload a video and tons of people will see it, right?"

Right…if you're Katy Perry.

Otherwise, your video is just another grain of sand on a humongous beach where billions of people are playing volleyball. According to YouTube's Fact Sheet, people are watching 6 billion hours of videos per month on YouTube and uploading hundreds of thousands of videos daily. In fact, every minute, 100 hours of video is uploaded to the site.[1] Does that mean that nobody will ever notice your tiny grain of sand on that big ol' beach? Not necessarily. It just means that you have to work extra hard to let people know it's there. Below, you will find several ways you can do just that.

But, wait! Before you start shooting videos, uploading and directing people to them, you need to define the purpose of your video marketing. After all, most of the 2 billion videos viewed daily fall under the category of entertainment. The majority of YouTube viewers are not looking for marketing content.

★ **HEAVYWEIGHT MARKETING** ★

Therefore, small business owners should ask themselves the following questions before firing up the video camera:

1) Can our audience be found on YouTube? I worked with a client whose Board of Directors said, "Our audience is older, they don't watch YouTube." What they really meant was "WE'RE older, WE don't watch YouTube, and don't understand the benefit of it." I went on to create 55 videos for this client's channel, which have received over 6,000 views to date. Clearly, their brand is engaging SOMEONE with its YouTube presence. It's not important whether or not the members of your organization are interested in YouTube, but it's imperative that the audience you want to reach is.

2) Who is our audience? Are you tired of asking this question yet? It seems to show up in practically every chapter of this book. That's not because I like repeating myself; it's because this is one of the most essential questions every marketer needs to answer. There is obviously a wide variety of people viewing all those videos, but knowing who YOU are specifically trying to reach will result in creating more focused videos that speak directly to your target audience.

3) What value do our videos offer? As mentioned above, most of the videos on YouTube involve people getting hit in the crotch with various objects, animals doing silly things and multiple other inane human shenanigans that can loosely be described as entertainment. Unfortunately, that's what most people go there to watch! Therefore, IF you choose to utilize video marketing for your company, it must be done in a way that is unique, fun, entertaining, educational and valuable to your viewer. You need to offer viewers a good reason to give you their attention.

Oh, and keep your videos short, preferably 2–3 minutes in length. You'd be surprised how long a 5-minute video can feel, especially if you're watching on a phone.

4) What are we hoping they will do after viewing? Simply going for brand awareness is fine, as long as everyone's on board with that objective. If, however, you've got a call to action in mind, that needs to be crystal clear to the viewer. Whether you want people to call a phone number, visit a website, or show up at your store, let viewers know exactly what's expected of them.

5) Do we have a sales channel set up to funnel interested prospects through? This relates to the previous question. If viewers are interested in your offering, you had better direct them to a place where they can complete the transaction when they're ready to do so.

6) What keywords are people using to find what we're offering? Knowing what words and phrases your customers are searching to find your company, product or category will help your videos get found. Once you have a list of keywords, optimize your videos for search engines by adding them to the areas listed below.

Three Hot Spots for Relevant Keywords:

Video Titles—Keep your titles short and snappy. They should tease, entice, provoke, or give a glimpse of what benefit awaits the viewer. Similar to your email marketing subject lines, you want your video titles to be too good to pass up. Browsing other people's videos on YouTube will give you a good idea of what works and what doesn't.

Video Description—The first thing that should go in the description box on every video is your company's complete website URL. You must include "http://" in order to create a working hyperlink. Sometimes people will view your video on YouTube, and sometimes they'll see it on another social media platform or a blog. Wherever your video shows up it will include at least a snippet of your description, so you want your web address to be visible right away. Beyond that, create a keyword-rich description that sums up your video's content.

Keywords Field—Under the video description box is a Keywords field. Use as many words and phrases that relate to your offering and your industry as you can. As you're typing these in, YouTube will offer some suggestions of its own. Feel free to use any of their relative terms that you haven't thought about. After all, they have a pretty good idea of what users are searching for.

Once you've got a few videos on your YouTube channel, you've got to spread the word. Be sure to promote your channel on all of your marketing collateral: include the URL in your email signature and your e-newsletter; post videos on Facebook and on your blog; tweet links to your videos, and take every opportunity to direct your prospects and customers there.

Remember, when promoting, do not simply say, "Check out our videos," or "Check us out on YouTube." Give people a reason to watch your videos by letting them know the benefit they will receive from viewing them. For example, "Visit our YouTube channel for free photography tips," or "Check us out on YouTube to learn how to start your own organic garden."

There have been some amazing success stories attributed to YouTube, including the discovery of Justin Bieber. Sure, as of late he has downward-spiraled into tabloid-fodder trainwreckland, but for a moment he was the planet's biggest teen-pop phenom. The children's choir that closed out the 2011 Oscar ceremony was discovered on YouTube, and flown out from

Round 2 - Tackle Your Tools

Staten Island to Hollywood for their big performance. Brands such as Snickers, BlendTec Blenders, Old Spice and Volkswagen have all experienced massive viral video success in the recent past by creating unique, compelling, humorous videos that people want to watch and are inclined to share.

So, getting back to my conversation with my prospect, yes, I suppose there is a chance that a video on YouTube COULD be seen by "tons of people." But more likely, it's simply another piece of content marketing that—if executed properly—could be a great way to engage, entertain and educate your target market.

★ 30 ★

AN INSTAGRAM IS WORTH A THOUSAND WORDS

At 200 million users (and growing), Instagram is the current heavyweight champion of social photo sharing. While other social platforms can boast a greater number of users, none have affected amateur digital photography as much as Instagram has. Instagram is a mobile-based photo-sharing app that allows users to take photos and share them across a variety of social platforms. Instagram's "big idea" was originally its filter feature, which allows users to apply a variety of filters to their photos, turning even the most mundane cell phone pic into a work of art.

Another distinctive feature was the square photo format, which was a throwback to the look of old Kodak Instamatic and Polaroid photos. The filter feature has been usurped, adopted, and appropriated ad nauseam by other photo platforms, so it may not be unique to Instagram anymore, but they are still credited with being "first" in the space. And, as any entrepreneur knows, that's a covetable position to be in.

In 2012—a mere two years after launching—Instagram was acquired by Facebook for a billion dollars in cash and stock. So, not only is Instagram one of the hottest social platforms going, but its rapid ascent from scrappy startup to billion-dollar buyout is a storybook fairy tale fueling the dreams of a million starry-eyed entrepreneurs across the globe. Several months after the purchase Instagram extended their mobile-only platform to the desktop, allowing users to create an online portal they can access from a computer—which looks a lot like Facebook's Timeline design.

★ **HEAVYWEIGHT MARKETING** ★

So, what's the allure? In two words: eye candy. Instagram capitalizes on the power of visual storytelling through still images and 15-second videos, allowing users to enjoy beauty, art, escapism and easy engagement. In addition to its point, shoot and upload simplicity, Instagram offers the pleasure of scrolling through an endless photo album without the confusion of Twitter. And, unlike Facebook, the platform is still new so it's not choked with the clutter and noise of a billion users. According to a study from Forrester Research, Instagram represents by far the best platform for marketers to interact with consumers. Looking at 2,500 posts on seven social networks, Forrester found that engagement on Instagram was roughly 60 times higher than Facebook.[1]

In another study, analytics company Curalate tracked Instagram activity around the hashtag #NYFW during New York Fashion Week. It found that the top ten branded Instagram accounts—a mix of brands, stores and magazines focusing on fashion and makeup—drove 2.5 million interactions in the course of a week.[2]

Instagram delivers high interaction rates with brand content for three main reasons, Forrester says. First, it has fewer users and less content so brand posts don't get lost in the shuffle. Second, Instagram doesn't filter out brand posts the way Facebook does, so fans and followers actually see content from brands they follow. And finally, Instagram's user base skews younger than Facebook and Twitter, which is helpful because younger users typically engage more with brands on social sites.[3]

Getting Started with Instagram

Just like any social platform, many of the same rules and strategies apply regarding setting up your account.

Round 2 - Tackle Your Tools

Name—Obviously, you want your user name to be the same as your personal or business name. One thing I've found to be a bit frustrating is the lack of available names. I've searched for a dozen names I wanted to use and they were all taken. Yet most of the accounts were either squatters with zero activity, or forgotten accounts from people who got caught up in the wave of Instagram hysteria back in 2011, only to peter out and drop out a few months later. I even read a story about parent-company Facebook taking back user names from inactive accounts for their employees to use. Bottom line, good user names are hot property on Instagram so if yours is available, snatch it up—even if you don't plan on using it right away.

Profile Picture—This is tiny, so make sure yours is bold and arresting. Since all of your Instagram content is image-based, your profile pic plays a lesser role than it does on Facebook and Twitter. However, it's still important to consider its impact from a branding perspective. And, hey, if you can create an image that immediately conjures your brand with a 40-pixel square, you're doing something right!

Bio—You've only got 150 characters to work with in your bio, so if you've ever needed to create a concise elevator pitch, it's right here. Your bio section is also the only place an actual outbound link will appear, so when filling out your profile, be sure to include your company's website URL.

Content—When creating content with Instagram, consider yourself the creative curator of your brand's museum. Don't just use the platform as a photo dump like some lazy people on Facebook do with their albums. Boooring! Instead, think of your images as art. Try hard to creatively convey everything about your business to the world, even if it isn't in a typically visual category. When shooting, ask yourself whether your images would stop users in their tracks as they scroll through the feed.

HEAVYWEIGHT MARKETING

That doesn't mean you can't mix it up by including photos of products, people and events in addition to your artsy imagery.

★ ★ ★ ★

Typical social nomenclature of Like, Share, Comment and Follow is used with Instagram, as well as the etiquette surrounding engagement with other users. To "like" a photo, you can either double-tap it or click the heart/like button, and the comment button allows you to join the conversation. You can tag your photos, which is similar to Facebook and alerts the person or company you tagged, and you can add captions and #hashtags to your photos, which are the primary way to ensure your content shows up when people are searching on the platform.

According to social superstar Gary Vaynerchuk, "Hashtags are the doorway through which people will discover your brand; without them, you are doomed to invisibility."[4] Unfortunately, this results in posts containing unsightly rows upon rows of hashtags either in the photo caption area or the comment section. This certainly doesn't help the aesthetics of the platform (at least Twitter's hashtag mania is limited to 140 characters), but the only way to search is via user names or hashtags so they do serve a purpose.

King of the Passive Consumption Platforms

There are a surprising amount of limitations to Instagram, which essentially reduces it to a passive, media consumption platform. Unlike every other social media platform, there's not a simple re-post function (or, "regram," in InstaParlance). In order to share someone else's photos, you need to capture a screen shot to re-post manually, or use a third party app designed to provide a regram option. You can, however, post your photos to other sites like Tumblr, Facebook, Twitter, Flickr (really?) and Foursquare, all of which have native sharing capabilities, thus giving your photos an opportunity to escape the closed loop of Instagram.

Instagram photos do not contain outbound links so, unlike Pinterest, they cannot be used as e-commerce drivers to send traffic to your website. In order to drive shoppers to your physical or virtual storefront, you have to include a call to action in your photo caption or comment section. And, while you can include your URL in your caption, it won't be

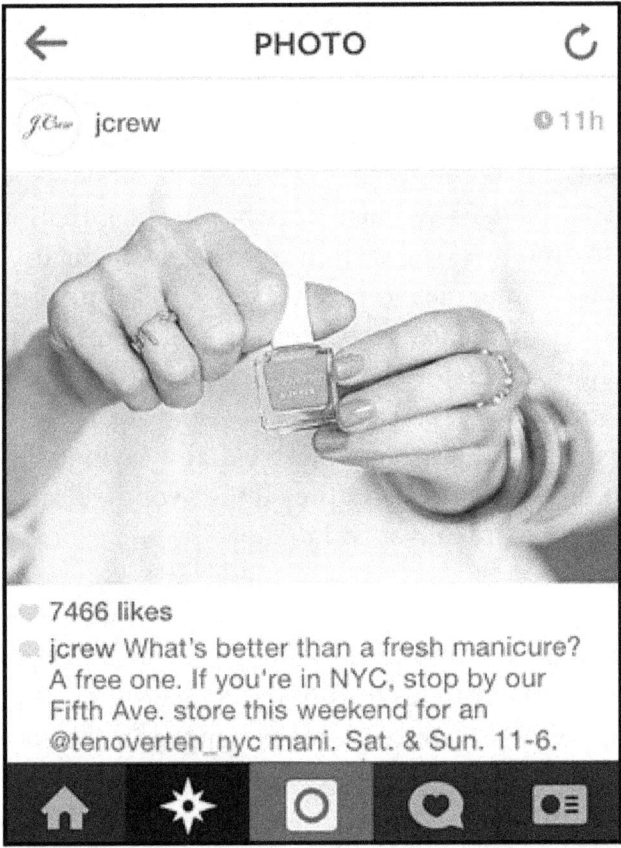

In this Instagram post, J.Crew drives traffic to their physical store

clickable. In order to track the effectiveness of Instagram-as-traffic-driver, you can include a specific code or discount for shoppers to redeem at time of purchase.

★ HEAVYWEIGHT MARKETING ★

When it comes right down to it, Instagram is kind of a one-trick pony: point, shoot, tweak, post, comment, like, repeat. And THAT was worth a billion big ones? Apparently so.

> *"Instagram followers reward the art of photos. And brands that respond with beautiful, emotion-filled photos of their products and their customers truly unlock the visual and emotional power of Instagram, and in turn drive the desire to purchase." —Kate Harrison, Forbes*

Harrison touches on a key point in her quote above. Marketing needs to concern itself with ROI (return on investment), in order to justify time and money spent. For years, social media advocates have been saying that, while it's difficult to directly calculate ROI from social media use, it's still essential for companies to be on the hot social platforms. The theory is that if brands go where their audience is and build relationships, share stories and have conversations, casual users will become loyal brand customers. This theory gets a little more abstract with Instagram, essentially saying: show your audience pretty pictures and they'll visit your website or store of their own accord and spend money.

While I think that's a bit of a stretch, it's really just another form of building brand awareness. Companies routinely spend hundreds of thousands of dollars per year on print ads featuring pretty pictures with logos slapped in the corner, and they are expecting the same results: carve out a little space in consumers' minds so they will remember us when it comes time to go shopping. When you think about it, perhaps the theory is not so far-fetched after all.

Round 2 - Tackle Your Tools

Tools and Tips to Help Marketers Inspire and Engage

Three months after Instagram opened their program up to advertisers, they wrote a blog post discussing some of the brands that were doing great things on the platform (the list included General Electric, Chobani Yogurt, Nike, GoPro, Warby Parker, Ben and Jerry's and a few others). The subtext of the post was, "Brands: get more creative!" and they offered five tips to do so.[5]

The numbered tips below are directly from Instagram's blog post, while the commentary following each tip is mine:

1) Be true to your brand

Some business categories are inherently visual, therefore a natural fit with Instagram. Others will have to try harder to develop a visual style that works on the platform. Determining how you want people to perceive your brand is an essential step in any business. In the case of Instagram (and any other social platform), understanding your brand parameters helps to guide the type of content you share with your audience.

2) Share experiences

Sue B. Zimmerman, aka the InstagramGal, is very active on the conference circuit. She loves to photograph herself with customers, clients, authors, celebrities, peers and colleagues. This gives her Instagram feed a very personable feel and shows that she is very friendly, outgoing and social in the offline world as well as online. People enjoy seeing themselves online. Photographing shared experiences, posting them to the web and tagging the images is a great way to build community by getting people to like, comment, share and participate with your content. *(We talk more with Sue B. Zimmerman in the next chapter.)*

3) Find beauty everywhere

As mentioned earlier, Instagram is based mostly around visuals. Personally, I have found that it inspires you to see the world with new eyes. Back when I was blogging on a regular basis, I approached each day with what I called a "blog mentality." This meant seeking daily moments, events and lessons that could be transmuted into blog posts. These days, I'm on the lookout for "Instagram moments." Using this app forces you view your surroundings through a creative lens. It motivates you to notice the beauty and art of everyday moments, and challenges you to capture those moments while you can. Sure, many users simply use it as another platform for posting the same old poorly-lit, blurry, sadly-composed snapshots and bathroom-mirror selfies that they post to all the other platforms, but Instagram fancies itself a creative platform and should stimulate users to treat it as such.

4) Inspire action

Certain brands work hard to inspire action in their audience. Nike, with their "Just Do It" mentality, prompts you to get off the couch and get active. Natural food brands aim to get people eating healthier with tips and recipes. Outdoor lifestyle brands like Patagonia inspire you to treat the earth's environment with respect. Other brands focus on smaller actions such as getting people to like, comment, follow, visit their website or go shopping at their store. Sure, there's a slight difference between inspiring activism and inspiring consumerism but both can be okay as long as they are done intermittently with taste and tact.

5) Know your audience

This tenet is not just helpful for creating effective Instagram content, but it's a core principle of operating any business. Knowing who your audience is, where they are and what they will find valuable is essential for success with any marketing effort. This also means knowing whether or not your audience can even be found on Instagram. Sure, most marketing experts love to encourage business owners to adopt every platform that pops up, but there are so many tools available and only a limited amount of time to utilize them. If connecting with your audience through photographic art and visual storytelling will benefit them and you, then by all means jump in. If not, then you're better off not wasting your time.

Case Study: Will Shoot for Food

Who would've thought social media innovation would come from a company known for selling frozen peas? Birds Eye frozen foods made news—and possibly history—for creating the "world's first pay-by-picture restaurant." To promote its new Inspirations product line, Birds Eye opened a pop-up restaurant in London called The Picture House which served two new entreé items, Chicken Inspirations and Fish Chargrills. Diners could "pay" for their meals by taking photos of their dinner, tagging them with #BirdsEyeInspirations, and posting them to Instagram.

Since "foodstagramming" is a thing, Birds Eye even held food-photography workshops to help users improve their snapshot skills, then had a photo competition during the restaurant's limited run. This is a great example of an unexpected company creating massive social buzz, press and goodwill—free food!—by using social media in creative ways to help launch a new product. Well done, Birds Eye.

Future Outlook

As mentioned earlier, Instagram is currently enjoying its sexy-Marlon-Brando-as-rebel-on-a-motorcycle phase: hot, young, vital and in demand. But if you have ever paid attention to the life cycle of anything, you know that Instagram's batshit-crazy-Marlon-Brando-showing-up-on-set-without-pants period is lurking in the distance. At least that's what Forrester Research is predicting, and hey, if anyone knows cycles, it's the companies that spend their lives tracking them.

> *"Instagram delivers best-in-class social engagement rates for brands today, but it won't last. Marketers must use Instagram now, before it changes the rules—and they must be ready to move on to another social site when Instagram's phenomenal engagement rates disappear."*
> —Forrester Research Report

The killjoys at Forrester Research are basically telling us to enjoy it while we can. They predict Instagram will only deliver impressive levels of engagement for a limited amount of time. As more marketers and users descend on the platform, it will become more crowded and therefore more difficult for companies to stand out. This may force the photo-sharing service to filter its content to ensure users are served up only those posts most relevant to them, which will probably affect brand content negatively. What's more, Instagram needs to generate revenue from marketers, and could begin to limit organic reach intentionally to help drive sales.[6]

The social media graveyard is littered with formerly-smoking-hot platforms that could not maintain relevance—and certainly not it-level status—as time marched on. Facebook is the latest bloated Titanic making so many changes, shifts and bids for relevance that users can hardly keep up. In the future, the Facebook-owned Instagram could very well fall victim to the same issues.

If you're thinking about adding Instagram to your marketing mix, don't ponder too long. The time to hitch your brand's wagon to the youthful star that is Instagram is right

Round 2 - Tackle Your Tools

now, while its back is still strong enough to support your weight and the thrill of its glory days are not yet viewed through the rear view mirror.

For your weekly dose of #creative #poptastic #eyecandy, follow Nikolas Allen on Instagram @nikolas_allen.

★ 31 ★

INTERVIEW WITH THE #INSTAGRAMGAL

Sue B. Zimmerman aka the #InstagramGal

Lifelong entrepreneur Sue B. Zimmerman runs a seasonal boutique, SueB.Do, on Cape Cod. SueB.Do is a product line of preppy fresh clothing, jewelry and accessories representing the beauty, fun and character of the Cape. A couple years back, Sue B. noticed her teenage daughters using Instagram and was intrigued enough to adopt it for her own use. Oddly enough, this didn't horrify her daughters and send them scurrying to a different platform, although they did have slight misgivings when Sue B. started positioning herself as the local Instagram expert.

★ **HEAVYWEIGHT MARKETING** ★

Sue B. started using Instagram as a social platform for her business, posting photos of her customers and products, and images from trade shows and events. In one summer, SueB.Do's retail business increased by 40% after using Instagram to connect with customers and potential clients. Experiencing the power of Instagram firsthand, Sue B. unleashed her own knowledge and successful theories and began to educate her fellow entrepreneurs on how to use Instagram successfully for their business. Thus, the #InstagramGal was born.

When I first heard Sue B.'s story, I was intrigued by the growth figure she was touting. After all, anyone working with social media has become accustomed to parroting the same old "Social media are impossible to measure" story. Yet Sue B. was claiming to have increased product sales by 40% simply by posting pics to a mobile photo-sharing app? I was curious enough to reach out for some clarity.

Despite a schedule that has her buzzing like a worker bee, Sue B. was gracious enough to answer the following questions:

Nikolas Allen: First off, how did your teenage daughters react when Mom hijacked their favorite social platform?

Sue B. Zimmerman: At first they didn't think I knew what I was doing, but when I told them the sales at my store SueB.Do increased over 40% I proved them wrong. They weren't too fond of me teaching Instagram, especially to their friend's moms.

NA: Marketing is often difficult to track, especially social media marketing. You tout the growth figure of 40% for SueB. Do after using Instagram. How did you track your company's 40% growth accurately enough to directly attribute it to Instagram use?

SBZ: My store is only 10' × 12' and we check out each customer with my iPad. We ask everyone how they heard about us and what brought them in the door. When they said Instagram, we tracked it and did the math.

NA: What time period did you use to measure this growth spurt?

SBZ: One summer selling season. My store is seasonal from Memorial Day thru Labor day. I also sell at Direct to Consumer venues on the Cape and the GeoTag feature is a huge way to lead people to my business wherever I am selling.

NA: To get the most out of Instagram, you need to have an account. Does that mean your business audience (the customers responsible for the 40% growth) was already using the platform?

SBZ: My growth was due largely to the seven gals who work for me. Part of their job description is to check in on FourSquare every shift and upload a pic, tweet twice per shift, upload to Facebook and post two Instagram pics. Because all the teenage/college gals have 500–1000 friends on Instagram, it was their collective efforts that helped increased my sales. I call them my buzz agents and they are all a part of my visual content strategy.

[Author's Note: Now that, my friends, is a social strategy! If you employ Millennials, they're going to be checking out their social media feeds all day anyway, so you may as well make it part of their job description. Leaders who leverage the social connectivity of their staff will reap rewards that will benefit the entire business.]

NA: How were you recruiting and/or reaching non-Instagram-users so they could engage with you and your content—and therefore become customers?

★ HEAVYWEIGHT MARKETING ★

SBZ: We have a big sign in front of the door at our store that tells people to follow @suebdo.capecod, use the hashtag #SueBDo when posting, and GeoTag the post, because the UGC (User Generated Content) is invaluable. When your fans create content on your behalf then you know you have attracted ideal customers and fans. Some of my customers are only on Facebook. We always share our Instagram pics from SueB.Do to our Facebook fan page, and some of our customers see our Instagram pictures there and come visit from the post.

NA: I see that SueB.Do's website does have e-commerce capabilities. Regarding your 40% sales increase, did the larger percentage of that come from online sales or instore sales?

SBZ: All in store. We have a website, but we do most of our sales from our store and Direct to Consumer venues and now from Instagram.

NA: Have you experimented with any unique Instagram-only codes, offers, coupons or third-party add-ons for driving traffic or tracking sales?

SBZ: I recently discovered an app called Heartbeat, which is an iPhone app that lets you post pictures of products to Instagram, multiple Facebook pages, Tumblr, Pinterest, and multiple Twitter accounts at the same time. Each picture links back to a simple Buy Now page, making it really easy to buy directly from social media. I'm able to track how many people click through to the buy page, so I can tell which pictures generate the most interest. Heartbeat is perfect for product-based businesses that are trying to get more out of the time they spend on social media.

NA: I've heard you talk about including Calls To Action in your Instagram photo captions. How have you been using these?

Round 2 - Tackle Your Tools

SBZ: I use CTAs to mostly to get people to sign up for a webinar, an opt-in, or a course I am teaching. I change the custom bit.ly in my bio depending on what my goals are. Sometimes I lead people to my YouTube channel because I want to grow my followers there too.

NA: Speaking of YouTube, I see you're quite active on other social media platforms. Have you been able to attribute business growth to those platforms the way you have with Instagram?

SBZ: I have ALWAYS been active on social media. My brain thinks in Instagrams and tweets. I think they are all connected. I often speak about connecting your social media buttons. Since Instagram is highly integrated with other platforms (Facebook, Twitter, Foursquare, Tumblr, and Flicker) it's my fave.

NA: What percentage of your time do you devote to planning, running and growing SueB.Do, these days?

SBZ: SueB.Do comes very easily to me. I have had this brand seven years now and my store is on its fifth season. I know exactly what my customers buy and like. A lot of it has to do with my keen, observant eye to trends, which has been my secret sauce since I was a young entrepreneur. I started my first business hand-painting boxer shorts and grew it to a million-dollar business when I was 22 years old.

NA: SueB.Do is seasonal. Where do you put your business focus in the off-season?

SBZ: My focus is on my Insta-Results course. This is an online course teaching Instagram to people who want to gain new followers, attract new customers, or reach a hyper-focused target market and convert them to paying clients. The course offers step-by-step tools and strategies for people to start increasing traffic to their site right away.

NA: Instagram is hot—and still growing—but it could easily go the way of Flickr, Hotmail or MySpace. Where does the #TheInstagramGal and @TheInstagramExpert go from here? How will you diversify?

SBZ: I am a multi-passionate entrepreneur and have had 18 businesses. I am the queen of reinvention and knowing when to transform into the next opportunity. I have been successfully doing this for 30 years.

NA: In your website video, you say you teach people how to "get more followers, find the ideal audience and make more money." What are your current favorite tips that you think will help people do that?

SBZ: Be authentic, humanize your brand, lead with giving, and hire a team that aligns with your values.

NA: Any other experiences or insights you would like to share with your fellow entrepreneurs?

SBZ: I lead with giving value and investing in relationships first—always have, always will—and the money ALWAYS follows. I also don't get caught up with what other people think of me. I have always done what I am passionate about with purpose and have attracted an engaging tribe because of my focus. My success has come from my gut and intuition, not data. I follow my heart and passion and it has always lead to me living a life with purpose and content.

NA: Thank you so much for your time, Sue B., and I wish you #InstaAmazing success in all your business endeavors!

Round 2 - Tackle Your Tools

To learn more about Sue B. Zimmerman, find her online:

Boutique: www.suebdo.com
Website: www.suebzimmerman.com
Insta-Results: www.insta-results.com
Instagram: @suebzimmerman
@theinstagramexpert
@suebdo.capecod
@suebjewels
@the.daily.ig

★ 32 ★

FACEBOOK IS DEAD, LONG LIVE FACEBOOK

I'm going to take a wild guess and assume that you're already familiar with Facebook. Everybody in the free world is. Heck, at over a billion users, even people in the not-so-free world have Facebook accounts. While it's still the granddaddy of the social media world, a lot has changed over the past two years in terms of using Facebook for business.

Facebook was built for personal use. Their mission has always been to help make the world more connected and open. During the social network's halcyon days (between 2008 and 2012), it was not only a great way to connect with friends and family, but also a powerful free-marketing platform with unlimited reach. Business owners were able to set up brand pages to connect with and market to their audience. Paid ads were also available—which has allowed Facebook to become a multi-billion-dollar business—but most users adhered to the old adage: why buy the cow if you can get the milk for free?

Well, in 2012, Facebook started pinching off the udder to their free-milk machine. They restricted organic reach of content published from brand pages to about 16 percent. In December 2013, another round of changes reduced it even more.

"Organic reach of the content brands publish in Facebook is destined to hit zero. It's only a matter of time."
—Marshall Manson, Social@Ogilvy

★ **HEAVYWEIGHT MARKETING** ★

According to a Social@Ogilvy analysis of more than 100 brand pages, organic reach dropped to 6 percent by February 2014, a decline of 49 percent from peak levels in the previous October. For large pages with more than 500,000 Likes, organic reach hit 2 percent in February, and Facebook sources were unofficially advising community managers to expect it to approach zero in the foreseeable future.[1]

So what changed? First, the space was getting way too crowded. With so many brands publishing, pushing, promoting, and polluting the newsfeed with commercial content, the "personal" aspect of the platform was getting diluted.

While Facebook would love to tout their reach-squelching motives as altruistic—trying to keep the endless stream of content limited to things people actually care about—there's an obvious financial incentive for their actions. The remedy for reduced organic reach is paid reach. Business owners can pay to "boost" and promote their posts and pages, which may be the only way their content will be seen by fans who have liked their page.

These developments have enraged business owners, who have gotten quite comfy with the free gravy train that was yesteryear's Facebook. But can you really complain about being charged to reach your audience? Advertising is a pay-to-play game. It always has been. Just because social media has introduced a new communication dynamic between businesses and consumers doesn't completely change the foundation of advertising. Besides, you're using a free platform that reaches billions of people around the world, and you're gonna complain that you have to spend money to actually sell to these people? Really?

In my experience, small business marketers have grown way too accustomed to using Facebook as their primary source of marketing. A laziness has set in that deters them from seeking out other viable alternatives. This is just as dangerous to your business as allowing any one client to become your primary source of revenue—which companies often do. Because if and when your relationship sours, you're left scrambling.

It's Not You, It's Me...Wait, Maybe It Is You

After organic reach plummeted, a few companies made news for deciding not to use Facebook for marketing. Just before Facebook's much-anticipated IPO, automotive manufacturer GM caused a ripple when they announced they were pulling a 10 million dollar ad spend because it wasn't reaping the results the company hope for. That's not too surprising. After all, how many people do you know who shop for new cars on Facebook? However, the minute someone says a specific tool or tactic is not working, you need to ask whether they were using it properly.

> *"If GM has the perfect media mix and they're struggling to find advertising return on investment with their Facebook ads, it would be interesting to know how often they tested, iterated and played with the format before deciding that it was simply not an effective ad platform for them."* —Mitch Joel, TwistImage

Testing and iterating aside, if a company is dropping ten mil on advertising and they're NOT seeing an adequate ROI, it would be idiotic to keep throwing money away, despite what all the armchair analysts have to say. Another automaker took the opposite approach: after noticing a decline in Facebook's organic reach, Ford accelerated its advertising spend.

> *"We've found that Facebook ads are very effective, and they're most effective when we strategically combine them with great content and innovative forms of storytelling*

★ HEAVYWEIGHT MARKETING ★

rather than a straight media buy." —Scott Monty, former Head of Social Media, Ford

If GM's ad pull caused a wave, then food delivery company Eat24 created a tsunami by becoming "the first company to leave Facebook" after getting fed up with the new pay-to-play scheme. Like GM, they stopped their ad spending, which was around one million dollars, but they went a step further and deleted their business page which had 170,000 fans. They got tons of mileage from their humorous, high-profile "breakup letter," which was written in the tone of a jilted lover and quickly went viral. The following is a short excerpt from a rather long blog post:

> "When we first met, you made us feel special. We'd tell you a super funny joke about Sriracha and you'd tell all our friends and then everyone would laugh together. But now? Now you want us to give you money if we want to talk to our friends. Now when we show you a photo of a taco wrapped with bacon, you're all like 'PROMOTE THIS POST! GET MORE FRIENDS!' instead of just liking us for who we are." —Eat24

Many of Eat24's fans, peers and fellow marketers applauded the bold move, and it garnered an enviable amount of press. But, because this is the internet, there was plenty of ire, outrage and criticism spewed in the company's direction as well.

> "Basically, the Internet exploded. People laughed, people cried, people yelled at us in all caps. A lot of people supported our decision to leave Facebook, but some people just got really pissed off." —Eat24

Round 2 - Tackle Your Tools

Like GM, Eat24's detractors suggested that they "weren't using Facebook properly." This misguided sentiment suggests that EVERY advertising platform can be effective IF you use it properly. While this may or may not be true, it does not mean that you absolutely have to utilize every available platform, especially if you have tried it and came to the conclusion that it doesn't work for you.

Facebook's communications director Brandon McCormick even chimed in with an official response to the breakup letter:

"Hey Eat24, I was bummed to read your letter. The world is so much more complicated than when we first met—it has changed. And we used to love your jokes about tacquitos and 420 but now they don't seem so funny. There is some serious stuff happening in the world and one of my best friends just had a baby and another one just took the best photo of his homemade cupcakes and what we have come to realize is people care about those things more than sushi porn."

Even more humorous than Eat24 getting tons of press for breaking up with Facebook, was that they got more press at the one-month-later mark. The food delivery service published a post-breakup article on their blog, which got picked up by news outlets that wrote headlines like, "One Month Later, Eat24 Stands By Its Breakup With Facebook," and "What Happens When You Break Up With Facebook: Nothing."

These bloggers and reporters had an incredulous tone, as if they were expecting to be writing different headlines after the unprecedented exodus: "One Month After Breakup, Eat24 Shutters Its Doors," "Eat24 Starves After Leaving Facebook,"

★ **HEAVYWEIGHT MARKETING** ★

or "Facebook to Eat24: We Told You So." Not quite. Here's an excerpt from Eat24's one-month follow-up post:

> "We closed our Facebook page, and absolutely nothing happened. The sky didn't cave in. Hell didn't freeze over. Tuesdays are still exclusively for Tacos. Everything is pretty much exactly the same as it was when we had a page. The only difference is now we don't have to think about things like optimal headline length, preview image resolution, and the proper ratio of cats to cheeseburgers to maximize virality. Other than all our new found free time, not much has changed. We're doing just fine. Thanks for asking!" —*Eat24*

This entire episode indicates that a lot of people out there—consumers and marketers alike—cannot fathom a company NOT having a Facebook presence. But believe it or not, Ladies and Gentlemen, even the Almighty Facebook is optional when it comes to marketing your business.

Elvis Has Left the Building

Speaking of people leaving Facebook, another story surrounding the company is the loss of its "cool" factor. "Facebook is no longer cool!" shout the online news outlets with glee. First, stories emerged that Millennials were defecting in droves. I mean, who wants to be on the same social platforms as their parents, right? Not to mention Facebook's biggest growth rate of late has been users in the 55+ age range. Lame-O!

The stories began in 2012. Even the *LA Times* reported on Facebook's declining popularity: "Facebook itself is no longer an adolescent. At 8, it's getting long in the tooth for a social network. And for some teens, the novelty has worn off."

Round 2 - Tackle Your Tools

"Facebook is just not the big fad anymore," said Kim Franklin, a 15-year-old from Gaithersburg, Md., who does not have a Facebook account and prefers social media site Tumblr. "It was like everybody was constantly on there, but now not so much."

Then the age range of the Facebook dissidents increased and statistics started pointing their pie charts and bar graphs at college students who were finding social alternatives to Big Blue.

> "(In 2014) digital consultancy iStrategy Labs released a study that draws from Facebook's Social Advertising platform to glean exactly how many young users have left the social network in recent years. The resulting estimates are pretty staggering. According to iStrategy, Facebook has 4,292,080 fewer high-school aged users and 6,948,848 college-aged users than it did in 2011." —Christopher Matthews, writer and reporter for TIME

Heck, even the friggin' President of the United States was overheard at a diner discussing Facebook's dwindling mojo amongst the youth of America. "It seems like they don't use Facebook anymore," said President Obama while having a coffee clutch with Millennials in order to determine the best way to reach them about the Affordable Health Care Act.[2] While you can bet the Feds still ended up using Facebook to promote the Act, they surely sought out other more relevant (i.e., cool) platforms to spread the word.

> "Facebook may not be the cool social network anymore—all the recent buzz has been about Instagram, Pinterest, and other niche networks—but Facebook is still the site most Millennials are on. Some 93% have a

★ HEAVYWEIGHT MARKETING ★

Facebook profile, according to Ypulse research, and it's for that reason that they'll continue to use it. Nearly all of their friends are on it, so they feel the need to be on it to keep up with what their friends are doing." —ypulse.com

Writers, bloggers and newshounds love to write about the Great Facebook Exodus, but there are still way more people using the platform than leaving it. It just seems that "Young Adults No Longer Use Facebook" makes for a more interesting story than reporting on Facebook's latest billion-dollar earnings report or most recent algorithm adjustment.

Personally, I'm over Facebook, and I'm neither a Millennial nor a college student. I'm tired of the endless stream of invites to events I'll never attend—some of them coming from friends in a state I moved away from six years ago (way to target your audience, folks); I'm tired of the infinite requests to like someone's new page from which the level of value I will derive remains dubious at best (IF Facebook even decides to serve their content in my newsfeed); and I'm over the armchair activists who blast post after post about society's injustices as if changing the world can be done in front of a computer screen between viewings of cat videos, family photos, and the latest meme du jour. But those of us moving away from the network are mere drops in the bucket compared to the ocean of users still addicted to the infinite dopamine drip that is Facebook.

Besides, here's the flipside of the story: cool is overrated. Cool is ephemeral. Cool is that shiny new object waiting to be supplanted as soon as something cooler comes along. Cool is only hot until it's not. Then cool becomes cold. Some companies strive to be cool, others strive to be useful. There's a difference between utility and appeal. It seems that in the past decade, Facebook's has morphed from shiny new object into the ultimate utilitarian communication platform.

Round 2 - Tackle Your Tools

"Facebook doesn't need to be cool. It doesn't want to be cool. It actively works towards to the total opposite every single day. Facebook wants to become an essential part of your life. Something you don't need to think about. Something so useful, you'll never want to leave it." —Pete Wood, guest columnist for TheDrum

Know What's Not Cool? Ad Fraud

Another story that has been giving online advertisers pause is the rampant perpetration of ad fraud in the digital space. In Facebook's case, it occurs when advertisers pay for ads hoping to generate legitimate page likes and increase their fan count with people who are interested in engaging with their content. Unfortunately, many of these likes that advertisers are being charged for come from click farms in developing countries. Click farm employees are paid $1 per 1,000 clicks of the Like button, which basically generates a bunch of fake likes from low-quality fans who couldn't care less about the content brands are posting to their pages. In many cases, the result of purchasing ads is a larger number of likes with minimal engagement on the page.[3]

When my first book, *Death to the Starving Artist*, came out, I purchased a couple different rounds of Facebook Ads before and after the holiday season. Using Facebook's excellent targeting tools, I zeroed in on a customized and highly-specific audience in different areas of the world. My objective was not to increase likes on a brand page, but to drive traffic to my book's website in an effort to generate direct sales.

Running ads rejuvenated my excitement in Facebook, which had long since cooled. Not because I was interested to see what my friends were posting, but because I was eager to check the status of my analytics! According to Facebook, my campaign was

★ **HEAVYWEIGHT MARKETING** ★

going according to plan. I opted for PPC (pay per click) rather than PPM (pay per 1,000 impressions), so every time people clicked on my ad—which they were allegedly doing—my click rate increased while my budget depleted. Sweet, right? Wrong.

While I was burning through my ad budget, I was a little dismayed to see that ad clicks weren't converting to book sales. This could be due to several things, and could even have indicated that my landing page needed work. However, things really got weird when I checked the analytics of my website against my Facebook reports. My website was not reporting traffic coming from Facebook. If and when it did, it would be 1 or 2 visits, certainly not the 25 that Facebook was claiming.

At the end of the pre-holiday campaign Facebook reported that I had around 200 clicks, yet my website reported more like six visits. I was seeing the same thing happen during my post-holiday campaign, so I cancelled it mid-run. After all, you remember Einstein's definition of insanity: doing the same thing over and over again, but expecting different results. I'm no genius, but I'm not insane either. Until I'm working with GM-size budgets, which would allow me to create far more robust campaigns than simple PPC ads, I'll be putting my advertising dollars elsewhere in the future, thankyouverymuch.

There's an eye-opening video by Derek Muller, a "science communicator" who runs popular YouTube channel Veritasium, in which he shines a light on Facebook's fake-like epidemic. Like many advertisers, Muller was intrigued by the low engagement on his posts—even after racking up a high fan count through ad spends. Having a scientific mind, he started experimenting by creating bogus pages, purchasing ads and tracking where his likes were coming from. This allowed him to see by region who was—and wasn't—engaging with his content.

Round 2 - Tackle Your Tools

The video is fascinating and Muller comes off as a smart and likeable character, but that didn't stop people from attempting to debunk his theories. Blogger Jon Loomer, whose audience consists of "advanced Facebook marketers" (hmm, if I were an investigating detective, I would say Mr. Loomer has very good motive to poke holes in Muller's theory), wrote a detailed post that directly addressed the ad fraud video. While Loomer praises Muller's video for the conversation it started, he disagrees with the conclusion it draws—which is that Facebook ads are a waste of money.[4]

Unfortunately, Loomer's arguments are not nearly as compelling as Muller's, and his main beef is that Muller's study was done in 2012. OMG, like, that news is *so* two years ago! Loomer's post (written in February, 2014) claims that the ad targeting tools have improved a lot since 2012. But all that really means is that fake likes have been an issue for a long time, and the majority of Facebook advertisers are finally waking up to the problem.

> *"I will not deny that there is an issue with fake profiles, bots and spam accounts on Facebook. There is a problem. When you spend money on ads to get likes, you expect them all to be real people. Facebook does need to clean this up the best they can. But understand that the problem is not unique to Facebook. And it's a problem that will never be completely eliminated." —Jon Loomer*

Just as with any argument, there will be two sides to the story. There are business owners who swear by Facebook and claim they get results from their advertising and engagement on their page. Then there are those who claim the opposite.

★ HEAVYWEIGHT MARKETING ★

So, who should you trust? Well, just like I recommended in the Google+ chapter, it's best to form your own opinion. Take a hard look at the results you're getting from the time, money and effort you put into maintaining your Facebook marketing strategy. If it's working for you, keep it up. If your resources would be better spent elsewhere, perhaps you should take a cue from Eat24 and stick a fork in it. Cuz for a rapidly expanding group of users, students and business owners, Facebook is done.

*"It will work.
I'm a marketing genius."*
—Paris Hilton

★ 33 ★

WHY BRANDING MATTERS FOR SMALL BUSINESS

When hearing about "brands," many people think of the big players like Coca-Cola, Nike, McDonald's and Apple. One of the most common misconceptions about branding is that it is strictly for huge corporations who have large enough budgets to spend money on it. That's far from the truth. Since many entrepreneurs and small business owners don't understand the nebulous concept of branding, they don't understand how essential it is when it comes to differentiating their small business from their competition.

In order to make sure we're starting on the same page, let's get clear on what a brand is: your "brand" is the public perception of you, your company, your product or your service. Your brand is intangible. It exists in the mind of your audience and is influenced by every single touchpoint, every encounter, and every experience related to your company. Gather up all the mental perceptions regarding your business that are floating about in the collective consciousness of your customer base, and you've got it—Your Brand.

Therefore, "branding" is everything your company does (or doesn't do) to positively (or negatively) reinforce this perception. In other words, whether proactively or inadvertently, your brand is being created, influenced and evaluated in the minds of your audience at all times. Your brand is not static, like your logo; rather, it's fluid, mercurial, dynamic. One bad experience is all it takes for your brand to be tainted. Conversely, one good experience can create a brand evangelist singing the praises of your company. Therefore, any and every chance that you have to positively influence the perceptions of your audience is going to help you create a stronger, more meaningful brand.

Essentially, your company's brand is the same thing as your company's reputation. Once you realize this, it only makes sense to run every company action and message through your brand filter by asking, "How will this affect our reputation?" This will help you consistently make decisions that are on-brand.

Let's face it, the bigger your budget, the easier it is to get your message out to people. Big businesses can afford to spend truckloads of money on marketing, advertising campaigns and product launches. They can cast a wide net, offer a wide variety and maximize their revenue and profits through volume. Small businesses don't have that luxury, so it's even more important for them to define what they want to stand for in the minds of their customers, and articulate their unique value through concerted branding efforts. Small business owners have to be a little more creative when figuring out who they want to reach and how they want to differentiate themselves to the consumer in a relevant and memorable way. Champion brands are built slowly by creating one positive customer experience at a time.

How to Build a Champion Brand

The good news is that successful brands are not dependent solely on big budgets. There are plenty of other things small businesses can do to create champion brands.

Create Something Amazing—The obvious would be to offer an absolutely amazing product or service. With so much mediocre junk out there, it's really not that hard to go the extra mile and do things BETTER than your competitors. The problem is that it's a lot easier and cheaper to be mediocre, so that's what the average business settles for.

I built an e-commerce website for the herbalist Amy Rachkowski, who runs a company called Wise Mountain Botanicals. Amy has an impressive selection of herbal extracts, tinctures and skin care products that she harvests, distills, packages, labels and ships right from her spare bedroom. Two of her standout products are a Spicy Fire Cider immune tonic, which is so zesty-delicious it should come in a sippy cup instead of a dropper bottle, and a Cocoa Ginger Mint lip balm that sounds (and tastes) like it could double as an amazing cake frosting.

Amy has managed to create an entire line of high-quality wellness products that look completely professional, work like a charm and turn first-time customers into dedicated fans. Wise Mountain Botanicals products are sold in local stores and online through a few different websites. The challenge facing Amy—and all small businesses attempting to grow—will be to expand the reach of her distribution while scaling the company efficiently as the demand grows. A great brand must begin with an amazing product or service. There will still be a long road ahead to become successful, but if you start at amazing, your subsequent journey becomes a lot easier.

Untouchable Customer Service—Most companies who tout good customer service are providing nothing more than lip service. Instead of *saying* how much your customers matter, go out of your way to show it at every point of contact. This is harder than it seems because companies are made up of people and people have fluctuating personalities and moods. Even the greatest customer service rep is going to have the occasional bad day.

★ HEAVYWEIGHT MARKETING ★

There's an office supply store in my town that offers a prime example of abysmal service. Lucky for them, they're the only game in town; if they had even the slightest competition, beyond the back-to-school aisle of the local drug store, they would surely have gone out of business long ago. The employees never acknowledge your presence when you arrive; even when you're standing at the cash register ready to make a purchase, you practically have to wave your money at them to get their attention. The products are haphazardly strewn about the store with no discernible organizational logic. Their inventory is limited, so when you go there looking for something specific, they usually don't have it, BUT they tell you they can "order it for you." Awesome. Well, guess what Buddy? I can order it too. Online. And that way I could avoid stepping foot in your sorry store and giving you money you don't deserve.

Actually, I stopped going there years ago. My girlfriend still shops there occasionally—and she complains about it every time! I tell her to either quite patronizing them or quit complaining. By continuing to support their business, she becomes complicit in perpetuating their shoddy charade. I'm a big proponent of supporting small business, but that doesn't mean I'll patronize any biz just because it exists. Every small business must work hard to earn my loyalty—and the loyalty of every other customer they hope to bring through their doors.

Most customers don't enjoy being confrontational. They don't want to create a commotion about the poor service they have received, so they clam up and neither the staff nor the management realize. Instead, upset customers will complain to friends, they'll post vitriolic rants on Facebook and seething reviews on Yelp. They'll write blog posts, case studies and books that paint specific companies in an unflattering light. If these companies are not tuned in to exactly how they are failing their customers, they will never realize how much negligent employees, failed expectations and deplorable attitudes erode their brand.

A customer-centric culture must be built into your company's DNA if you truly expect your fantasy of untouchable customer service to become a reality.

Unique or Memorable Personality—I saw an ad for a real estate company that had six very typical headshots of their agents and the seventh photo was a full-body shot of a man in a kilt holding a "Sold" sign. Instead of a simple email address like the rest, he had his own Web URL: AgentInaKilt.com. Now, there's probably a whole swath of people who would refuse to buy their home from a man wearing a skirt, but that's okay. He doesn't have to appeal to everybody—no brand should aspire to that—because he will appeal to "his people." People who are fun, kooky and bold enough to appreciate his unique approach in a very staid industry.

How many pizzerias do you think there are? Innumerable. Okay, now how many of those have delivery drivers dressed in superhero costumes? One. Galactic Pizza in Minneapolis. Galactic Pizza is committed to running a business that's good for the earth. The restaurant is powered by renewable wind energy. Pizzas are made with organic ingredients when possible, and mozzarella cheese from cows not treated with the hormone rBGH.[1] The packaging is made from recycled or biodegradable materials, and pies are delivered—hot, fresh, and delicious—in electric vehicles driven by those aforementioned superheroes. Galactic Pizza is a pizzeria that wants to save the world. By living that mission in a fun, unique way, the company has created a memorable brand personality that stands out in a crowded market.

Expertise—There's nothing more comforting than putting your trust in the hands of an expert. Whether you're getting the brakes in your car replaced, receiving a Swedish massage, or looking for an elusive tool at the hardware store, it's a great feeling when the person you're dealing with exudes confidence and deep knowledge within his or her field.

Have you ever dealt with a retailer or service rep who seemed utterly incompetent? It's frustrating. Consumers want to do business with people who know more about a specific subject than they do. That doesn't mean they want to be talked down to, or made to feel inferior, but they do want to be comfortable deferring to the expertise of the person with whom they're interfacing.

I enjoyed a family reunion in Sonoma, California, which is the heart of wine country in the West. Our group of 15 people ate at two different restaurants. At the first, the unflappable waitress answered all our questions about wine and food with authority and élan. At the second, the jittery waiter was reaching for answers, guessing and coming up short. Where do you think we'll go next time we're in town?

Four Essential Brand Attributes

When attempting to hone your own brand, the following attributes will help you to define and articulate your company's unique assets:

Focus—Zero in on your company's strengths. What do you do better than your competition? What One Thing would you like to stand for in your customer's mind? Don't try to be everything to everyone. Instead, stay focused on the best attributes of your brand. At the same time, notice where you're falling short and aim to improve your company's weak points.

Clarity—Keep your message on point. Resist the urge to throw too many messages into your marketing. Once you figure out what you do best, or what sets you apart, hammer that point—and only that point—home in every marketing vehicle you use. Remember the print ad for the fitness center we looked at in Chapter 19? Use that as a reminder to keep your message simple, and always choose clarity over clutter.

Communication—Make sure everyone in your organization is on the same brand page. Communicate to your employees the importance of delivering on your company's brand promise. Communicate to your audience how your company will solve their problems and make their lives better. Remember, communication is a two-way avenue, so listen to your customer's compliments as well as their complaints and take action on each and every one of them. This may require someone to be responsible for social media monitoring. After all, it's a lot easier for customers to vent online than to share their feelings with you and your staff, so make sure you've got ears to the ground via all channels.

Consistency—Once you figure out what you want your company's reputation to be, you must make certain that your message, your image and your actions are consistently influencing that perception across all platforms. Every point of contact your customer has with your company needs to reinforce the singular promise of your brand. Don't worry about getting bored with your own message. As an insider, you will see it a lot but there will be an ongoing influx of new customers who will be seeing it for the first time. Remember Thomas Smith's guide to effective frequency in Chapter 1? That may have been written 129 years ago, but its core idea still rings true today: consumers need to see your message many times in order for it to register. Be sure to keep it consistent.

★ HEAVYWEIGHT MARKETING ★

As you can see from examples in this chapter, a big budget is not the sole requirement when attempting to build a memorable brand. After all, it takes more than money to create something meaningful. It takes creativity, willingness, communication, effort and a true desire to hone in on the most unique attributes of your offering in order to stand apart from other companies competing in your field.

Some of the clients I worked with had a hard time even saying the word "brand," much less considering what their company brand would be if they embraced the concept. I chalked that up to fear of the unknown. If you don't know what your own singular, special or unique points are, how can you possibly share them with your audience? It can also be scary to turn a discerning eye towards your own business. What if you realize that your business is boring, commonplace, or unremarkable? Then you've got to dig deeper.

Whether branding yourself as an entrepreneur or the company you have created, there will always be some singular facets that are unmistakably and irrepressibly YOU. Once you discover them, be sure to embrace them and share them with your audience. Because, in order to stand out, you've got to brand out.

★ 34 ★

WHAT'S IN A BRAND NAME? EVERYTHING

It never ceases to amaze me how many companies put such little effort into naming their business. Living in northern California, where many small towns dot the landscape, I see an abundance of offenders in every little town. The majority of small business owners in this area seem to use the following naming equation:

Name of Town + Type of Service = Our Business Name

I call this the "Yellow Pages Mentality," as if the only criterion for the name is to be found easily in the phone book. I would call it the "Search Engine Mentality," but I'm pretty certain that most of the offenders named their business before the domination of Google and proliferation of smart phones. The so-called logic in this naming anti-strategy is that if a motorist is rolling through Mt. Shasta, California and she gets a flat tire, the first company that will appear when she flips through a phone book or pulls out her iPhone, is the Mt. Shasta Tire Company, making it her obvious choice.

Branding is about communicating your company's point of difference, and the problem with a generic name is its inability to differentiate one business from the next.

"The most important branding decision you will ever make is what to name your product or service. Because in

★ HEAVYWEIGHT MARKETING ★

the long run, a brand is nothing more than a name." —Al Ries, author 22 Immutable Laws of Branding

There is an art gallery in Mt. Shasta that is actually called, The Gallery. You cannot get anymore generic than that. Galleries are about art and art is all about creativity. Yet, this utter lack of creativity frustrates me every time I drive by the place. Now, if The Gallery was the ONLY gallery in Mt. Shasta, its name, although insipid, would at least make some sense. If an artist said, "I'm having an art show at The Gallery in Mt. Shasta," her audience might know where her show is. But, that is not the case. There are at least half a dozen galleries within a six-block radius of The Gallery.

Before we continue, allow me to state for the record that I visit The Gallery frequently and consider its owner to be a friend. My critique in no way reflects my thoughts or feelings about her personally—I think she's a wonderful person and a tireless entrepreneur. This is strictly biz-talk as it relates to effective branding principles.

The Gallery's owner purchased an existing business with its name already in place. Although she has acknowledged that the name is underwhelming, she decided against changing it outright. However, in order to inject a little more clarity, she added the prepositional-phrase tagline, "In the Black Bear Building," which is—you guessed it—the name of the building The Gallery is located in. Is that any more helpful? Minimally. Now the name speaks to the "what" of the business—it's a gallery—and it speaks to the "where" of the business—it's in the Black Bear Building. What's missing is the most important part of what a brand name should convey: the "why" of the business.

More specifically, there is zero indication of what type, style, genre or category of artworks is featured, so the potential customer has no idea "how" a visit might enrich their lives, or "why" they should even make a point to stop in for a visit.

Case Study: Brainstorm in Action

Since it's easier to come up with complaints and critiques than it is to come up with solutions, I want to run you through a little exercise that shows how one might dig deeper when brainstorming the perfect name for a business. If I were tasked with creating a better name for The Gallery, here is the thought process I would use to get there:

First, you need to be familiar with the company's offering. In this case, The Gallery contains a large percentage of Native American works, and an equally large percentage of what I would categorize as New Age, angelic, or esoteric works. I love the word "esoteric." It means "likely to be understood by few," which describes many of the ideas and topics explored in the New Age community. So let's hang on to that word for sure.

Next, let's think about art that explores and celebrates Native American culture. Now, in my opinion, Native American peoples are very grounded; they are in tune with the cycles of nature and connected with the earth, the land, and the ground. Aha: terra firma.

While brainstorming, you can continue jotting down as many descriptive words as you want until you feel like you've got some strong ones to work with. Once you've chosen some descriptive words you want to experiment with, try out several variations. In this case, I've focused on "esoteric" and "terra firma," and came up with the following mashup:

Esoterra Fine Art Gallery

★ HEAVYWEIGHT MARKETING ★

Okay, I like that, but it may still be a little unclear. That's where a clarifying tagline comes in. It could be as simple as "Native American and New Age Art." Or it could be a little more intriguing like, "Art That Bridges Heaven and Earth," "Art Spanning Heaven and Earth," or "Celebrating Art From Heaven and Earth." Again we're playing upon the esoteric New Age angle with "heaven," and the grounded Native American angle with "earth." After more tweaking and deliberation, perhaps the final result is:

Esoterra Gallery
Works of Fine Art from Heaven and Earth

This combination is intriguing and evocative. It would definitely make certain art lovers want to stop in the gallery to investigate. When seeking the perfect name, you will create many variations. The key is to come up with something you love that is not already copyrighted or in wide use.

After my brainstorm, a quick Google search indicated that "esoterra" is currently the name of a magazine, a DJ, a mythical land in fantasy fiction, and probably several other things. That doesn't automatically mean you couldn't use it. Let's say it wasn't copyrighted, and the URL esoterragallery.com was available. In that case, it would be up to you as to whether you wanted to commit to claiming this name and building your brand around it. If not, keep brainstorming. There's plenty more names where that came from.

I believe that many business owners, especially in small towns, lack a larger vision. They don't think about creating a brand that is going to excite and intrigue people outside of the county they're in. I'm sorry, but a gallery called "The Gallery" is NEVER going to make a dent in the national, or even regional, art world.

3 Primary Functions of a Brand Name

Your business name needs to do a lot of heavy lifting. It needs to communicate clearly and efficiently what your company does, set your company apart as different or distinct, and do it all in an appealing and memorable way. Therefore, your name should be chosen carefully with one or more of the following functions in mind:

1) Describes What You Do—Anybody encountering your business for the first time needs to comprehend what your company does the instant they read or hear your company name. That's not always easy, and many times it leads you right to the literal, generic names you want to avoid. If you come up with a name that is great but not very descriptive, it's okay to add a clarifying tagline that clues people in to your business category.

When I launched my marketing consulting business in 2010, the name "BAM!" came to me in a flash of inspiration. The letters stood for Branding And Marketing, which spoke to the service I was offering. However, the average person wouldn't have known that, so I added the clarifier, "Small Biz Consulting." The name was bold, it spoke to the aggressive brand I wanted to create, and it even informed the boxing theme that I threaded through my visual identity, my brand voice, the names of my service packages—and even the title and theme of this book.

If you do decide to use a non-descriptive name with a descriptive tagline, eventually your audience becomes familiar enough with your brand (that's what you're hoping anyway) that they drop the tagline and just use the main name. After my consulting biz took off, I would run into my clients around town and they would gleefully shout "BAM!" and some would even mime throwing a punch. There was something about the powerful simplicity and familiarity of the name that people picked up on and had fun with.

★ HEAVYWEIGHT MARKETING ★

"Either the name has to say inherently everything about you, or you have to actively invest the name with everything you want to stand for." —Allen P. Adamson, author of BrandSimple

Both of the options in the above quote are challenging for different reasons. Let's say you go the first route and seek a name that "says everything about you." Examples of this might be Furniture World, Toys "R" Us, and Radio Shack. These names are all fine and dandy as long as you don't diverge from your main offering. And, from a branding perspective, it's best that you don't deviate from your specialty. Therefore Furniture World needs to be all furniture all the time. The minute they want to get into home remodeling or kitchen appliances, there's a disconnect.

Toys "R" Us faced this dilemma when they wanted to skew younger, and they made the right move: rather than trying to work baby products into their successful toy store, they created an entirely separate brand called Babies "R" Us. As for Radio Shack, progress was not on their side. In our internet and iPod world, radios have become a relic of a bygone era, rendering their name obsolete. In 2009, the company made a half-hearted attempt to rebrand themselves as "The Shack," which never really stuck. Taking a different approach in 2014, Radio Shack decided to stick with the name, but update and remodel the interiors of all their stores—rebrand from the inside out, as it were. They announced the change with a clever commercial during the 2014 Super Bowl® that played on 80s nostalgia and became an audience favorite with Gen Xers like myself who vividly remember all the pop culture icons shown in the spot.

If you haven't seen it, I encourage you to Google it. Google? Now there's a name!

Round 3 - Buff Your Brand

When Google launched in 1997, their name was meaningless. Although it was a play on the actual word "googol" (a mathematical term for the number represented by the numeral 1 followed by 100 zeros), most people had never heard that word. The company had to work hard to build meaning around the name, or as Adamson said earlier, "invest the name with everything they want to stand for."

Now, 17 years later, the Google brand represents a mega-tech conglomerate with its hands in search, advertising, social media, video, robotics, venture capitalism, data-mining, computer hardware, software, wearable computers and self-driving cars. Heck, the name has even become a verb (it currently equates to "search," but is slowly moving towards "ravenously omniscient and slightly evil corporate overlord"), which is not only the sign of a strong name, but also indicates sheer mass-culture acceptance.

2) Differentiation—If your name does not allow you to stand out in your industry, you're going to have a hard time convincing prospects why they should patronize you over your competition. It's hard enough to come up with a name that describes what you do, but finding one that also hints at your company's point of difference is even more difficult. That shouldn't dissuade you from trying, though.

One of my favorite things about the explosion of tech startups and mobile app companies launching at an exhaustive rate is the seemingly infinite pool of names the founders are pulling from: StitchFix, ThinDish, Dropbox, Silverpop, Jawbone, GitHub, Gnip, Goonj, Splunk, Shazam, Kaggle, Quirky, Tencent, ZipDial, and the list goes on and on.

While many of these names are fun and catchy, good luck trying to tell me what they DO, much less how they differ from each other. But I will say this: they are ALL more interesting than adopting an obvious choice like Cupertino Tech Company, St. Louis Electronics, or The Fashion Store.

There's a retail store in my area that has concocted a solid name for a very cool business idea: Alpine Originals. The first part of their name speaks to the mountainous region where their business is located. Sure, "alpine" is used a lot in our area and other similar regions, but it's still less obvious and overused than "mountain" or, God forbid, "Mt. Shasta." The second part of the name speaks to what they sell, which is 100% hand-crafted art, jewelry, gift items, specialty foods and body care products from artisans and craft persons in our immediate area. They sell original works from original people and have managed to speak to that difference in their business name.

Now, compare that with their competitors directly across the street that sell souvenirs, novelties and gift items of a more mass-produced nature. Their name? All That & More. If you didn't know the business category they were in, good luck trying to figure out what they're actually selling. Even if you did know they were a gift shop, there's nothing about the names that speaks to the company's point of difference. It's kind of like saying, "We do it all!" And if any company claims to do it all, you can bet that they don't do any of it very well. Nobody can. Recently, signs have appeared in the windows of All That & More shouting about a "Going Out of Business Sale." A failed business is the death of a dream and I don't wish that on anybody. However, I can't help but wonder how significant a factor the company's lack of differentiation played in their eventual downfall.

3) Favorable Association—Your brand name needs to be appealing and appropriate to your audience. For a death metal band, Cannibal Corpse is a great name. For a funeral home, it's probably not. Some brand names are immediately appealing even if you've never heard of them before. For someone who

Round 3 - Buff Your Brand

finally starts washing her own laundry, Snuggle fabric softener is a no-brainer. Other names have to work a little harder to create positive associations in consumers' minds. Can you imagine New Yorkers wanting to eat at a sandwich shop called Subway when it first came out? I've never ridden a NY subway but I can't imagine it's all that pretty, and I surely wouldn't want to associate that perception with my dining experience. However, Subway has done a great job of creating a positive association that calls to mind a healthy, delicious fast food option rather than a filthy, crowded, noisy underground transit system.

What many long-standing brands have over newer brands is the benefit of legacy. For brand names such as State Farm Insurance, Ford Motor Company, Heinz ketchup and Skippy peanut butter, positive associations have built up over time. Some of these names have been around for several generations. As youngsters grow up and move out on their own, they tend to gravitate to the names that are familiar to them. They remember having Cheerios in the pantry, A&W root beer in the fridge, and Glad trash bags under the sink. There's nothing quite as strong as positive childhood memories, so any brand that's trying to break through in today's world has to not only create a name that's descriptive, catchy, effective and memorable, but work extra hard to create favorable associations and build positive brand experiences every step of the way. Like I said earlier, your name needs to do a lot of heavy lifting. Be sure to choose a name you love so it is worth all the effort.

Naming is not simply a creative exercise. Your name is one of the most critical of all your branding signals (everything used to represent your brand to your audience). It is the ultimate conjurer of images and associations, and needs to be treated

★ **HEAVYWEIGHT MARKETING** ★

as such during the naming process. The best names are built on strong, clear, simple objectives. Whether you are naming your company, your product or service, don't just aim to create a name that is easy to remember: aim to create a name that is hard to forget.

★ 35 ★

SUCCESSFUL MARKETING STARTS WITH STRATEGIC POSITIONING

The American landscape photographer Ansel Adams once said, "The secret to a good photograph is knowing where to stand." Obviously, Mr. Adams understood the importance of positioning. The same is true of small business: you need to be clear on where you want your company to stand in the minds of your audience. Otherwise, you will waste time and money sending random marketing messages that fail to properly position your offering in the minds of an ambiguous audience.

When launching a business, many entrepreneurs are so eager to share their offering with the world, they skip over some of the early research and planning necessary in the formative stages (I've been guilty of this myself). Instead of taking a slow, methodical, strategic approach, they charge out of the gate, sharing their excitement with anyone and everyone, focusing on quantity of audience rather than quality. This approach finds business owners careening around like a wayward billiard ball, as opposed to darting towards a targeted bullseye.

Creating a positioning statement for your business allows you to identify and define the following:

- Your product or service
- Specific business category
- Target audience
- Primary benefit of your offering
- Your main point-of-difference in relation to competition

★ HEAVYWEIGHT MARKETING ★

The positioning statement is not for public consumption; rather, it's an intra-organizational battle cry that creates a foundation for the branding and marketing messaging you create for your company. Only when you are completely familiar with the above points can you craft messaging that hits the mark.

First, let's take a closer look at each of the included elements. Then we'll examine the formula that helps pull all the elements together into a concise positioning statement.

Target Audience—Who are you trying to reach with your marketing? If you say "everyone," you have not given this essential question enough thought. Think about what segment of the population is most likely to respond to, connect with, or benefit from your offering, and start there. Consider their demographics (gender, age, location, marital status, occupation, etc.) and their psychographics (goals, desires, fears, objectives, etc.), and create up to three Ideal Buyer Profiles that will help you to think of your audience as real individuals, rather than a faceless crowd of consumers.

Creative agencies do this a lot, sometimes creating multiple profiles depending on how varied the audience is. You can even have some fun with this by pulling images of people from magazines, giving them names and applying characteristics based on your data and research. Some might avoid this exercise for fear of perpetuating profiling, generalities or stereotypes. As long as the customer profiles you create are based on real-world experience and research, this can be a very helpful way to "get to know" your ideal customer. Heck, you can even use existing customers as representatives of certain audience segments:

> *Brenda runs a deep tissue massage therapy practice. Her clients are not there for "ooh-aah" spa-like relaxation; they are there to work through serious structural issues, or what Brenda*

calls "body projects." One of her long-time customers, Ed, is retired from a life of working road construction for CalTrans. Ed is totally old school. He's too manly for yoga, getting him to do regular stretching has been a Herculean task, he doesn't use a computer, and while he prefers to communicate via phone, Brenda has been training him to text. While Brenda serves a wide variety of distinct customers—just like most businesses do—Ed fits one of her ideal profiles. He is the perfect litmus test to determine how Brenda can best serve the entirety of her audience. Now, Brenda may have ten Eds in her customer base, or she may have one. Either way, with every new business decision, marketing message or deployment tool she implements, Brenda needs to be sure that Ed is comfortable so she doesn't alienate him in the service of others.

So, who's your company's Ed? Once you identify him, look for a few more people who stand out as representational of your diverse audience and think of them when crafting your marketing materials.

Company, Product or Service—Determine whether you are positioning your company as a whole, or positioning a new product or service you are bringing to market. For most small businesses, it makes sense to focus on one position statement for the company, whereas larger companies who regularly bring new products to market may wish to create new positioning statements for each new product.

Business Category—Try to get as detailed as you can with this. It may feel natural to simply list the broad category that your business fits into, but make an effort to dig down and flesh out a more descriptive representation of where your company or product falls in the marketplace. Doing so will help you to carve a narrower niche, further differentiating your business from your competitors.

★ HEAVYWEIGHT MARKETING ★

For example, rather than "Health and Fitness," consider all aspects of your offering and work them into your category, such as "Premium fitness and wellness centers offering personal trainers, physical therapy, chiropractic, group fitness classes and full gym and spa amenities for a full-spectrum health experience."

Key Customer Benefit—Often times, the most difficult part of positioning (and marketing in general) is determining the most meaningful benefit that your customers derive from your offering. Usually, there are several reasons why people buy from you, and your job is to figure out what those are—in order of priority—so you can pinpoint the most effective benefit to speak to in your messaging. Once you do this, your job of marketing becomes a lot easier.

A Helpful Guide: In Chapter 9, The Motivational Value of Stiff Competition, I list 10 questions to ask your customers to determine how they perceive your brand. You can hypothesize all day on how people benefit from your offering, but there's nothing like direct feedback from your customers to provide true insight.

Your Competitive Alternative—Who are the companies that offer your customers an alternative to buying from you? In order to know how your company is different, you need to know something about your competition. You will have both direct and indirect competition that you will need to be aware of. If you run a bakery, any other bakeries in the area will be your direct competition. But if you want to position your bakery as a go-to breakfast spot that serves fresh donuts, pastries and espresso, your indirect competition will be any other establishment that serves breakfast. You'll have to give the morning crowd a great reason to choose your bakery over all the other cafés, coffee shops and convenience stores.

When you consider this, you can see why it's essential to provide a true point of difference and meaningful customer benefits to a clearly defined audience. Otherwise, your customer will perceive you as just another option, instead of the first, best or only option.

The Brand Positioning Statement Formula

Once you've considered all the above elements, apply your own info to the appropriate spots (items in parentheses) in the following formula:

To (Target Audience), (Your Company, Product or Service) is the only (Category) that (Key Customer Benefit), unlike (Your Competitive Alternative).

Here's a fictitious example so you can see the formula in action:

To (busy pet owners), (Pristine Pet) is the only (mobile pet washing service) that (is on call anytime, anywhere) unlike (the brick-and-mortar pet hotels that offer cleaning services).

As for the Key Customer Benefit, it might be difficult to come up with one that only your company is offering. Feel free to reword slightly if needed: instead of "only," perhaps you're the "first," "best," or "fastest." Remember, the positioning statement is for internal use, not for public consumption. Leave out the biz-speak and corporate jargon, and use simple language that everyone in your organization can understand and repeat. You can use the template above as many times as needed, meaning you may have a main positioning statement for your company and separate, unique statements for any new product, service or market segment that you wish to introduce.

★ HEAVYWEIGHT MARKETING ★

Let the statement be your guide as you zero in on your audience, choose the best marketing vehicles to reach them and craft a meaningful marketing message that speaks to the benefits of your offering while differentiating you from your competition.

This can be a challenging exercise, but it will behoove you and your company to make the effort. Crafting an accurate positioning statement will make it easier to create successful marketing messages for your company that are consistently on point and, better yet, effective.

★ 36 ★

GETTING YOUR EMPLOYEES ON THE BRANDWAGON

Every time I visit Ramshaw's ACE Hardware in Mt. Shasta, I am approached by an employee inquiring if I need help within a minute. No matter which department I meander to, another helpful worker pops out of nowhere with their friendly inquiry. I mentioned earlier that many businesses that tout great customer service are merely blowing hot air, but Ramshaw's ACE Hardware is not one of them. The company brands itself as "The Helpful Place," and that brand promise is fulfilled every time a customer walks into the store. Not just once or twice, and not just on random days. Every. Single. Time.

Some shoppers may find it annoying to be smothered by overly obliging employees, but as a marketing maven, I view business transactions through an acute Customer Experience lens, so I find it quite impressive. After all, it's one thing to tout your company as a helpful place but another thing entirely to effectively integrate that pledge into the company culture. Sure, it could be less difficult for solopreneurs or little shops with a couple employees to maintain an acceptable level of service, but the minute your company head-count exceeds double digits the challenge multiplies exponentially. I started wondering what ACE Hardware's secret was, so I went in and talked with General Manager Bill Ramshaw to learn how management has been so successful in getting their employees to live the ACE brand.

★ HEAVYWEIGHT MARKETING ★

A Little History

Bill told me that Ramshaw's ACE Hardware was started in 1945 by his grandparents, who ran it for 22 years before joining the ACE Corporation in 1967. Even back then, ACE knew the value of good service and set out its intention to be "the most helpful place in the world." In the 50s and 60s, it was not possible for small shops to meet the minimum order requirements set by large manufacturers, so several independent shops came together under the ACE banner and became a supply chain for all their affiliated outposts.

Unlike most corporations that answer to stockholders and board members, ACE is a cooperative buying group. This means that the individual dealers own the company and act as its governing board. While each store location carries the ACE name and follows suggested advertising programs, each store stands alone as an independent business.

Recipe for a Great Workplace

While Bill didn't elaborate on his specific techniques, he offered many vital insights about running a business that has flourished for nearly 70 years. Here are some key takeaways from our conversation that business owners and managers may want to consider when inspiring their own teams to "be the brand":

Respect the Family—They say that businesses are a lot like families, and that metaphor is never more accurate than when running an actual family business. A healthy family dynamic is evident at Ramshaw's ACE Hardware. Bill feels that this strong, familial bond trickles down to everyone in the organization and is one of the factors that makes it a great place to work. Even if your business is not bonded by blood, working and communicating as a cohesive "family" unit will create an allegiance strong enough to adhere through thick and thin.

Engender Pride—Healthy profits are essential to any successful business, but they cannot be the sole focus of the company. Exceptional companies need to have a common purpose based on shared values, and they need to operate with integrity. The goal is not just to create a successful company, but rather a great organization that people are proud to be part of.

Ditch the Drama—If you've ever had a Thanksgiving dinner devolve into a perfect storm of kinfolk chaos, you know that not all families sprout roses and rainbows. While it's not always possible to keep the workplace completely drama-free, Bill says his team makes a concerted effort to keep turmoil out of the workplace.

Protect Your Peeps—The old credo stating that the customer is always right was clearly written by…a customer. Bill knows that the customer is NOT always right, which is why he chooses to back up his employees 100%. Family creed requires standing united with your tribe when threatened by antagonistic forces. It would do any business well to abide by the same creed.

Practice Reciprocity—Business owners are also consumers, and they can learn a lot about service from all the companies they patronize. What are other companies doing right? What are they doing wrong? Which ones make you feel like your patronage matters? Which ones do you dread going to? When it comes to running your own business, Bill suggests helping every customer the way YOU want to be helped, treated and served when you walk into someone else's store.

A few ingredients I would like to add:

Communication—Sure, communication plays an integral role in many facets of business, but I'm specifically referring to the need to communicate your company's brand promise to your employees. Inform them of the niche your business aims to carve in the marketplace and the perceptions you hope to cultivate in the minds of your audience. Many of the newer companies coming up today place heavy emphasis on company culture. When hiring, they place equal importance on ascertaining whether prospective employees will "fit in" and thrive in their culture as they do examining their skillsets.

Team Effort—Since branding occurs at every touchpoint, it must be made clear that branding is the job of every department, not just the marketing department. Encourage your employees to embrace the company brand, cultivate it, and live it. This request illuminates the significance of building a meaningful company your employees will be proud to champion.

Empowerment—There's nothing more frustrating than dealing with an ineffectual employee rendered impotent by strict company policy. Take a cue from one of the most prestigious hotels in the world—the Ritz-Carlton—and empower your employees to make decisions on the company's behalf. Every employee of the Ritz-Carlton has access to a budget of $2,000 per day per guest to "delight or make it right."[1] Your company may not have Ritz-size resources, but that's not the point. Adopt the practice of empowering your employees and they will work that much harder to ensure consistent customer satisfaction.

Accountability—If employees are not aware that their roles and responsibilities extend to brand advocacy, their lack of it can always be blamed on ignorance. Make certain your employees know the role they play in the branding of your company. Have frequent meetings where you discuss successes, failures and areas of improvement as it applies to your branding efforts. It's easier to track progress when everybody knows exactly what they are responsible for.

Consequences—Implement both rewards and consequences for delivering, or failing to deliver, on your company's Brand Promise. PayPal has been struggling to maintain its position in the mobile commerce wars. When former company president David Marcus realized that most of his staff wasn't even using their own company's payment app, he fired off a scathing email ordering employees to "use PayPal or find another place to work."[2] Consequences don't have to be that severe but I'm guessing PayPal usage among employees improved after Mr. Marcus sent his missive.

In today's feeble economy and hyper-competitive marketplace, proactive branding efforts are imperative. The challenge is making certain that the brand you aim to cultivate is clearly represented at every touchpoint your customer encounters. Externally, this includes your various branding signals such as website, advertisements, storefront, vehicles, etc. Internally, this means your employees need to get on the brandwagon. Your entire staff needs to understand the important role that each and every one of them plays in the brand perception of your company. They need to live your brand, whatever it may be, every single day.

Remember, branding is not just a marketing buzz word. It's real and it matters. Creating a positive brand experience encourages customers to perceive your organization as a company that provides real solutions to their problems, and is worthy of their loyalty. Failing to pay proper attention to your branding efforts means those same customers may seek solutions to their problems through the offerings of your competitors instead.

★ 37 ★

YOUR BUSINESS NEEDS TO TELL A BETTER BRAND STORY

Business owners can no longer compete in a frantic marketplace by merely shouting more "me-too" marketing messages into the cacophonous din of commerce. Any business hoping to connect with today's overstimulated, attention-deficient society needs to go beyond simply existing. Instead, they need to seduce the imagination, pluck the heartstrings and pique the interest of their audience through the power of storytelling.

Many of the clients I've worked with over the years as a marketing consultant were afflicted with the same problem: lack of a strong brand story. Most small business owners simply don't take the time to craft a compelling story, a unique hook, or a remarkable "it" factor to set them apart and make them stand above the competition. New companies spring up and the owners shout "we need a website!" without fully considering the story or content that will attract, impact and engage their customer. A website is merely a tool. Sure, it can be a powerful tool, and a great place from which to command your brand's online presence. But to build a truly successful website, it needs to include a compelling combination of concepts, words, images, ideas, and an interesting story behind the product, service or company.

Finding Your Hook

In music, the magic ingredient to a hit single is an irresistible hook—a lyrical chorus or melodic phrase that burrows into your psyche and takes up permanent residence. This is annoyingly evident when you hear a catchy song that you hate, yet the hook gets stuck on repeat in your brain for days on end. It's even more apparent when you hear a song you haven't heard in years, and by the first chorus you're singing along as if you just heard it yesterday. Much like writing a hit song, your business needs to come up with a catchy hook of its own. The kind that will get stuck in the minds of your audience and play automatically the minute they have a need or desire for your offering.

The key to finding your hook is focused reflection. Take a hard look at your business and determine what makes your product or service worthy of discussion. Then write a "hit single" for your business. The easiest way to determine popular talking points is to monitor the feedback from your audience. What things come up repeatedly? Why do people say they enjoy patronizing your business? What are they saying about your business in emails, blog comments or social media channels? Of course, in order to glean this info, someone in your organization needs to be responsible for monitoring your communication channels.

Some of the story categories that came up while consulting with my clients are listed below, which may inspire you to find unique and appropriate hooks for your own business:

Community—I worked with a local retailer who had a unique problem: they already had all the customers they needed! In fact, most of the year, they were operating over their capacity. So the question became: what marketing solutions would serve them if they were not trying to attract more customers? In their case, they also wanted to alter their overall brand perception. After digging deeper, I learned that this organization was spending ten times more on community donations and sponsorships than they were on advertising. They were also working with local farmers and doing what they could to promote all things organic, fair trade and sustainable.

However, nobody knew about these things because they were doing it all pretty quietly. Sure, there's a certain nobility to anonymous do-gooders, but hey, if you don't blow your own horn, there's no music! The solution here was to tell the Community Story with integrity and disseminate it through various channels in an effort to educate, inform and influence the company's brand perception in the minds of their audience.

There are several large companies that do a great job telling a Community Story. Starbucks is well known for providing insurance plans for part-time workers, which is not only generous but quite uncommon. The company also touts its Fair Trade practices and produces rich-media content of CEO Howard Schultz visiting with coffee farmers. Eyewear company Warby Parker donates eyeglasses to those in need with every pair they sell. They also partner with non-profits that offer training to low-income entrepreneurs who want to sell eyewear in their own communities. Toms shoes created a One-for-One® policy, donating footwear to kids, families and communities in over 60 countries. Of course, this story angle only works if you and your staff are truly active members of your community. If not, it's best to seek your hook elsewhere.

Fantasy—I was once contacted by a prospect needing a website for her line of shabby-chic furniture. Her company reclaims and refurbishes home decor items, producing pieces that have a well-traveled, vintage look. At the time, her online marketing efforts had consisted of posting numerous photos to Facebook with no description, no titles and no names. While these pieces were indeed distinctive and attractive, they certainly didn't speak for themselves. With a product like that, a little fantasy would go a long way. An easy way to inject fantasy would be to personify the pieces. Give them a narrative voice that shares their well-traveled past and builds an alluring story around their existence. Make your customers fall in love with the rich, fantastical history of these products, so they want to bring them into their own homes to continue the journey.

A great example of this is the J. Peterman catalog, which takes brand storytelling to supreme levels. The creative copywriting throughout the catalog transforms a typical home-shopping experience into a magical journey. Speaking of magic, Disney is another brand that has built an astoundingly successful kingdom by selling magical fantasy to generation after generation. Another supreme fantasy brand is Victoria's Secret, which hires some of the most beautiful women in the world to sell lingerie to women who want to feel just as sexy as the supermodels featured in the company's advertising, catalogs and fashion shows.

Men have their own reasons for liking the brand. When was the last time a straight man actually wanted to watch a fashion show on TV? When it featured the Victoria's Secret Angels. And you know that gawky gaggle of teenage boys walking circles in the mall so they can pass Victoria's Secret's window display twenty-three times? That's no accident, and you can chalk it all up to fantasy.

Personality—I worked with a designer who creates user interfaces for mobile and web apps. He was building an online portfolio of his work and, while his design skills are fantastic, his writing style is rather dry and technical. He hired me to help him inject some personality into his brand. Sometimes it's important to create a voice that actually sounds like the owner, leader or figurehead of the business, and sometimes it's okay to create a unique "character" or personality that stands on its own. We chose to do the latter and create an irreverent, distinctive brand voice so his prospects, clients and web visitors would enjoy spending time on his site not only for his expert design skills, but also for his memorable brand voice.

Round 3 - Buff Your Brand

He ended up getting hired by a growing tech company that has created a product to compete directly with Google's search engine—an audacious goal if there ever was one. My client's design skills are surely what secured him the job, but the quirky personality of his brand voice exhibited throughout his excellent online portfolio certainly aided his campaign for the position. Remember, you've got to brand out to stand out.

Even companies in typically staid industries such as insurance have realized the power of personality. Insurance company GEICO, which is actually an acronym for Government Employees Insurance Company (you can't get any more stodgy than that), has done a fabulous job of giving their brand a funny, youthful, hip voice by creating their cheeky little Brit mascot, The Gecko. More recently, their commercials have veered into abstract, bizarre humor that feels very fresh and modern. Even if The Gecko isn't featured, the brand's irreverent personality still shines through. The impressive thing is that GEICO has never abandoned their core marketing message, which has always been, "15 minutes could save you 15% on your car insurance." Their creative agencies should be commended for concocting endless humorous scenarios around which to base that one core message year after year after year.

Progressive Insurance is another brand that has captured the hearts of their audience with adorkable mascot Flo, a plucky, geek-chic adventurer who's up for anything. Flo's post-ironic exuberance is a perfect counter-balance to our snarky, self-aware youth culture, which could be why she has struck a chord. Unfortunately, a little Flo goes a long way, and seeing her ubiquitous retro mug is becoming more annoying than endearing. And don't get me started on her tone-deaf "singing" featured in Progressive's radio spots that play after every third song while listening to iTunes radio. Just like *Scooby-Doo* introduced Scrappy-Doo to inject a fresh burst of energetic mayhem to the

★ HEAVYWEIGHT MARKETING ★

gang, and *The Brady Bunch* introduced Cousin Oliver to shake up the family dynamic towards the end of the show's dominance, my prediction is that by 2015, Progressive will introduce another character to take the reins when the public grows weary of Flo's perky personality.

Human Interest—When it comes to storytelling, nothing can pique the attention of your audience like a good human interest story. In the previous chapter, I mentioned Alpine Originals, the retail store that sells hand-made products from over 100 artists and artisans. The owner of that store is sitting on a treasure trove of stories! Every artist has an exclusive story to be told, and each product has an origin story that speaks to a unique creative process. Small-batch production, hand-made products, and boutique brands are becoming increasingly popular with discerning consumers. Focusing their brand story on the people involved in this movement could help Alpine Originals stand apart because it offers a great counter-story to the mass market, low-quality, discount mentality of the big box retailers.

Many businesses tend to be faceless entities, especially if their customers primarily interface with them online. I can't tell you how many websites I've visited that have no element of humanity, no representation of the diverse individuals running the business behind the virtual portal. Therefore it's a treat when I come across companies that feature their staff prominently on their website, with good photos and imaginative bios. Of course, the creative sector excels at this, but any business category can benefit from sharing something a little unexpected about the humans involved in their business operation. That might be the people running the company, its extended partners and collaborators, or the customers and communities being served.

Unique Idea—This is pretty rare, but sometimes a company will bring a product or service to market that is so innovative, different or unique, that IT becomes the story! Here's one example of such a story: the co-founder of Twitter, Jack Dorsey, steps away from his day job to launch a credit card processing platform that turns your iPhone, Android or iPad into a point-of-sale merchant account. The company is Square, and while the story is intriguing, and his Twitter connection provides instant cachet, it's the product that blows people away. The Square card reader is portable, easy and convenient, and I've been raving about it to everyone I know who might benefit from being able to accept credit cards. You know you've got a great story when your audience shares it of their own accord, and that's exactly the kind of brand evangelism you want to inspire with your company's story.

Many unique business concepts are cropping up lately, especially in the service realm. A lot of them are based around the idea of bringing their service to you, which is a great way to cater to a busy audience. I've seen mobile pet washing services that come to your house and clean your dogs, and mobile mechanics who come work on your car rather than forcing you to bring it into an auto repair shop.

Companies like Airbnb and Uber, which have both been growing rapidly, are unique because they allow everyday people—who may never thought of becoming entrepreneurs—to make extra money providing a service to consumers. Homeowners can sign up with Airbnb to offer temporary lodging to travelers, and Uber can turn any upstanding citizen with a clean car and good driving record into a temporary chauffeur.

As with many innovative ideas, both of these ideas are facing resistance. Needless to say the hotel industry is not amused with Airbnb's recent rise to power. A friend of mine was making money renting out a spare room through Airbnb until the city caught wind of it and ordered her to cease and desist. They said because her house was in a residential zone, not a commercial one, she was not allowed to operate "as a hotel." Uber is being flogged by both taxi commissioners and limousine associations in various states, proving that innovation is indeed a great thing—until it ruffles the feathers of the Old Guard.

Get Your Story Straight

Once you've got a grasp of what makes your business special, it's time to zero in on your Big Idea. When determining the unique brand story you want to tell, you need to make sure everyone in the organization is on the same page. There may be differing opinions as to what your company's main talking points should be. It's essential to work together so everyone feels connected to the message. If you don't get your story straight, it will not be told properly or consistently, resulting in a muddled brand that's ineffective in connecting with your audience.

Now's a good time to add that your story needs to be authentic. Nothing kills brand perception quicker than building your story on a lie. When that lie is discovered—and it will be—your company will crumble like a house of cards. This happened in 2012 to ersatz health-food brand Kashi (which is actually owned by global food powerhouse Kellogg's), when it was discovered that the cereals they marketed as "all natural" contained high levels of GMO ingredients.[1] This caused a scandal that eroded consumer trust, and sent their brand value plummeting. Once you play your audience for fools, it's nearly impossible to regain their allegiance.

The rule of authenticity applies to personal branding as well. Author James Frey sold a bajillion copies of his book *A Million Little Pieces*, after Queen Oprah raved about it on her TV show. Later it came out that Frey had fabricated much of his book, a memoir that chronicled his struggle with addiction.[2] Oprah brought him back on her show for a very public tongue-lashing after the scandal broke, and his golden-boy author status was forever tarnished.

More recently, former PayPal executive Scott Thompson was hired as CEO of Yahoo just prior to Marissa Mayer's reign. Unfortunately, Thompson stated on his resume that he held a bachelor's degree in "accounting and computer science," which was only half true. He did have a degree in accounting, but a quick call to his alma mater revealed that the school didn't start issuing computer science degrees until four years after Thompson graduated.[3] Oops. When the scandal first broke, Yahoo stood behind their man, calling his blunder an "inadvertent error." However, after enough pressure, the company reversed their supportive position and Thompson was ousted after only four months on the job.[4] See kids, even top tech execs embellish their résumés, but it's still not a good idea.

Bottom line: people love a good brand story, but you must be sure that yours is not merely a fairy tale.

Spread the Word

Now that you've agreed on the unique story your company has to share, it's time to determine the tools you will use to spread it. Ideally, you will implement the channels you are already utilizing. However, it may be necessary to adopt some new communication channels if they will improve your ability to spread the word.

Company Blog—Obviously, your own online properties are the best place to start telling a better brand story. If you keep a company blog, try to determine how your story can be parlayed into multiple articles revolving around the essential talking points of your topic.

As for the retail client I mentioned above in the Community section, they could create blog posts about the people and organizations that benefit from their donations and sponsorships, or about the various small farms they work with to ensure fresh organic produce throughout the year. These stories would offer a great opportunity to educate the public about the company's values while at the same time building awareness about who and what they support.

For the computer app designer, creating blog posts featuring case studies about the individual design projects would offer an opportunity to further flesh out the personality of the brand voice. This would give potential clients more insight into his creative process and showcase his expertise in a more comprehensive way than a mere photo portfolio.

Website—If you don't maintain a blog, tell your story on your company website. Make sure your brand story is told through more than just words. Think about how your story can be communicated though images, colors, video and overall feel of the site. Give your story prominent real estate, whether that's on the Home page, the About page, or the Our Team page. The objective is to communicate the essence of your brand to every visitor, regardless of how much time they spend on your site.

Social Media—You cannot ignore the power of social media as a significant platform for disseminating your brand story. In order to be truly successful with social media, your company needs to build media production into its DNA. One or more people need to be responsible for building an ongoing library of text, photos and videos, and every company function, event or milestone must be viewed as a media opp. That doesn't mean you try to get the attention of a media outlet to come and cover your event; it means that your company BECOMES a media outlet and captures, creates, and crafts original content to be doled out to your audience.

Tell visual stories with photos on Pinterest, Instagram and Tumblr. Engage and entertain with video on YouTube and

Vimeo. If producing full-fledged videos seems daunting, you can start with shooting micro-vids on your mobile phone using Vine, which has a six-second limit, or Instagram, which limits you to fifteen seconds. Share a combination of media via your Facebook and Twitter profiles that provides insight, value, entertainment and education.

One of the most creative and helpful applications of the above tools I've seen recently is from Lowe's Home Improvement. They started a Tumblr blog called Lowe's Fix In Six that is populated solely by six-second Vine videos they bill as "a collection of clever improvements that make life at home a little easier." All the videos are stop-motion animation that showcase "fixes" to common quandaries such as storing Christmas ornaments, organizing unruly spools of ribbon, removing water stains from your shower hardware, and keeping squirrels from raiding your bird feeder. These helpful little gems are brilliantly executed, artistically pleasing and surprisingly valuable. Best of all, they help enforce Lowe's brand as the home improvement experts.

Press Releases—In the previous section, I suggested your business becomes its own media outlet. However, that doesn't mean you completely eschew traditional media in your marketing strategy. You should also put the power of the mainstream press to work for you by submitting frequent press releases communicating any newsworthy activities your company is involved in. Of course, traditional media are far more selective with what they cover, so it's best if your press releases focus on a community benefit or human interest angle that is actually considered news and not just promotional puffery.

Even if the main focus of your release isn't about your brand story directly, you can still summarize your story in the boilerplate section of the release. Just as any solid foundation is built one brick at a time, every press release the public reads about your company is another brick that helps to build, alter, or reinforce their perceptions about your brand. Since your brand exists primarily as a collection of perceptions and feelings, it's up to you make sure your foundation is solid by keeping those perceptions and feelings positive.

Packaging—I drink protein shakes on a daily basis and use frozen fruit from Willamette Farms. Right on the back of the package, they have a section called "Our Story," which starts off like this: "Here in Oregon's Willamette Valley, glorious sunshine, billowing clouds and misty rain combine with deep, rich soil for growing the most incredible berries in the world." It goes on from there to paint a glorious picture about the farmers working together to grow, pick and freeze the fruit with loving care. As a consumer, reading this story makes me feel connected to the origin of the product more than I would if I grabbed a bag of Dole frozen blueberries.

Packaging offers prime real estate for storytelling. Smaller boutique food brands understand this and use it more frequently, and to greater effect, than the mammoth mainstream food brands. The reason? Small-batch food production begins as a labor of love. The people producing these products have an authentic desire to create an alternative to what's already available on the market. They're targeting consumers who respond to authenticity, who care about the origin of their food and the integrity of the ingredients used. Plus, these companies don't have budgets for extensive advertising campaigns, so by including their story right on the packaging, they are turning the product itself into an advertising vehicle that tells their story to one customer at a time.

Let's face it, mainstream food brands are all about cheap ingredients, maximum profits and massive scale. People who grab Heinz ketchup, Eggo waffles, and Oscar Meyer bologna off the shelf don't give two hoots about where it was produced or what it's made with. They just want something cheap, tasty and familiar. Therefore, Heinz, Eggo and Oscar Meyer don't care about creating stories of authenticity, nor do they need to use their packaging as mini billboards to convert customers who have never heard of them. Instead, they spend hefty budgets to hire advertising agencies, who are responsible for creating stories that will get consumers to choose one product over another.

When it comes to crafting stories to build brands, some companies opt to tell true-to-life tales and others choose to engage the imagination with fiction. Both can be effective (as long as your "fiction" is not actually a fib-filled version of truth), but I suggest you ascertain which route you wish to take before setting out, so you don't get confused by your own plot line along the way.

Storytelling is a powerful technique that has been embedded in our culture for thousands of years. When done well, it has the ability to differentiate your company and its offering, earn the attention and interest of your target audience and build loyalty between you and your customers. Taking the time to craft a compelling brand story and communicate it to your target audience through a variety of channels will help ensure that your small business lives happily ever after.

★ 38 ★

DOES YOUR BRAND SUFFER FROM MULTIPLE PERSONALITY DISORDER?

One of the recurring themes that came up when consulting with clients was the importance of consistency in all aspects of branding and marketing. Creating a visual identity for your company both online and off can take lots of time, thought, effort and money. In many cases, the identity comes together piecemeal at various stages of the company's life cycle. First you might get some business cards, then a website, maybe a brochure, eventually some storefront signage, and so on. Usually, your company's multiple branding elements get created by different designers, produced by different vendors, and purchased at different times. Before you realize it, you've stitched together a big, green Frankenbrand that displays more personalities than Sybil.

I'd like to share a couple examples of signage that indicate the companies could be suffering from Multiple Brand Personality Disorder.

Shown on the following page is Couch Critics, a local movie and game rental business. Full disclosure: I am both a loyal customer of this store and friends with the owner. My intention is not to smear the company's name but simply to offer a great visual example of a double identity that could be confusing to anyone paying attention. Couch Critics moved their operation into this location from their former location across town. The sign on the roof is a holdover from their old location. It's red,

★ HEAVYWEIGHT MARKETING ★

gold and black and combines classy cursive script with a bold sans serif font. The vinyl window lettering is their new logotype and features a mix of fun, playful, kid-friendly fonts in bright orange and yellow.

Inconsistent logos and signage shows lack of a solid brand identity

By having both on display, Couch Critics appears noncommittal, like they want to start dating someone new, but haven't quite broken up with their current partner. Now, is this violation of The Rule of Consistency going to cause people to go elsewhere for their movie and game rental needs? Probably not. But the minute you start doing things halfway, or aiming for "good enough," is the minute your competition gets the jump on you.

Lightweights don't become champions by training only when they feel like it. They train every day. Initially, they're aiming to reach their potential; in time, they're training to keep their edge. On one hand, Couch Critics has an advantage because it's the only stand-alone video store in town. It has outlasted two other local shops that shuttered—victims of a changing era. On the other hand, competition for video entertainment has never been more fierce: in addition to the local movie theater and grocery store rental station, consumer have unlimited options via Netflix, Hulu, YouTube, Amazon, cable and video-on-demand, allowing everyone with a computer, tablet or mobile device to access any movie, anywhere, any time.

Even perennial behemoth Blockbuster Video chose to throw in the towel rather than face those odds, causing a million Gen Xers to shed a single nostalgic tear. In order to stand strong in a competitive marketplace, it's more important than ever to present a consistent, unified brand identity that consumers are able to recognize and identify with, building their own associations with it.

. . . .

Multiple brand personalities at work: Two different signs for the same store

This is a successful local store called Soul Connections, a New Age retail emporium that's a big hit with tourists. From the exterior signage you would think that these are two different stores. Upon closer inspection you realize they simply have two different signs. When Soul Connections first started, they occupied one retail space, and the sign shown on the right was displayed over the entrance. When they expanded into the space next door, they locked the initial entrance, and hung a new, and completely different sign, over the new entrance.

So, is their original sign even necessary anymore? It's not their official logo and it's over a doorway that is no longer functional. As far as I can tell, all it's doing is creating confusion. In fact, the store just took over a third space that was abandoned by a used book store, which will add yet another non-functioning doorway to the expansive footprint of Soul Connections. Will they add a third sign as well to create even more confusion?

The many faces of Soul Connections

Business is booming for Soul Connections, and they are doing a lot of things right, so my critique may seem like I'm splitting hairs. But in the world of small business marketing, there's always room for improvement.

To be fair, let me state for the record that I do understand that new signage is expensive, and that the current roof signs at both of these establishments are necessary for optimal street-traffic visibility. The resulting effect of Multiple Brand Personality Disorder is that all these disjointed company logos never really gel, and so they do not end up standing for anything

Round 3 - Buff Your Brand

meaningful in the minds of the audience. When it comes to branding, the ultimate goal is to spark immediate recognition, thereby opening the floodgates of positive associations.

Picture this scenario: You're on vacation, driving through a strange town. It's 9am and you're craving a triple latté.

Now, you could take a chance on the little coffee shack that has a sign promising "Expresso," but you figure, if they don't know how to spell it, they sure don't know how to brew it. Then you see it—that beautiful, round, green logo with the happy mermaid and the familiar blocky, white letters that spell out "Starbucks Coffee." BAM—you're in there! Why? Because, the minute you saw their brand signal (the familiar logo), you trusted them to deliver on their brand promise (a delicious trip-latté). Now, on the other hand, if the logo you spied was a purple rectangle with "Starbucks Coffee" in a yellow script font, it would either not register mentally, or you would be slightly confused. In fact, you might even backtrack to the "Expresso" guys.

To be clear, we're not talking about corporate vs. non-corporate in this scenario, and it doesn't matter what you may personally think of Starbucks. We're talking about the difference between sending signals that merely say something (coffee), vs. sending signals that mean something (the Starbucks Coffee Experience).

Of course, creating a meaningful brand goes well beyond the logo on your storefront signage, and we've covered many ways to build a strong brand throughout this book. But, ideally, the minute consumers do see your logo on signage—or anywhere else for that matter—it should trigger all the positive mental perceptions and associations that have accumulated over time. This is quite similar to the "conditioned reflex" work that Russian physiologist Ivan Pavlov is known for. If Pavlov's dogs heard different sounds every time they were fed, they would never

★ **HEAVYWEIGHT MARKETING** ★

learn to associate any particular sound with the reward of food. Likewise, if your customers encounter an inconsistent variety of visual stimuli, they will never learn to salivate for your tasty brand morsels.

Five Steps to Brand Consistency

1. Know what you want to stand for in the minds of your customers (e.g., widest selection of spiritual merchandise, great recommendations from a movie-obsessed staff, consistently delicious coffee in a comfortable environment).
2. Create a visual identity that expresses what your brand stands for.
3. Be consistent with every application of your visual identity.
4. Be consistent with the delivery of your chosen brand promise.
5. If you choose to rebrand at any point, go all in and update everything.

Your long-term objective is to send familiar, consistent brand signals that spark immediate and positive associations in the minds of those who encounter them. If your company's visual identity is a careless, morphing mish-mash of styles, colors and ideas, the only thing you'll be sparking is mass confusion, or worse yet, general apathy. In a hyper-competitive marketplace, either one of those could be the kiss of death for your business.

★ 39 ★

HOW TO CREATE A TRUE BRAND EXPERIENCE

In June of 2012, as schools were letting out, Boston-area English teacher David McCullough, Jr., created quite a buzz with his commencement speech in which he blithely informed all the graduates, "You are not special." His bold proclamation seemed to fly in the face of every single parent, teacher, mentor and guru who claims that "specialness" is our own birthright; that, simply because we exist, we are special. The point Mr. McCullough was raising was that if everyone is special, than no one is special. In his mind, being special is not an automatic right—I exist, therefore I am special—but rather a status that each of us has to earn through hard work, deeds, actions and accomplishments. In short, we need to prove that we are worthy of being considered special. If everyone is starting on the same level playing field, then everyone has an equal opportunity to rise above the rest based on the intensity of his or her efforts.

Whether you agree with Mr. McCullough's theory or not, he definitely raises an interesting point that can equally apply to small business owners: if you think that just because your business exists consumers should support you, then you deserve to fail. In most cases, consumers have multiple options, so it is your responsibility as business owner to "prove" to customers that your offering is special enough to earn their support. Let's face it, the majority of shopping activities and brand interactions we encounter on a daily basis are rather un-special indeed. In fact, most businesses operate purely in Perfunctory Mode,

★ HEAVYWEIGHT MARKETING ★

with the seemingly sole objective of completing commercial transactions, thank-you-come-again.

Most of the time, this is acceptable. After all, I don't necessarily want strobe lights, flashpots and dancing girls every time I duck into the grocery store for a quart of soy milk. However, other times I'm aching for more than just a business transaction, more than just an exchange of my cash for their product. Sometimes, it's nice to be surprised, excited, shocked, wowed, inspired or impressed by a memorable experience.

Before you dismiss this as dramatic hyperbole, ask yourself, "When was the last time I was truly surprised by a company?" As a consumer, how often are you roused from your weary, robotic trundle long enough to actually notice an unexpected detail, a memorable moment, or an innovative idea in action? More than likely, the answer is, "Not often enough."

Like a Virgin

I lived in five states and three different countries before the age of 18. Suffice it to say, I've done my fair share of air travel. Yet when I stepped onto a Virgin America airplane for the first time in 2008, my inner Austin Powers was immediately engaged. It was all I could do to suppress my urge to shout "Yeah, Baby, yeah!" repeatedly as I strutted down the aisle towards my seat.

The sexy cabin lighting—glowing neon purple and hot pink—made everyone on board look like extras in a Prince music video. Hypnotic electronic music pulsed through the cabin at a volume that aroused the ear of the casual EDM fan without repelling those who prefer JPR. The rich, sumptuous decor felt hi-tech and modern. And those seats! Multiple rows of plush black leather and smooth, shiny white plastic resembling an army of recycled Stormtroopers. Embedded in each headrest was a video monitor with enough content options to keep passengers glued to their screens throughout the duration of the flight. Instead of a typical airplane, this felt like a traveling nightclub.

I was blown away by how different the Virgin experience was from every other plane I had flown on. You may not have the resources (or the cheeky élan) of Richard Branson, but as a business owner, it's your job to create that elusive experience for your customers. The question is, "How can this be done?"

Areas in which to apply your own creative solutions:

Atmosphere—People love the feeling of being transported to another time or place, if only for the brief moment they're in your space. Go beyond the basics to create a unique in-store atmosphere that aligns with your business concept, name or category.

Chozu is a Japanese-style bathhouse in Ashland, Oregon, that looks like an ordinary house from the street. The minute you step into the backyard bath gardens, you are transported to a Zen-tastic sanctuary of bamboo, lava rock, and lush greenery that feels like another world. This serene atmosphere is perfect for a business that promises a brief respite from the responsibilities and stress of everyday life.

Don't forget to consider all of the senses: sights, sounds, tactility, tastes and smells contribute to the overall atmosphere of any given location. When Starbucks added breakfast sandwiches to the menu, CEO Howard Schultz would visit stores and, instead of smelling the rich aroma of freshly ground coffee, he was assaulted by the acrid stench of burnt cheese. His knee-jerk reaction was an attempt to ban the offending menu item because it was ruining the atmosphere of his beloved institution. Since it was a popular menu item (i.e., good revenue generator), the company decided to invest in new ovens instead, decreasing the chances of burning the cheese.

★ HEAVYWEIGHT MARKETING ★

I experienced my own version of this at a restaurant called Grilla Bites in Redding, California. Initially, I was thrilled to discover a fast-food restaurant that served healthy vegetarian and vegan fare, and I would stop in for veggie burgers and smoothies whenever I was in the area. Until one fateful visit when I stepped in and was overpowered by the pungent reek of ammonia. Apparently they were cleaning during dining hours and it smelled like they had doused every existing surface with bleach. I've never been back since. All I have to do is think of the place and my nose twitches in disgust. Sure, I can appreciate a clean restaurant but wait until you close before drowning the place in toxic chemicals, fer cryin' out loud.

Quality—In our disposable, mass market, Made-In-China society, it's pretty rare that we buy something that doesn't disintegrate inside of a month. So many companies are focused on ways they can cut costs and trim budgets that quality is right up there next to the Borneo Pygmy Elephant on the endangered species list. When people actually do discover a quality product, they stick with it and become vocal brand ambassadors. The trouble with maintaining a high standard of quality is that it costs more for both the vendor and the consumer. This ends up narrowing the target market to people who appreciate quality, can afford it, and are actually willing to invest in it.

Therefore, marketers must learn how to speak effectively to that audience, telling a story of quality in a way that attracts, differentiates and converts. Let your competitors aspire to be the JCPenney, Dell or Hyundai of your industry while you aim for a brand perception more akin to Nordstrom, Apple or Jaguar. Pursue quality at every turn, and you will attract a loyal audience of equal caliber.

Efficiency—Creating a leisurely atmosphere is great, but sometimes it's about moving bodies through the door as quickly as possible. This, too, can create a favorable experience. After all, if your checkout process is redolent of the DMV's waiting room, it's time to streamline.

The Rule of Efficiency applies to phone-based customer service as well. Have you ever tried to talk to a real person at AT&T? Good luck! You have to carve out an hour of your day just to work through an infuriating maze of automated runaround while being subjected to distorted classical muzak—the soundtrack to your own personal hell. This exercise in futility is what finally led me to ditch AT&T for a local internet provider.

Thankfully, there are some companies that do understand the importance of efficiency. One day during the holiday season, I was trying to cram some quick online shopping in before an early client meeting. I completed an order for some yoga pants from Vickerey.com and was going to order a yoga mat from a different site. Then I realized the yoga mat I wanted was also from Vickerey.com and if I had ordered the pants and the mat together, I would have qualified for free shipping. Instead, I would now have to place two orders and pay for shipping twice! Unacceptable.

With the clock ticking closer to my meeting time, I decided to try Vickerey's customer service line, although at 7:20 a.m., I highly doubted I would reach anybody. I was wrong. Two rings later, a real person came on the line and within five minutes he solved my problem and sent me on my way. Yoga crisis averted. Client meeting punctual. Never underestimate the power and delight of efficiency when delivering your brand experience.

Organization—One of my clients opened a brand new restaurant in a town that was experiencing a cultural revival. After building the website, creating the printed collateral, designing the advertisements and watching the progress as they built out the physical space, I was eager and excited for my first experience at the new culinary hotspot. During my inaugural visit, my excitement morphed quickly to befuddlement as I watched the disorganized, poorly-trained staff fumble about haphazardly as if still trying to establish a process. Nobody knew whether they were offering counter service or table service—not even the staff. Do we come order at the counter, or do we take a seat at a table? Are these workers milling about waiters or table bussers? Do we pay when we order or after we've eaten? Can we take a seat on the patio or do we have to check in first?

Adding insult to injury, I ordered a vegan dish directly from the chef with whom I was shooting the breeze prior to eating. The grilled portobello burger looked lovely and arrived with a handsome side salad. Ah, but what were those white specks in the homemade dressing the salad was swimming in? Parmesan cheese! Vegan fail. Mind you, the restaurant actively touted "vegetarian- and vegan-friendly fare" in their marketing. While they had no problem talking the talk, it was clear they didn't walk the walk. Details, people, details.

I wrote it off as growing pains, but unfortunately, they never got much better over time. The mistake they made was building a restaurant around a great chef without hiring an equally great front-of-house manager to inject some organization into the proceedings. Their menu is unique, their food is good, but their brand experience is a confusing clusterfudge.

Make things easy. Make things intuitive. Don't make people think too hard just to figure out what the heck they're supposed to do. People have enough stress in their daily existence and if your company's product, service or in-store experience injects a little organization into your customers' lives, they will love you for it.

Round 3 - Buff Your Brand

Attitude—Have you ever been in a foul mood, only to be elevated by an encounter with someone whose attitude was positively infectious? The opposite can be true as well: you're flying high until an encounter with a cranky, clueless or incompetent boob sends you crashing down to earth.

More than once, I've gotten in a kerfuffle with a waiter or barista who had messed up my order (I realize I may seem like a high-maintenance restaurant customer, but I don't understand why receiving exactly what I order is so freakin' hard), and they have actually tried to argue their way out of their own mistake. Seriously? It doesn't matter who's at fault. What matters is that the wrong is made right—with a positive attitude.

There's a drive-through coffee chain called Dutch Bros., with several locations in the Western U.S. Unlike most coffee spots that cater to the breakfast and daytime crowd, Dutch Bros. is open late, making them a great destination for night-shift workers and the after-dark party crowd. The company understands its audience, too: their baristas are always upbeat, cheerful and conversational.

Whenever I have visited the chain, regardless of time or location, the employee on hand has reached out with some form of "So, what are you guys up to tonight?" while crafting my order. This tells me that congeniality and conversational aptitude are built into employee training. Sure, it helps to seek vivacious, friendly people when hiring, but in order to guarantee consistency and excellence with your chosen brand attributes, they must be embedded into your training protocol and company culture.

As you can see from these customer tweets, I'm not the only one whose impressed by Dutch Bros.' positive attitude:

★ **HEAVYWEIGHT MARKETING** ★

> Always impressed with the phenomenal customer service I receive at @DutchBros.
>
> — John Franck (@johnfranck8) **March 12, 2014**
>
> @DutchBros service always on point. i could be in a terrible mood, and they just make me so happy<3 #makesmyday
>
> — 1133556990 (@RacecarLaMar) **March 10, 2014**
>
> Shout-out to @DutchBros for the always having outstanding customer service and BTW their #coffee is great too!
>
> — Jose Ochoa (@JoseOchoa15) **February 6, 2014**

Dutch Bros.' outstanding customer service inspires plenty of love on Twitter

They say that attitude is everything, and while that may be an overstatement, I know for a fact that in a world of impatient idiots, egocentric clowns and vitriolic trolls, a positive attitude can go a long way.

With so many of your competitors gliding comfortably along on cruise control, what would it take for your company to fire up the rocket boosters and leave those Sunday drivers in a cloud of turbo-scented dust? Gather your staff, pull out your Thinking Caps and brainstorm on ways that you can improve the brand experience for your customers.

You might improve simple details, you might pursue grandiose innovations. However you choose to actively rise above the perfunctory pack, your actions and investments will surely pay off in improved customer satisfaction, increased word-of-mouth and stronger brand loyalty. Hey, maybe you are special after all. But the only way to get people to realize this is by acting like it.

★ 40 ★

RESISTING THE SEDUCTION OF LOW PRICE

You've probably heard the age-old maxim, "You get what you pay for." While there will always be exceptions to every rule, the reason this phrase has become ingrained in our lexicon to the point of becoming cliché is because it contains more than a modicum of truth. In fact, at least 40% of the web-design projects I secured as a marketing consultant were rebuilds of the company's initial site. Why did they need rebuilding? Because they were built by friends, amateurs or former employees who offered a price that could not be refused. You know what else could not be refused? The harsh reality that every one of these sites ended up being ineffective to the viewer, inaccessible to the owner, and downright hideous to boot. But, hey, at least they were cheap! Low price points seduce business owners in two directions: buying and selling. Let's examine the attraction and risk of both.

Buying Low

The magic equation in business is Revenue - Expenses = Profit. Therefore, the more you control your overhead and reduce your expenses, the higher your profit margin. While I do understand the allure of a small price tag when building and growing your business, basing your purchasing decisions on price alone is a short-sighted strategy. Sure, it appears to be good for your company's bottom line, but choosing the low-price option should be considered a temporary solution, because that's usually what it will end up being.

★ HEAVYWEIGHT MARKETING ★

I'm not suggesting that business owners spend money they don't have, rely on credit cards, or become indebted to bankers so they can invest in business solutions (been there, done that, still making payments). But I am suggesting they always consider the long-term investment over the quick fix. There are certain areas—which will vary by business—in which it's more feasible to scrimp, and certain areas in which to spare no expense. For instance, you may not need to decorate your office with Jonathan Adler when Ikea will suffice.

You may, however, wish to invest more strategically in areas that are essential to your business. That might be hiring and retaining top-notch talent, manufacturing and distributing product, developing and protecting your technology infrastructure, or positioning your company with marketing strategies that help you build a champion brand.

I'm not a financial consultant, so managing your company's finances and choosing where to spend them is on you. However, based on my experience working with scores of business owners and "wantrepreneurs," I've seen how many of them would rather buy cheap than buy smart. While frugality is not without merit, it's also important to understand the difference between an expense and an investment—and to consider the long-term risks and rewards of each.

Selling Low

The other side of low-price seduction comes into play when pricing your products and services. There's an equation at play here as well that depends on whether you are reselling products you have purchased elsewhere, selling something you have produced yourself, or selling a service—which often includes passing expenses and operating costs on to your clients. The equation looks something like Your Cost + Markup - Expenses = Profit.

Round 3 - Buff Your Brand

This equation may seem easy, but don't be fooled: determining the right price for your offering is one of the hardest things about running your own business.

Resellers—Reselling items you have purchased seems easy enough, right? After all, you probably received bulk or dealer pricing, so you slap on a comfy markup and you're off to the races. The tricky part is determining what type of brand you want to build. Are you positioning your company as a discount store, a middle-of-the-road establishment, or a high-end brand? You need to make this decision early because once you choose a spot on the pricing food chain, you can either stay put, or slide downward. Rarely are companies able to reposition themselves as a high-end brand after occupying a low or mid-range position.

JCPenney is a recent example of this. When Ron Johnson took over in 2011 as CEO, he attempted to increase the relevance of the brand by giving the discount store a hip makeover. He revamped the store layout, created in-store boutiques filled with up-and-coming designers, and attempted to do away with their frequent deep-discount sales in favor of everyday low prices. While Johnson's vision was grandiose and his efforts impressive (in theory anyway—they never got a chance to play out long-term), customers barely recognized their beloved discount store and refused to accept the changes. After only 18 months on the job and consecutive quarterly losses, the Board freaked, ousted Johnson and reinstated their previous CEO—yanking him from retirement to captain the S.S. Penney, recharting its course straight back to Discount Island from whence they came.

Makers and Producers—While artisans have been producing hand-made products for centuries, the digital revolution has made it easier for makers and producers to build a business around their products. The internet has allowed people to sell their wares online, build brand awareness regardless of location,

★ **HEAVYWEIGHT MARKETING** ★

and drive both foot and web traffic to their stores whether physical or virtual. Consumers have developed a renewed interest in quality, hand-made products and the phrase "Made In U.S.A." has started to hold meaning again.

> "Mom-and-pops are engineering entire business strategies devoted to locally made goods—everything from toys to housewares. And it's not simply patriotism and desire for perceived safer products which are altering shopping habits. The recession, and still flat recovery for many Americans, have created a painful realization. All those cheap goods made in China and elsewhere come at a price: lost U.S. manufacturing jobs. A growing pocket of consumers, in fact, are connecting the economic dots between their shopping carts—brimming with foreign-made stuff—and America's future." —CNBC

From fashion to furniture, messenger bags to bicycles, and wine to cupcakes, aspiring entrepreneurs are growing the small business landscape. At some stage of the business journey, all these makers and producers have to determine where to set their price points in order to create the appropriate brand perception they're aiming for, and to generate enough profits to create a sustainable business. Price your goods too high and you never attain critical mass. Price too low and you can't create a profitable business.

Over the years, many of my consulting clients have been artists or creative entrepreneurs. Now there's a group that is notoriously challenged when it comes to pricing their work (I'm an active artist myself, so I understand this challenge first-hand). More experienced artists have a better grasp of where their price points should be, but that doesn't mean their work will sell consistently—especially in a soft market. Newer artists often pull

Round 3 - Buff Your Brand

prices out of thin air, hoping that if they price their work low enough, it will sell.

Makers and producers often make the mistake of thinking that they simply need to recoup the cost of materials and a little extra for their time. They fail to realize they also need to cover rent, insurance, taxes, electricity, and all the other bills and expenses that are adding up while they're holed up in the workshop or studio making their product. Remember, it's not about selling a few belts, candles or handbags, it's about building a viable business that will allow you to live the life you want to live.

Pricing properly is tricky and each scenario is different. While I'd love to offer you an easy, one-size-fits-all equation to apply to your business, there's no such thing. Sorry. However, there are some steps below that should prove helpful when deciding where to position your brand in the marketplace.

Services—If you think pricing products is challenging, try pricing intangible items, which is what those in the service industry have to do. When I started BAM! Small Biz Consulting in 2010, I had a frantic brainstorming session where I crafted all the different service packages I would provide my clients: The Spar Session, The One-Two Punch, The 3-Round Showdown, The Lightweight, Featherweight and Heavyweight Champion, etc. These packages contained a variety of different services that I *assumed* my clients would want, and I created prices that were a mixture of thin-air guesstimates, industry experience and the desire to create a premium brand.

Needless to say, my first year was a real eye-opener. There was definitely a gap between what I thought clients wanted (and the work I wanted to do) and what they thought they wanted (and were actually willing to pay for). I never really set out to be a website designer, but that's what the overwhelming majority of my clients were seeking, so I adapted. Of course I wanted every client to opt for my fully-integrated, multifaceted marketing strategy, implementation and management packages. But a large majority of my clients opted to eat from the a la carte menu as opposed to the all-you-can-eat buffet. The key is to be flexible enough to shift your service according to demand, without being a pushover who caves to your clients' every request.

A huge part of selling services is educating the client. While they may be an expert in their field, you are the expert in yours and that's why they hired you. With intangible services, clients need to understand exactly why they're paying so much for something they can't see, touch, eat, wear, park in their garage, or display on their mantle. One of the biggest hurdles to overcome (both for you and your clients) is the perception that you are simply selling your time. That often seems like the easiest solution: you charge X dollars per hour, the job took Y hours, therefore $X \times Y$ is your billable. Wrong!

One of my heroes of the consulting world is "Million Dollar Consultant" Alan Weiss. He has plenty of choice words for those "amateurs" who "trade dollars for hours," because one of his core beliefs is that true wealth is not a surplus of money, but of time. After all, what good is having money if you have no time to enjoy the life benefits it affords? Therefore service providers need to create a high level of perceived value around their offering and communicate that value to their clients.

While all three of the above categories contain distinctive challenges, they also share common elements that need to be considered when it comes to setting prices:

The State of the Economy—It seems like we've been in slow-recovery mode since the economic crash of 2008. While some of the bigger cities seem to have bounced back, fringe areas are still feeling the squeeze. I'm based in a tourist town up in the rural stretch of far northern California and I've been hearing local biz owners complain about the sad state of the economy for the past six years. Factor in our crazy weather patterns—our ski park didn't even open last winter due to lack of snow, which meant zero tourist traffic—and business owners have plenty to be concerned about. It's no wonder their first instinct is to slash prices.

What the Market Will Bear—This is directly related to the previous point. In a strong economy, people are buying luxury items, frivolous toys and premium brands so the market can bear higher price points. When the economy tanks, consumers become smarter shoppers. They reduce spending habits to essentials, they seek better quality, and they opt for long-term investments over short-term splurges. Consumers may not stop spending completely but surviving a soft economy requires a little more finesse. Know what's happening in the marketplace and be flexible enough to adjust your value proposition accordingly.

Who Your Audience Is—Understanding your target audience is an essential element of your marketing strategy. When you really know who your customer is, you can speak to his values, concerns, fears, dreams and goals. The Walmart shopper is a different breed than the Neiman Marcus shopper and vice versa. While these examples occupy extreme ends of the spectrum, it gets trickier when targeting the middle ground. That's why it's important to find your niche. It's nearly impossible to have a meaningful conversation with someone you don't know. Getting to know "your people" will allow you to connect on common ground and communicate shared topics of interest.

Getting the Most Bang for Your Marketing Buck

1) **Plan Ahead**—Most of the business owners I have dealt with over the years have been driven by a passion for their topic

★ **HEAVYWEIGHT MARKETING** ★

of expertise. This is excellent, but it often leads entrepreneurs to operate in "Ready, FIRE! Aim" mode. If your passion compels you to set up shop before you determine a solid, consistent, long-term plan on how to get customers through the door, you'll end up spending more time scrambling for business than running a business.

2) Start With Your Message—The secret to an effective marketing strategy is using the right tools to reach the right audience with the right message. All three elements must be in place, working in sync, and it starts with a meaningful message. Know how your offering is unique, who will benefit most from it, and how they will benefit. Articulate that information with a crisp, concise benefit statement to deliver through your myriad vehicles of outreach: website, advertising, public relations, social media bios, interview talking points, etc.

3) Allot Marketing Budget—There are certain fixed costs to running a business and marketing should be one of them. However, based on my experience with clients, this is not a common viewpoint. If you plan on taking a vacation, you allot a vacation budget. If you want to send the kids to college, you start a college fund. If you plan on running a successful business, you dedicate a certain percentage of your revenue to your marketing initiatives. Occasionally, you'll hear about a company that builds a grassroots following because their offering is so cool, unique or desirable. The founders will boast about how they barely spent any money on marketing, yet their company still took off. While that scenario does happen, it's pretty rare and is not a route I would recommend hoping for. Don't use marketing as a knee-jerk solution to jump start slow sales. Allot a percentage of revenue to your marketing efforts and use it. Always.

4) Easy Does It—You don't have to invest in every solution at once. Look for the most accessible ones to start with. These could include social media strategies, online review sites and business listings, networking, building your email list, creating a referral program, and generating positive word-of-mouth with an affordable strategy I like to call "Be Awesome Marketing." You achieve this by—you guessed it—being awesome. However, don't assume that you can get by forever on "free" online tactics like those listed above. Social platforms are wonderful for connecting with your audience but should be considered just a few arrows in your marketing quiver, not the golden harpoon that's gonna render paid and traditional tactics obsolete.

5) Think Cost-Effective, Not Cheap—When purchasing business solutions, your goal should be to get the most value for your investment, not just the lowest price. When you feel ready to invest in a big ticket item such as a website or an ad campaign, shop around a bit and compare the level of value each vendor is offering for the price. And be relatively certain (there's always a little risk involved) that the big ticket item you're considering is going to be the most appropriate tool to reach your audience. When selling your own products or services, your goal should be the same—to provide the most value for your customers' investment.

In our Costco society, we have become obsessed with getting the cheapest price. In some cases, opting for the cheap or free option may indeed offer a perfect temporary solution. However, don't be surprised if this solution ends up costing more money in the long run when the original investment falters, fails or proves otherwise insufficient. This is true whether you're talking about marketing solutions, furniture, garden tools or any of the gimcrack garbage available for a pittance at the nearest big-box retailer. Remember, nobody likes a cheapskate, not even your business.

★ 41 ★

DO YOU INNOVATE OR IMITATE?

It's not easy for companies to be as innovative as Apple or to create a product that explodes in popularity like…the Snuggie. Nevertheless, business owners still must apply an innovative mindset to their every undertaking. History has shown that it's not the public who pushes for major innovations. Instead, it has always been forward-thinking inventors and entrepreneurs who take the initiative to explore new ground, thereby leading the way for the rest.

The public was content with the horse and buggy, they weren't clamoring for automobiles. Music fans were satisfied with the Sony Discman, they weren't asking for a pocket-size device that could hold thousands of songs. And couch potatoes weren't revolting over the fact that their blankets didn't have sleeves. Thankfully, Henry Ford, Steve Jobs, the Slanket guys (the Slanket was actually the original blanket with sleeves, and the Snuggie is a more recent and popular improvement on the concept) and countless other innovators have not settled for "business as usual."

Innovation is the application of better solutions that meet new requirements, unarticulated needs, or existing market needs. Innovation belongs to those who continue to ask themselves if there's a better, easier, more unique way of doing something. This can include ground-breaking, revolutionary ideas, but it doesn't have to. In fact, holding innovation up to this standard is the reason it can seem daunting, intimidating or just plain inaccessible. You

★ HEAVYWEIGHT MARKETING ★

know the saying, "Shoot for the stars and you just may hit the moon?" That's the way I like to look at innovation: if you aim for "innovation" and your efforts only reach "improvement," you're still better off than most of your competition.

There are naysayers who claim that the term "innovation" is tossed around so much that it has started to lose its true meaning. This may be due to the explosion of startups and entrepreneurs in the tech world, every one of them promising that their Big Idea is destined to put a dent in the universe—even if it is just another photo messaging app. Disregard the semantics bullies and adopt innovation as a core value of your business. Whether you plan to change the world, or simply change an outdated product, process, technology or idea, innovation can be applied anywhere at any scale.

Innovation at Work

Even simple innovations like pop-top lids on soup cans make life a little easier

I was buying soup at the grocery store recently and was thrilled to discover that my favorite brand of soup, Amy's, had

Round 3 - Buff Your Brand

implemented those pull-tab tops that alleviate the need for can openers. My first thought was, Hallelujah! They probably just saved five years of my life that would have been wasted rummaging through kitchen drawers and wrestling with crappy can openers that weren't made for left-handed people like me.

My second thought was, what took them so long? Cats have been enjoying this convenience on their food cans for years, and it's just now making its way to the soup aisle? Regardless, pop-top soup cans provide a welcome improvement to the unarticulated need for an easier, faster way to get your soup outta the can and into the pan.

There's a company called Quirky that crowdsources new product ideas and inventions. They allow community members to vote on their favorites and bring to market the products that get the most votes. They sell the products online and distribute them to brick and mortar stores around the country.

Quirky's top-selling product is called Pivot Power. You know how typical power strips have several outlets placed real close together? That makes it hard to fit a bunch of bulky plugs side-by-side so you end up skipping an outlet or two, which defeats the whole purpose of multiple outlets.

Boy Genius: Pivot Power inventor Jake Zien

The inventor of Pivot Power, Jake Zien, was a senior in high school who realized there had to be a more efficient design for a power strip. He created a multi-plug power strip with six pivoting outlets that accommodate plugs and adapters of all shapes and sizes. The success of his product proves that there were plenty of other people who were wrestling with the same power-strip problem. Of course, since the success of Pivot Power, the market has been flooded with multiple imitations of the concept from different companies. That's the difference between innovators and imitators: the former see opportunity where no one has gone before, and the latter sit back and wait for something to become a success before taking action.

I mentioned the tech sector earlier, which is where innovation is really running rampant. The proliferation of online applications, services and solutions accessible from your mobile device has essentially transformed your smartphone

Making homes smarter: Nest thermostat and iPhone app

into a multi-faceted remote control from which you can operate and monitor your life. One recent success story involves Nest, a company that reinvented the household thermostat, of all things.

Nest founder Tony Fadell was one of the key players on Apple's iPod team, and he applied a similarly beautiful minimalism to a smart thermostat that learns the desired temperature patterns of your household. The Nest app allows you to adjust temperature settings in your home from wherever you are. For their second act, Nest introduced Protect, a completely reimagined smoke and carbon monoxide alarm that is both work-of-fine-art beautiful and ridiculously simple to operate.

Sometimes when innovating, there are missteps. Case in point: shortly after its introduction there were problems detected with the Protect smoke alarm, forcing a recall and putting production on hold. Hey, no one said innovation was easy. In early 2014, three years after redefining what thermostats are capable of, Nest was acquired by Google for $3.2 billion, proving that innovation really does pay.

Perhaps your company is not improving packaging techniques, inventing new products or reimagining household utilities, so let's hone in on our main area of focus—branding and marketing your business. Can you adopt and apply an innovative marketing mindset to your business? Absolutely. Simply start where you are and determine where you would prefer to be, while also taking a closer look at what you've been doing and how you've been doing it.

The Problem With "Me-Too" Marketing

If you examine several advertisements by different companies in any given category, it's often difficult to tell one business from the next. That's because many companies simply resort to imitation marketing. This is when business owners look around at what's working for other companies in their category and then tout the same old features and the same old solutions to the same old problems. Whether the reason for this is lack of time, knowledge or desire to make the necessary efforts doesn't matter. Companies that resort to "me-too" marketing will never stand for anything meaningful in the minds of their prospects or customers. In that case, customers make decisions based on convenience of location, or even worse, on price alone, which essentially reduces your offerings to commodities. If you didn't intend to enter the commodities business, you need to define and articulate your meaningful difference to your audience so they perceive your offerings as unique, valuable solutions to their problems.

Four Steps to Memorable Marketing

In the four steps below, we cover features, advantages, benefits and delivery. When assessing your own product or service, you may find many features and several advantages. That's great. Then you'll just have to determine which are most meaningful to your customers and focus on those. For the sake of simplicity, in each of our examples below I have chosen one feature, advantage and benefit per product.

1) Focus on Features—The first step is to understand your offering completely. What are the features of the products or services you are bringing to the marketplace? I like to call this the "What" of your business and, while it's a great thing to figure out for your own purposes, features are generally not interesting or compelling enough to use as a marketing angle. Unfortunately, companies do it all the time. I've seen way too many ads featuring bullet points of everything the company offers. My immediate response to this is, "So what? How will all these bullet points benefit me, and why should I patronize your list of bullet points over your competitor's?" If your marketing messages have been focusing on the "What" of your business, it's time to dig deeper.

Round 3 - Buff Your Brand

Pulling from our three examples of innovation above—Amy's soup cans, the Pivot Power flexi-strip, and Nest's smart thermostat—the features from those offerings might look something like this:

- Soup cans with pop-top lids
- Power strip with six pivoting outlets
- Self-programming thermostat that "learns" your schedule

As you can see, features are pretty bare bones. They're simple, obvious even. That's okay. Features are only your starting point. The next steps are where things start to get interesting.

2) Assess Your Advantages—Next you need to determine how the features of your offering put you in a favorable or superior position. If features speak to the "What" of your business, advantages speak to the "Why," as in why these favorable aspects are important. The more competitive the marketplace, the more common it will be for multiple companies to be offering similar products and services. How many restaurants do you think there are in Houston? How many art galleries are located in Miami? How many clothing boutiques exist in Chicago? It's imperative to understand where your company stands in relation to your competitors, what things you do differently and how those things give you a competitive advantage. If we were to examine the advantages of the bullet-point features listed above, they might be:

- Easier and faster to open cans with no extra tools
- Every outlet can be utilized with ease
- Smart thermostat adjusts to customer's unique lifestyle

Keep digging until you have a solid list. The more advantages you uncover, the more opportunities you have to differentiate your offering. "When you're trying to differentiate, there's going to be this gut sense [of] 'is this right?'" says Nest's Tony Fadell. "If you're not having doubt, then you're not pushing it hard enough, or you're not looking at the details close enough. You need to be feeling that doubt every single day." While doubt can be a strong motivator, be sure to keep it in check so it doesn't paralyze your progress. After all, it's not until the next step that things start getting juicy.

3) Boast About Your Benefits—All your unique features and competitive advantages won't mean a thing until you are able to communicate exactly how those attributes will benefit your audience. Of course, this means you need to know your audience and understand what's important to them, what motivates them, and how your offering will improve their lives. Most consumers won't respond to a checklist of tech specs, nor will they typically be seduced by marketing jargon. But all consumers will respond to clearly articulated benefits that directly address some aspect of their lives. When you break it down, there are only a handful of general problem areas that strike a universal chord:

- Saving time
- Saving money
- Making things easier
- Making things more enjoyable
- Improving safety or security
- Improving health or well-being

Within those general areas, however, there may be a million specific scenarios to which customers may apply your solution. The more specific you can get with your solution, the more targeted your niche audience will be. Continuing with our three examples, what might be some of the benefits of their stated features be?

Round 3 - Buff Your Brand

Pop-top soup cans that are easier and faster to open with no extra tools might shave a little extra time off a busy professional's already-short lunch break. It might mean a hiker can exclude one extra item from her backpack—a bulky can opener—as she takes on the Pacific Crest Trail. The pop-top might even offer a safer can-opening experience—a feature I would certainly have appreciated 25 years ago:

> *I was 20 years old, working part-time at a nursing home serving meals to the residents. One night, I was running a little behind on food prep. As the oldsters filed into the dining room, eager to enjoy the social highlight of their long, solitary days, I wrestled with an industrial-size can of peaches. The feeble hand-held can opener, rendered ineffectual by the cylindrical steel behemoth, chewed away at the lid leaving random stretches of unpenetrated surface. Frustrated, I grabbed a nearby butter knife in an attempt to pry the jagged lid from its stubborn affixation.*
>
> *One steel tendon snapped, reluctantly releasing its grip from the can. Then another. With only one point of connectivity blocking hinged-lid access to a sweet bounty of fruit, the knife slipped and my hand shot forward, meeting a shark-like row of mangled metallic teeth. The angry, ravenous lid gouged an inch-long ravine in my index finger, severing nerves and nipping at bone. Too young and stupid to realize I needed immediate medical attention, I barely stifled a maelstrom of expletives, wrapped my shocked and gushing digit in a paper towel, secured it with a rubber band, and proceeded—dizzy and swaying—to serve a hundred hungry tenants, while trying hard not to drip blood in their meatloaf.*

A pivoting power strip that allows each outlet to be utilized with ease might alleviate the frustration of having to Frankenstein a bunch of power strips together—some of which STILL contain vacant outlets—just so all your bulky adapters have a power source. It might provide a little organization in your home office, which can easily become an unruly spaghetti junction in this era of electronic-device overload.

A smart thermometer that learns your schedule, adjusts its heating and cooling temperatures to your lifestyle, and is easily accessed via your smartphone will help you save both money and energy. After all, how many times have you come home to realize you forgot to turn the heat down before you left, and spent eight hours heating an empty house? Another benefit of the Nest thermostat is that it simplifies your life. It's easy to install and the simple "turn up" or "turn down" motion is all it takes to teach the unit your preferences, without any complicated programming.

4) Determine Your Delivery—Now that you have uncovered the features, benefits and advantages of your offering, it's time to address your delivery. While there are seemingly infinite tools and tactics available, the number decreases to a more manageable size once you start honing in on the most effective ways to reach your ideal audience. Therefore your selections will be determined by who your audience is, where they can be found, and the budget you have to reach them with.

In the three examples we've been threading through this chapter, innovation was implemented in the idea and execution stages. When it comes time to market these products, Amy's, Quirky, and Nest will most likely use traditional online and offline channels. Yes, there seems to be a new social media platform every month that sends marketers into an excitable tizzy, but jumping on every shiny new object is not always an efficient use of your time. In many cases, tried and true methods are perfect at the delivery stage.

Typically, "delivery" refers to the tools used to disseminate your marketing message, but it could also mean delivery of

Round 3 - Buff Your Brand

your product itself. I've read about some innovative forms of product delivery lately in an sector not known for its eagerness to reinvent: the music business.

As a long-time musician, I've enjoyed keeping tabs on the ongoing struggle the music industry has faced in adapting—with great reluctance—to the digital age. It has been 15 years since the industry was blindsided by Napster at the turn of the new millennium. Since then, record companies have lumbered, dinosaur-like, towards new models of distribution. Only recently have they finally started to surprise with innovative ways of releasing new music to the public. These two examples are a couple of my recent favorites:

A couple weeks before the official release of his debut album, red hot EDM producer Skrillex released an app titled "Alien Ride." The app was supposed to simply be a video game similar to the Atari classic, Asteroids. However, it also contained a folder with 11 hidden objects, which turned out to be song files for his new album. Fans who downloaded the app began to see songs unlock on a specific date, with a new song unlocking every 30 minutes.

For another space-age music release, John Frusciante, former guitarist for Red Hot Chili Peppers, loaded his latest solo album onto a satellite and launched it via rocket ship into orbit. A couple days later, his record company released a free app that allowed fans to track the satellite's journey. Of course, the app also contained locked music files and when the satellite approached a user's geographic location, the song files were unlocked, allowing fans to listen to the album for free.

Throughout this book, we discuss the importance of storytelling. Hiding your new album on a video game app or sending it into space on a rocket makes for way more interesting

★ HEAVYWEIGHT MARKETING ★

stories than simply crafting yet another press release about another musician releasing another album.

In this "seen-it-all" world, it's definitely a challenge to come up with something truly unique. However, that shouldn't stop you from trying. I'm not suggesting innovation has to be employed at every stage of the game, but I am suggesting it should be considered at some stage of the game. If you don't give it your best efforts, your business will unwittingly blend into the faceless cluster of imitators.

Companies that aggressively seek to innovate with their products, services, operations or marketing always rise above the pack. Some of them reach the stars and others merely reach the moon. In this increasingly crowded and competitive marketplace, either one of those is an enviable place to be.

★ 42 ★

FOURTEEN WAYS TO POSITION YOURSELF AS AN EXPERT

I'm thrilled that there are people who know more than I do. I never wanted to learn how to rebuild the engine in my car; I love good coffee but certainly don't want to grow, harvest and roast the beans myself; and while finding a great pair of jeans with a perfect fit makes me quite happy, I'm even happier that I don't have to know how to make them. I'd rather leave all that stuff to the experts. Your prospects and customers feel the same way.

Consumers want to do business with people they trust. In order to gain the trust of your audience, you must position yourself as an expert in their minds. The way you do this is through education. You must use a variety of methods and tools to educate your audience with information that demonstrates your knowledge and your expertise.

The first step in positioning yourself as an expert is knowing what you want to stand for. Your brand is a perception in the minds of your audience, so you need to determine what you want to be known for. Remember, experts are specialists, not generalists, so pick one area of expertise and run with it.

Fourteen Ways to Share Your Expertise With the World:

Maintain a Blog—Blogging is a great platform for educating your audience. Once you choose a specific topic, provide valuable information on that topic with regular posts and rich media content. Your blog is your home base, so all the tools you choose to employ should drive traffic back there.

With the rise of micro-blogging platforms such as Twitter, Tumblr, Plurk, Facebook—basically any platform that allows a status update—many people have bypassed long-form blogging in favor of social media activity. Some even say blogging is a dying medium. While this may be true of the first-wave bloggers who treated the medium as a daily journal, those in the business sector understand how essential blogging is to their content marketing strategy. One scroll through Twitter is all it takes to see that blogging is not dead, as most of the tweets in the stream contain links back to blogs, or websites with blog components. We talked about the pros and cons of blogging earlier, so I won't go into them here, but for my money, there is still no better, easier or cheaper way to disseminate your expertise and increase your search rankings than through frequent blog posts on your own website.

Guest Posts on Other Blogs—There are plenty of other people in your industry sharing ideas on the same topic you cover. Many of them are in need of additional content for their blog, so reach out to them. Offer to trade guest posts and cross-pollinate your audience. Before you submit a guest post, make sure you are able to include a photo, bio and link back to your own site at the end of it.

Speaking of backlinks, there has been a lot of talk lately about the death of guest blogging (sheesh, what is it with all these grim prognosticators?). Google's own Matt Cutts has even tackled the topic on several occasions, including this statement from January 2014:

> "Stick a fork in it: guest blogging is done; it's just gotten too spammy. In general I wouldn't recommend accepting a

guest blog post unless you are willing to vouch for someone personally or know them well. Likewise, I wouldn't recommend relying on guest posting, guest blogging sites, or guest blogging SEO as a linkbuilding strategy." —Matt Cutts, Head of Webspam at Google

Most guest posts are like Twinkies: zero value, tons of garbage. That's because people have been misusing the practice as a way to get their spammy links on as many websites as possible. So, if your objective is to cram your guest post full of links with the hopes of driving massive traffic to your site, forget it. However, if you are one of the few people still crafting valuable guest posts for respectable blogs that cater to the same audience you're trying to reach, guest blog posts can still be a legitimate way to share your expertise.

Comments on Other Blogs—I love this strategy. It's kind of like leaving bread crumbs of knowledge, opinion and personality that lead back to your site. The resulting traffic is more of a trickle than a flood, but I've earned followers, sold books, and made connections with people who enjoyed my comments and followed the trail back to my site. Commenting is easier and less time-consuming than writing guest posts, but you need to limit your focus to topics that are relevant to your area of expertise.

For max effectiveness, you need to make sure your photo shows up next to your comment and your name hyperlinks to the web property you want people to visit. Comment boxes allow you to sign in several different ways. Apps like Disqus and LiveFyre allow you to set up a profile with photo, bio, contact, etc. If you sign up through these apps, your profile photo shows up next to your comment, and your profile page is where people end up when they click your name. Once there, people can see all the comments you've made through the comment app, which gives them an overview of your expertise. However, getting them from your comment profile to your website is an extra step—which they may or may not take.

You can also log in via social media platforms like Twitter or Facebook. In that case, your corresponding profile pic shows up and your name links to your chosen social media profile. This is a good choice if you're trying to build followers. The final log-in option is to enter your name, email address and website URL, which is the best choice for driving people to your website. To make sure your photo appears by your comment when choosing this option, you need to set up a profile at Gravatar.com. This site allows you to upload a profile photo and connect it to your primary email address. Anytime you enter your email in a comment box log-in, it will pull in your connected image from Gravatar. You can even add several email addresses and connect them to different photos, which is handy if you're commenting on different topics and wanting to drive visitors to different web properties.

For example, in order to drive people to the website for my art marketing book, *Death to the Starving Artist*, I comment on art-related sites using a specific photo/email/website combo. I use a different combo when commenting on business and marketing blogs in order to drive people to the website for this book. If I'm not trying to drive people to my book sites but still want to build brand recognition, I just sign in with Twitter. Allow me to state for the record that in most cases—in the name of consistency and brand recognition—it's a good idea to use the same image and brand, company or personal name across all your web and social platforms.

This may seem like a lot of effort to offer your two cents on someone else's blog post, but a little work up front allows you to stand out amongst a large majority of anonymous commenters with their silly pseudonyms and generic thumbnail icons.

Social Media—There's so much advice out there about how to use social media for business (and I've written at length about it in the previous section) that I'll keep it brief and on point here. From the standpoint of showcasing your expertise, the rule is pretty simple: people should be able to immediately glean your area of expertise by a quick glance at your tweet stream or Facebook wall.

There are differing opinions on what constitutes the "perfect ratio" of personal to promotional posts, but what everyone agrees on is that too much of one or the other is a turnoff. If all your posts are promotional, you're not using the medium properly. If you are "all biz all the time" and tweet link after link to articles, blog posts and industry news—with zero personality included—people will think you're a robot. If all your posts are personal anecdotes, replies, musings and quotes, you're not offering much value to followers who are looking for deeper business insight or education.

So what is the proper ratio? Enough shop talk to show what you're passionate about, enough personality to show you're a human, and enough promotion to show that, hey—you've got a business to run!

As for your bio section, resist the temptation to summarize the entirety of your existence in three sentences. It drives me crazy when I see Twitter bios that read "Father, Son, Husband, Friend, Jesus Follower, Tinkerer, Tailor, Candlestick Maker, yada yada…" Does that mean you're gonna be tweeting about all that stuff? I sure hope not. If you are using Twitter as a business tool, your bio should tout the area of expertise you want to be known for. Remember, aspire to be a specialist, not a generalist. If you do include more than one thing in your bio, at least put your primary focus first. In other words, the only reason "Father" should be listed first in your bio is if you're a daddy blogger.

★ HEAVYWEIGHT MARKETING ★

E-books—A great way to turn your knowledge and expertise into an informational product is to write an e-book. You can produce one e-book that provides an educational overview of your preferred topic, or produce a series of e-books that tackle different topics within your industry. A great technique to educate your audience and grow your mailing list at the same time is to offer your e-book(s) as a free download in exchange for joining your mailing list.

If you prefer to use your e-books as a way to generate revenue, you can sell them from your own website using a PayPal plugin or an e-commerce shopping cart like WooCommerce. Another option is to sell your product through ClickBank, an online marketplace that provides an entire suite of features and services to digital marketers and product creators. ClickBank takes a percentage of sales, but if they can help you sell more product, they deserve it.

Another online publishing service is BookBaby, which is a great option if you need help formatting your e-books for different e-readers like Kindle and Nook. When selling from your own site, or even ClickBank, a simple PDF file will suffice. However, creating a file that will offer a positive reading experience across a variety of devices is tricky and may warrant outside help. Another cool thing about BookBaby is that they not only handle formatting, but also global distribution to the popular sites such as AmazonKindle, Apple's iBooks store, Barnes & Noble's Nook, Scribd, E-Sentral and others. Sure, you could spend time searching, uploading and filling out profiles on all these sites on your own, but for the low margin that e-books typically generate, your valuable time is better spent elsewhere.

Newsletters—If you're using e-books to get website visitors to join your email list, then you'll need to serve them with regular content after they've joined. Sending a monthly email newsletter containing links, tools and tips that educate and entertain your audience is a great vehicle for keeping them engaged.

I sign up for a lot of newsletters, especially from marketing bloggers, media sites and publishing companies. I also get some from traditional retailers like Macy's. The difference is clear: Macy's sends frequent emails packed with promotional messages and sale info, which would only appeal to the serial shopper. I do shop at Macy's but I go when I go and if I catch a sale, great. If not, no biggie. Therefore, their emails hold zero value for me. On the other hand, the newsletters I get from CreateSpace, the self-publishing platform that has allowed me to bring two books into the world, is filled with helpful tips on publishing, marketing and writing that any author or aspiring author would find beneficial. Sure, they also sell their premium services and tout new products, but it's sprinkled amongst the content and info that I find valuable.

We discussed email marketing in Section 2, so I won't belabor the point here, but I know from experience that it's still a viable tool for connecting with your audience. Just make sure your newsletters pass the "What's in it for me?" test by providing content that your audience is truly interested in.

Q & A Sites—There are lots of question and answer sites out there that allow you to create a profile and chime in with your expertise when people post queries. LinkedIn Answers used to be a popular spot because it was focused on biz-related questions. However, the company did away with the feature, upsetting numerous professionals who used it to find business prospects and leads. Currently, LinkedIn Groups is the next best thing on that particular site.

This feature allows you to join multiple groups in a variety of topics and share questions, answers and advice with other members

★ HEAVYWEIGHT MARKETING ★

of the group. This works best if you have a robust LinkedIn presence so people can view your profile with one click if they like your answers enough to learn more about you. Be warned, there's a lot of blatant self-promotion going on in Groups, which can be a turnoff. If you choose this avenue, make sure you're attempting to provide value and be tactful with your sales pitches.

Currently, Quora is the big kahuna of the Q & A sites. You need to create an account in order to access the site, which vets members pretty thoroughly, ensuring a sense of legitimacy. You can sign in through Google, Twitter, Facebook or email, then you're lead through several steps to set up your account, optimize your profile and allow you to get the most of the site. There are many topics of interest you may select, which customizes the content that shows up in your feed. One thing that struck me as odd when I joined is that there were some really old questions in my feed. The question at the top of the page was from 30 minutes prior, and the third question down was from 2010! Quora does have a solid reputation, and I've heard powerful stories from colleagues about great connections being made after posting thoughtful, thorough answers to queries on the site.

There are several other Q & A sites such as Yahoo Answers, Allexperts, and Answerbag, but the quality of the conversation on these sites is on the low side. Also, the topics are all over the map—which may be okay depending on the focus of your business—but most entrepreneurs may find the topical scope too broad. While investigating these sites, I saw the following question on Answerbag:

> "How should I get payback on my brother? He said he was going to make me look nice but shaved me bald. I was [thinking of] shaving a penis on his head."

Round 3 - Buff Your Brand

Uh, okay. Perhaps you run a salon and have some great advice on crafting phallic objects with a #2 clipper, but I doubt it. Unless your marketing strategy includes slumming with the hoi polloi, I would suggest being very selective with where you choose to offer your expertise. While Q & A sites offer multiple opportunities to share your expertise with an interested community of peers, colleagues and prospects, they also require an ongoing investment of time and human resources. Do your research, choose wisely and only put your efforts into tools that align synergistically with your business.

Speaking Engagements—There are two types of people: those who enjoy speaking in front of a group and those who would prefer to have a root canal. I happen to fall into the former category, which is to say I love it. I played in rock bands for 15 years, and to me, public speaking is the next best thing. I still get to rock the stage, but the context is a bit different. If you fall into the other category and would rather have your teeth drilled, then ignore this option.

Public speaking is a fun, dynamic way to get your brand known in the community and "prove" your expertise to your audience. Seek out professional organizations, business groups and chambers of commerce in your area who would find your topic relevant, and offer to speak at an upcoming meeting. Until you become an established name on the speaking circuit, you'll most likely be appearing for free, so start in your own community and work outward from there.

While I was running my marketing consulting business, public speaking was one of my go-to marketing tactics. I had several speaking engagements from which I earned great exposure, press clippings, hot prospects, customers and business partnerships. Between writing and rehearsing your speeches, and securing and delivering your presentations, public speaking can be a lot of work. Therefore you need to understand your objective at the outset, which is to generate business. As with all of these tactics, you need to provide value to your audience. After all, no one wants to sit through a 30-minute sales pitch.

Every group you speak to should consist of people who make up your ideal audience profile. Make sure you have business cards and collateral to pass out and a mailing list that interested parties can sign. Then, follow up like a champ. There's a short window of opportunity after a speaking engagement when hot prospects are excited and inspired to make changes or try something new. Be sure to reach out to them while your words of wisdom are still fresh in their minds.

Workshops and Seminars—With speaking engagements, you are often piggybacking on someone else's event. They do most of the organizing and heavy lifting and you show up to deliver the goods. The next level of commitment is to put on a workshop or seminar. I've worked with arts organizations to produce art marketing workshops and they have proven beneficial for the artists, successful for the organizations and fulfilling for me.

Workshops usually last several hours to a full day, whereas seminars are often multi-day events. Depending on your level of ambition, your company can either produce a seminar on its own, or you can pull several partners together who offer complementary information to create a full-spectrum offering that people would pay to attend.

At one point I was planning to produce a small business expo that would cover a variety of essential business topics from several different presenters. I was real excited about the idea until I started digging into the details and analyzing the risk-to-reward ratio. I like to think big, so the scope of the project quickly got overwhelming. Eventually, I realized that it was too big a project for a solopreneur like myself to be taking on. There are tons of successful workshops and seminars out there, so the model is a proven one, but you need to make sure you have the resources—both financial and human—to pull this off successfully.

Teaching—You've probably heard that cynical saying that goes: "Those who can, do. Those who can't, teach." However, I prefer the one that says: "If you want to learn something, study it. If you want to master something, teach it." I know several photographers, painters, artisans and business consultants who teach ongoing classes to students of all ages. Some have even become adjunct professors (teachers-for-hire) at colleges. While this is a great way to share your expertise, it has the potential to become its own career, which may or may not be what you're after.

However, there are many business owners who teach classes at their place of business, producing an extra stream of revenue. This makes even more sense if your core business sells products or additional services directly related to the classes, giving you the chance to upsell or supply your students with the materials they need for their class. I have had so many great teachers over the years who have made a profound difference in my life. I consider them experts, and I'm glad they decided to share their wisdom with me.

Videos—I'm currently working with a company whose product is in danger of become commoditized, so it places emphasis on its expert technical service as a strong selling point. We've been creating a technical how-to video series addressing common problems customers experience when setting up or operating their equipment. It's relatively easy to create a YouTube Channel and produce short videos based on your topic of expertise. You can drive people to your channel, or you can post videos on your website and share via social media. Wherever the videos are posted, be sure to use all your marketing channels to cross-promote them.

★ HEAVYWEIGHT MARKETING ★

Podcasts—Podcasting came of age in the mid-aughts and enjoyed a moment of glory until the wide adoption of social media stole its thunder. Podcasts are digital recordings in mp3 format that can be posted and played online, or downloaded to portable music devices. Instead of music files, podcasts are voice files that cover a variety of topics via talk-show-style interviews, creative ramblings, talking-head punditry, foreign language lessons, or whatever. You can share your expertise by creating a frequent podcast to discuss issues, news and trends in your industry. Some bloggers attach podcast versions of their blog posts underneath the written version for people who prefer listening to reading. The iTunes store is full of podcasts, both free and premium, and getting yours accepted into iTunes could add some serious distribution muscle.

At one point, I subscribed to several business, marketing and Spanish-lesson podcasts through iTunes, but I never found a time in my day that I felt like listening to an audio file of people talking. However, I see people promoting their podcasts every day on the web, so the format is still popular with many content producers, but you definitely want to make sure your audience enjoys consuming content in that format before going all in.

Television—The way people consume televised content in our modern age has become so fractured that the idea of sitting down to watch a TV show at its appointed hour seems downright quaint. But there are still plenty of television talk shows, entertainment, news and business programs that are seeking topics to cover and people to interview. I see authors and experts appearing on TV to promote their new works, discuss industry trends and events and offer input on hot topics du jour.

Even if viewers don't catch the show when it airs, video clips of your appearances can be repurposed for your website or various social media channels. Sure, it's a lot easier to film

Round 3 - Buff Your Brand

your own videos and throw them up on your YouTube channel, but being associated with a local or national station or program increases your level of credibility exponentially. The trick here is good PR. Whether you handle publicity yourself or hire it out, make sure to include local and national TV outlets on your list of PR targets.

Books—There is no better way to showcase your expertise than writing a book about a topic you specialize in. I might even be so bold as to say that books are the new business cards. When trying to earn someone's business, sending them a copy of your book, or using it as a leave-behind after a meeting, is a powerful way to stand apart from your competitors and convey your expertise. You can also sell your book through online channels, leverage it to get press coverage, use it as a contest prize or giveaway, and make back-of-room book sales at your speaking engagements or live events. Your book can become a multi-purpose, promotional powerhouse that can help your company build a solid brand and establish you as an expert in your field.

While many authors still go the traditional publishing route, the rise of self-publishing platforms has made it possible for anyone to circumvent the Old Guard and become a self-published author. Of course stigmas still exist. Many people dismiss self-published authors outright, assuming that if they weren't blessed by the gods of a traditional publishing house, they are not "real" authors. The reason for this is simple: when the barrier to entry is low in any area, quantity rises and quality suffers.

I've been turned down for reviews from publications and denied business from PR firms for being a self-published author. However, there are still plenty of people, firms and companies that will work with self-published authors, and it's up to you to actively seek them out. The best way to prove that you're a "real" author is to get your book into the hands of the people

★ HEAVYWEIGHT MARKETING ★

who truly matter: the prospects and customers who will benefit from your book. Get them excited, get them talking, and they start spreading the word for you. Who knows, you may build such a critical mass that the Old Guard will perk up their ears and take notice.

There is no shortage of ways to position yourself as an expert in your field. When choosing which of these tools and tactics to commit to, there are three criteria to keep in mind.

First, you want to determine which methods you most enjoy using. That's right, you've got to enjoy it—marketing should not feel like a chore. Second, you need to have time in your schedule to implement the tools you choose. Some people can kick out a 20-page e-book in less than a week, while it can take over a year to write a book. Maintaining a blog can take a few hours every week, while commenting on other blogs can be done in daily 15-minute blocks. Third and most importantly, you need to determine which method will best reach your audience. No matter how much you enjoy and have time for any of the above, if nobody is there to consume your expertise, you're simply wasting your time. It doesn't take an expert to know that wasting precious time is not a good branding strategy.

★ 43 ★

COMMUNICATE YOUR VALUE BEFORE AND AFTER THE SALE

I had been working with a new client for a few months and was real pleased with how things were going. She was a doctor who ran a private practice, and she had hired me to design a new website and take over her email marketing duties. The site was up and running, the email newsletters were being managed efficiently and I was billing her monthly for ongoing services.

Life was good. Or so I thought.

After receiving one of my invoices, my client called me up frustrated and took me to task for my billing. She felt my prices were too high, and didn't quite understand the cost-to-value ratio that she was receiving. After a long phone conversation, we managed to clarify the confusion and alleviate her frustrations. However, this scenario reminded me that communicating the value of your product or service does not stop once the sale is made.

Of course, when we signed the initial contract, my client was thrilled! She was one of those people I mentioned earlier who had a friend design her website—because it was cheap—only to have this friend go missing when her life got busy. My client was left with an unfinished site that she couldn't access. She got my name via referral and was excited when I came along and promised she would not have to concern herself with web updates or with planning, writing, designing, editing, linking, formatting, testing, scheduling, replying, and all the other factors involved in managing a successful email marketing program. I guess you could call this the Business Honeymoon Phase.

Since she's a busy professional who travels a lot, I wanted to provide full-service solutions that would allow her to focus on what she does best and not even have to think about the services I was providing. I thought I was being helpful by doing things quickly and quietly, hoping my client would notice (which proved to be my mistake) that I was going above and beyond in order to create the most effective online marketing strategies for her business.

In this case, the problem was that I was being too efficient and too stealthy. While I thought this was making my client's life easier, I found it was actually causing her frustration. Since she didn't realize all I was doing behind the scenes, she had a hard time equating my value with my cost when the monthly invoice arrived. You know the old saying, "out of sight, out of mind"? Sometimes that's a good thing, but in this particular instance it proved detrimental to my client relations.

Five Ways You Can Avoid This Fate:

1) Know Your Value—Products are a little easier than services to put a value on because the client is getting something tangible. However, they both need to be presented to the client as something that will improve the conditions of their business. In addition to knowing what's important about your offering, you also need to determine what is important to your customer. That's the intel you can use to help them understand the value of what you are providing. If they know that your efforts are simplifying their life, freeing up their time, saving them money, or earning them money, they will have an easier time justifying their purchase.

The value of your product or service will be determined by several factors, as we discussed earlier. Don't sell yourself short just to get business. Instead, do the necessary research so you know what else is going on in your industry and how your offering or solution is better, and therefore worth the cost you're charging. I had many prospects reject my business proposals because they thought I was too expensive. It was a little scary sometimes to see business slip through my hands instead of seeing a check land in them. But I knew that if I caved and gave in to a scarcity mindset I would never forgive myself. Prideful? Maybe. But you don't build a champion brand by groveling for scraps from the cheapskates of the world. Instead, you try to get better at qualifying your prospects and spend more time finding those who are willing and able to pay for your offering.

2) Communicate Your Value Before the Sale—Whether you're pitching your potential clients in person or marketing to them using any of the tools and tactics we've discussed in this book, be sure to focus on conveying the unique and valuable benefits of your offering. Think about how your customers' lives will be AFTER they buy from you and articulate the feelings, results, outcomes or improvements they will experience from the purchase. You hear a lot of talk about "pain points" in marketing, which is jargon for understanding what matters to your customer. What are they struggling with? What are they dissatisfied with? What would they prefer to be different in their lives or their business?

While talking with prospects about web design projects, I found that they usually wanted one of two things: empowerment or freedom. Either they wanted to be trained how to maintain the site themselves, which empowered them to be the master of their web domain, or they wanted to trust that someone else was taking care of their site, allowing them the freedom to not concern themselves with it. As soon as I determined which they

★ **HEAVYWEIGHT MARKETING** ★

wanted, you better believe I spoke directly to those desires in my pitch. After all, what do you think people value more, a website or empowerment? An online storefront or freedom?

Keep in mind, you'll be a lot more successful if you have a true desire to provide the best solutions to your customers' problems, needs or objectives, rather than simply trying to make the sale. Not only will you be less attached to the results, but operating from the desire to serve always trumps operating from the desire to close a sale.

> *After courting a prospect for several months, we finally agreed on a deal for a full-service, year-long project. This was an exciting challenge to see how I could handle a larger project and, at a low five-figures, it was definitely a deal worth celebrating. Not even two months into the project, the client started getting scared about implementing such big changes to their marketing efforts. In short, they got cold feet. They stopped responding to my communications and rather than explaining their fears and concerns, they took an ostrich approach—bury head in sand, hope threat retreats.*

> *After multiple attempts to move the project forward, I finally aborted my efforts to chase them. Here's the kicker: they still paid the full fee. Did I appreciate the money? Sure. But I would have appreciated it a lot more if I felt like I earned it by providing custom solutions that generated positive results for their business. My desire to serve was there, but instead all I did was close the sale. Some might think the easy money was awesome, but to me it felt a little bittersweet.*

Now, let's say your prospects are not quite ready to commit. When you boil it down, there are really only two reasons why that may be:

a) *They need more education*—That's your job. Throw them back into the sales cycle and continue to educate them as to the benefits of your offering. This could be done through a variety of educational tools like email drip campaigns, videos, e-books or content that lives on your website. One of my Realtor clients worked with a prospect for 17 years before finally selling the guy a house! Timing is everything, so work with your prospect until they are ready. Unless...

b) *They are not qualified*—When scouting prospects, make sure they fit the profile of your Ideal Customer. If you don't have an Ideal Customer Profile, create one (or two, or three). It will save you time and money spent chasing unqualified leads. When I started my consulting business, I would schedule personal meetings with everyone who contacted me about a project. Can you say "amateur"? I learned very quickly what a waste of time that was, considering the low percentage of meetings that produced paying clients. I began offering free 30-minute phone consultations instead, which proved a lot more efficient and allowed plenty of time to suss out the prospect's needs and level of commitment (although, you're never *really* sure until they cut the check).

The next lesson involved creating client proposals, which were not only detailed and verbose, but sometimes took up to four hours to prepare. Eventually I refined the process and knocked the prep time down to an hour. Once a client committed with a signed contract and a down-payment, I became a lot more generous with my time. The lesson? When digging for gold, don't waste time fawning over pyrite.

3) **Do the Work**—Congratulations, you made the sale! Now, do what you do best in a timely, friendly and professional manner in the way that you—and only you—can do it. I've been using examples from a freelance contractor's perspective, but "doing

the work" can apply to any business. It could mean showing up every day at the boutique, restaurant, gallery, clinic or spa with a smile on your face, ready to face each new day and each new customer with gratitude and positivity.

That real estate agent I mentioned earlier? After selling a house, she went to a local flower shop to purchase flowers for everyone involved in the sale. The proprietor actually yelled at her when she showed up before the order was ready! A customer is about to drop a couple hundred dollars on flowers and the business owner yells at her. Really? That's not what I call "doing the work."

As a business owner, you will find things will get challenging, difficult, frustrating, and overwhelming. When they do, you must remind yourself that you didn't start a business because you thought it would be a walk in the park. You launched a business because you created an offering that will make a wonderful difference in the lives of your customers. So do the work and smile as you shine your entrepreneurial light on the world!

4) Communicate Your Value After the Sale—Here is the lesson I learned from the whole ordeal with my frustrated client. Once the work is done—or as it progresses—keep in contact with your customers and let them know exactly what you're doing and how that is helping them meet the objectives you agreed upon.

You don't want it to seem like you're seeking praise or a pat on the back, but rather, you're keeping them informed out of respect because you care about them achieving their desired outcomes. Instead of hoping your client notices your excellent, efficient work, it's better to direct their attention to it in a professional way. By making sure they understand what you're doing and how it is benefiting them, you are securing their loyalty and making them less eager to search for another vendor, or a better deal, elsewhere.

5) Follow Up—When the original job, sale or assignment is complete, plan on following up to check in with your customers after the fact. The feasibility of this might depend on what business you're in. If you run a boutique, a gift store or a bakery, you may not be able to follow up with everyone who makes a purchase unless they join your mailing list or engage with you online. On the other hand, if you run a web design firm, an auto body shop, or any other biz that provides big-ticket items, following up after the sale is a lot easier because you typically glean more customer data when you sell someone a website than when you sell them a cupcake.

Checking in is an easy way to surprise and impress your customers. You might inquire how things are working out with your products or services and let them know you're there for them if they have any future needs. Make sure your follow-up comes across as genuine interest rather than you just trying to get them to spend more money.

For the purpose of following up, you should create a database of the people who patronize your business so you can continue to engage them after the sale. As for your follow-up tools, you have plenty of options—as we've discussed throughout this book. Some of the most popular are email newsletters, social media platforms, postcards and even the occasional phone call. Keep in mind that different customers prefer to communicate in different ways. Determining and using their preferred method will ensure that your communication is welcome and not intrusive.

Just because the check has cleared and the work is finished doesn't mean you forget all about your client. After all, you're not in business for the sole purpose of closing the deal. You're

★ HEAVYWEIGHT MARKETING ★

in business to build ongoing relationships that are mutually beneficial for yourself and your customers. By continuing to communicate your value before, during and after the sale, you are reinforcing the quality of your brand and increasing the potential of doing business together in the future.

★ 44 ★

BEING IRREPLACEABLE MEANS BEING DIFFERENT

In an earlier chapter, I asked when the last time was that a company truly surprised you. We discussed several examples, proving that, occasionally, it does happen. I had another experience similar to my Virgin American airline discovery during a recent road trip to Santa Cruz. While planning my trip down the California coast, I booked a hotel in South San Francisco, which was about the halfway point from where I began. Due to the hotel's proximity to the airport and myriad corporate office parks, I wasn't expecting much more than a place to sleep. In a wonderful twist of fate, I got much more than I bargained for.

The contemporary-Victorian-Asian-Pop design aesthetic of Inn at Oyster Point

★ HEAVYWEIGHT MARKETING ★

The minute I walked into The Inn at Oyster Point, my low expectations were blown out the window. I was immediately impressed with the crazy, fun and irreverent mish-mash design aesthetic, Pop Art–laden walls, community iMac in the lobby and friendly, attentive service by the attendant, who called me by name for the remainder of my visit.

The bizarre design mashup was done by interior designer Andrew Alford

This was not stuffy, upscale-executive chambers, nor was it bland, minimalist bargain lodging. It was Eclectic Boutique Hotel at its best. Everything about The Inn at Oyster Point shouted unique, non-conformist, fearless and bold—which is what every champion brand should aim for.

Intrigued by the bizarre décor, I did some research and discovered the Contemporary–Victorian–Asian–Pop Art aesthetic was by San Francisco–based designer Andrew Alford. I was so blown away by the singularity of The Inn at Oyster Point's brand, I shot an impromptu video blog post in the sitting room even though I was on vacation. In the video, I outlined some of the points that impressed me from a branding perspective, with hopes to inspire other small business owners to have fun with their brands.

Words to Live By

In their printed collateral, The Inn at Oyster Point had a few great quotes. I'll share them with you here because they deserve to be pondered. The statements that follow the quotes are my own.

"Always put in one controversial item. It makes people talk."

This quote clearly references some of the odd choices used in the hotel's interior design, but it could just as easily refer to your product line, items on your menu, or concepts in your marketing strategy. It could even be a guiding philosophy that you refer to as you make choices surrounding your business. You've probably heard the saying that any publicity is good publicity, and, while that's far from true, you DO want people talking about your brand.

Word of mouth is the best advertising you can get, but you want the buzz to be positive. After my first visit to The Inn at Oyster Point, I posted the video I made to YouTube, my blog and a couple other social channels. I tweeted about the hotel and plugged it on Facebook. Now, I'm writing about it in this book simply because I was so pleasantly surprised by my experience. With so many people active on social media, I'm certain I'm not the only one who's voluntarily promoting them, which is exactly the kind of response you want your brand to generate.

"Never interrupt someone doing what you said couldn't be done."

So many people work hard to find reasons why they CAN'T do something. Instead, they should be putting an extraordinary amount of energy into figuring out how they CAN do it. Innovation is difficult, finding ways to be unique is challenging, and creating an amazing customer experience is hard, but that

★ HEAVYWEIGHT MARKETING ★

shouldn't deter business owners from making the effort. The exterior of The Inn at Oyster Point emanates a pleasant, coastal vibe with a pastel palette of whites, soft yellows and grays.

The Inn was founded in 1990, and up until 2010, the interior matched the same easy, breezy vibe. After 20 years of pleasant-but-unremarkable design, I can't imagine everyone in the organization was too pleased when some crazed creative came up with the idea of going batshit loco with the interior design aesthetic. But someone was bold enough to start that conversation—and persistent enough to see it through to its conclusion. Boldness and persistence is what separates the Winners from the Losers, the Leaders from the Followers, and the Innovators from the Imitators. Which of these do you aspire to be?

"In order to be Irreplaceable, one must always be different."

Right across the way from The Inn at Oyster Point, there is a Marriott Hotel. When planning my travels, I could have chosen to stay at Marriott because I would have known exactly what to expect. After all, the Marriott has a fine, upstanding brand and offers a superb hotel experience. The only challenge for Marriott—particularly in a saturated industry and a sluggish economy—is they could easily be replaced by a half dozen other brand-name hotels. The Inn at Oyster Point, on the other hand, has created a one-of-a-kind experience that differentiates itself just enough to be irreplaceable. I took a chance by trying something new, and while that doesn't always work out, I'm pleased to say this time it did. I've already been back a second time, and next time I'm in the area, there is no question as to where I will stay.

There are many business categories that seem to be governed by rules that say, "You must do it this way." This leads to a glut of unremarkable companies and products that all look and feel similar. Branding is based on the idea of singularity, which means you need to create a perception that there is no other business or product like yours. To do this successfully, you must think outside the box—regardless of the business category you are in—and you must define and articulate the unique value your company provides. Only then will your business escalate from merely serviceable to truly irreplaceable.

★ ★ ★ ★

SCAN TO VIEW VIDEO

In this chapter, I mention that I shot an impromptu video* blog post while on vacation at Inn at Oyster Point.

To view video, scan code above with QR code reader. Free readers are available for download from your preferred app store. Enjoy!

*The BAM! Small Biz Consulting website mentioned in the video is no longer online.

★ 45 ★

WHY "JACK OF ALL TRADES" IS A POOR BRANDING STRATEGY

I live in an area dotted with small towns, where much of the community is self-employed. The reality of our economy is that most of us need to earn our living through multiple income streams. In order to create those streams, many people attempt to capitalize on as many of their skills as they can. The result is that people try to market themselves as multi-hyphenates, such as Artist–Life Coach–Chiropractor, or Massage Therapist–Housekeeper–Yoga Instructor, or Musician–Muralist–Handyman. This may seem like a good strategy because it increases opportunities for multi-stream revenue by covering many bases, right? Wrong. All this does is confuse your audience and create a muddled brand.

If your prospects and customers don't have a crystal clear perception of what your primary specialty is, they will not think of you when they are seeking solutions to their problems. A person needing a chiropractic adjustment is not going to call someone whose business card reads "Artist, Life Coach, Chiropractor." They are going to call an experienced practitioner who has earned a reputation for excellence in chiropractic healing.

Solopreneurs are not the only ones guilty of attempting to cash in with a jack-of-all-trades strategy. I see plenty of small businesses trying to be everything to everyone as well. Restaurants are particularly fond of attempting a culinary mashup. The following photo shows one of three Mexican restaurants in my

★ **HEAVYWEIGHT MARKETING** ★

town. Four if you count the walk-up burrito shack. As you can see by the sign, their list of "specialties" is a bit of a stretch. With three nearby competitors, perhaps they felt a need to play up their diversity, but would you really go to a Mexican restaurant for seafood? No. For the same reason you wouldn't order a burrito at a sushi bar. You wouldn't expect a steakhouse to be boasting about its tacos, would you? Even if they had a killer steak taco on the menu, from a branding perspective, it should be all about the beef.

Lalo's Mexican, Vegetarian, Seafood, Steakhouse

I had a speaking engagement at a Youth Entrepreneur Program event where students competed for cash prizes to launch their business concepts. A set of cousins won $500 to put towards their overly-ambitious idea, which was to start a two-in-one restaurant that served Italian and German food. They envisioned a place where you would "walk in and go to the left" to a side that would be decked out like Italy, and "go to the right" to a different side that would offer a full-on Wienerschnitzel-and-lederhosen experience. Holy overhead, Batman! I mean, kudos to these kids for thinking big right out of the gate, but maybe they should start with a pizza shack or a sauerkraut stand.

More recently, there was a long-standing family restaurant that finally closed its doors. I saw a large banner slung over its front balcony advertising the dream of its starry-eyed future occupants:

Glassy Junction Pizza and...Indian? One of these sounds like an afterthought

Pizza and Indian? Why would they attempt both? The art of perfect pizza takes a lifetime to master, and Indian food requires its own unique expertise. Besides, there are lots of other pizza joints in the surrounding area, yet there are exactly zero Indian restaurants. They have an opportunity to become THE go-to restaurant for authentic Indian food throughout the entire county, and instead they choose to cloud their focus by competing with all the pizza parlors. Oh, and how on earth did no one along the production chain catch that "cuisine" was misspelled? Maybe they should have just gone with "food."

Limited or Focused?

Some business owners may feel limited by touting a singular brand promise or narrow area of expertise. But what you may

★ HEAVYWEIGHT MARKETING ★

view as limiting will be seen by your audience as focused—providing it's something they care about. If your office supply store claims to stock the largest supply of rubber bands on the planet, you may not be faced with stampeding crowds every morning. When seeking the hook to hang your brand on, you need to be certain there's a demand in the marketplace for your unique selling point.

Pressed Juicery is a juice bar with 22 locations in California. They are expanding to the East Coast, with plans to open up to 15 stores in New York. CEO Hayden Slater understands the importance of excelling in one area and wants no confusion about what his company sells. "At the core of who we are, we are a juice company," says Hayden. Pressed Juicery doesn't do breakfast, they don't sell trendy wheatgrass shots, no power smoothies, just fresh-pressed juice.[1] Now that's focus.

Not all companies can have such a narrow focus to their offering, but they still become known for one popular item. Pinkberry has built a global franchise by focusing on frozen yogurt. Sprinkles is a dessert shop operating in eight states that serves cookies and ice cream, but is primarily known for its cupcakes. In particular they have created the "World's First Cupcake ATM," which dispenses freshly-baked cupcakes 24/7. Not only have they become known for their signature cupcakes, but have found a novel—and newsworthy—way to deliver them to their audience. Then there's Krispy Kreme, the company that has turned something as basic as a glazed donut into pure gold.

> *In 2002, I was living in Minneapolis and there was tremendous buzz and excitement about Krispy Kreme donuts opening a location in nearby suburb Maple Grove, MN. Krispy Kreme's signature item is a warm, glazed donut that disintegrates in a burst of deliciousness the minute it hits your tongue. Now, to me, a donut is a donut, but my fellow*

Round 3 - Buff Your Brand

Minnesotans were delirious! Lines formed out the door for days, weeks, months. The company expanded, opening three additional stores in the metro area and stocking their product at every store that had a grocery aisle.

Mere office workers became superstar VIPs for stocking breakrooms with boxes of golden, glazed goodness. Soccer moms ditched their traditional post-win ice cream runs for celebratory sojourns to Krispy Kreme. College students around the state added donuts to their dietary staples of pizza and beer. Donut tycoons prospered pushing donuts by the box for a profit on local street corners. The collective BMI of the state increased by three points in two years.[2] Six years after taking Minnesota by storm, Krispy Kreme had officially flooded the market. Finally, the gig was up; the sugar rush ended. By 2008, Krispy Kreme had closed all Minnesota locations, relinquishing their donut domination and sending customers back to the pastry display cases of Super Americas, gas stations and convenience stores across the land.

Okay, let's leave the food realm for now and compare a couple competitors that place their singular focus in different areas, even though their general offering is the same.

In Chapter 36, I profiled Ramshaw's ACE Hardware, which brands itself as "The Helpful Place." Not only is that a great brand promise, it also makes for a strong core marketing message. Focusing on that one unique specialty doesn't limit the amount of products or services ACE can offer; it promises prospects and customers that, regardless of what they are looking for, they will get the help they need.

There's another hardware store in town that promotes itself as "The Outdoor Headquarters." In this mountainous region of northern California, that is a legitimate niche to focus on. Again, this company can still provide all the necessary items one expects in a hardware store, but by calling attention to the fact that they specialize in outdoor gear, they are targeting a certain segment of customers who will think of them first when camping, grilling or ski season approaches.

Trying to cast a wide net and position your company as a solution to many problems is not as effective as taking a strong position on one unique specialty and touting that as your core marketing message. That doesn't mean that you can't offer ancillary products or services—of course you can. But they will exist under the umbrella of your overall brand.

Exceptions to the Rule

Of course, with every rule, there are exceptions. It's essential to maintain a singular focus when launching a business so the audience knows what you stand for. However, it seems that once companies build a heavyweight brand, they often want to leverage their strong name recognition and positive brand perception to venture into different industries. We talked about the diversification of Google in an earlier chapter. When they were founded in 1998, their singular mission was to "organize a seemingly infinite amount of information on the web." This goal—while indeed audacious—was impressive in its restraint. Their massive growth from scrappy startup to global, multi-industrial powerhouse has been equally impressive, if not a little disconcerting.

Virgin Group is another prime example. What started as a single record store, Virgin Records and Tapes in London, eventually grew to a business empire that has created more than 200 branded companies worldwide in 29 countries. The Virgin moniker is used by companies as varied as hotels, health clubs, casinos, bookstores, mobile carriers, holiday cruises, media companies, investment firms, financial services and wineries.

Round 3 - Buff Your Brand

Sony has taken a similar route. Started in 1946 as a small electronics shop in Tokyo, Sony has burgeoned into a thriving multi-conglomerate in the electronics, game, entertainment and financial services sectors.

Obviously, from a business standpoint, Google, Virgin and Sony are doing great, so they certainly don't need me telling them to stay focused. However, my point is that all that diversification came later. If they tried breaking into multiple industries from the get-go, there's no way they would have gained the same traction.

Now, let's get back to the Artist–Life Coach–Chiropractor for a moment. An important question that may have come up is: how DO self-employed multi-hyphenates market their myriad talents? By creating separate brands.

If people are trying to successfully market more than one service, they need to take the following steps for EACH of their specialties:

- Define and articulate their unique brand promise
- Create complete and separate brand identities and marketing collateral
- Find the appropriate target market in each category
- Market each different service to its own appropriate audience

Whew, that sounds like a lot of work. That's because it is! That is why it's best to zero in with singular focus on what you do best, and what you enjoy most. Then, as momentum either builds or stalls in your primary category, you can determine if it's necessary to implement your additional brands.

★ HEAVYWEIGHT MARKETING ★

There is certainly something admirable about being skilled in many areas, except when it comes to positioning your brand in the minds of your customers. In my experience, those who claim to do many things don't do any of them very well. When consumers are seeking real solutions to the needs and problems in their lives, their trust—and hard-earned money—does not belong to the Jack of All Trades. It belongs to the Master of One.

> *"A year from now you will wish you had started today."*
> —Karen Lamb

★ 46 ★

INTERVIEW WITH A MARKETING MAN: A DOZEN QUESTIONS FOR NIKOLAS ALLEN

When I was running my marketing consulting business (from December 2010 to March 2014), I was interviewed for a local business website called Interview Siskiyou. The site featured interviews with dozens of local entrepreneurs in our community for the purpose of introducing local business owners to the community. It was a great place for consumers to learn more about the companies they were supporting, and fellow biz owners to study up on their competitors.

I believe these questions touch on some key points of running a business so I have shared them with you here. Please remember that I am not currently offering consulting services, so this is not a thinly-veiled sales pitch. The answers are written in present tense and, while they certainly applied at the time of the interview, they may not at the time of this writing. If nothing else, the following discussion will offer a few more insights from the journey that lead to this book—which I sincerely hope you have found enjoyable, enlightening and inspiring.

"May you succeed beyond your wildest imagination!"
—Nikolas Allen, author, Heavyweight Marketing

★ HEAVYWEIGHT MARKETING ★

Interview Siskiyou: What made you want to start BAM! Small Biz Consulting?

Nikolas Allen: I spent 15 years as a creative in the advertising field in Minneapolis, MN. Half that time was working as an employee at various companies and in-house agencies, and the other half was working as a freelance graphic designer, art director and creative director for companies large and small.

I moved out to California in 2008 and tried to launch an art and apparel business that never took off. The recession was hitting hard and I was seeing so many vacant storefronts, closing businesses and struggling entrepreneurs—including myself! I decided that instead of using my knowledge, experience and passion for branding and marketing for my own business endeavor, I would be serving a greater purpose by using it to help others grow their business.

In a flash of inspiration, I conceived my marketing consulting business, BAM! (which stood for Branding And Marketing) Small Biz Consulting. My objective with BAM! was to help business owners determine how their offering was unique, then create meaningful marketing messages that would resonate with their audience. As my business grew, I helped many clients in several states to define their ideal audience, determine the most effective marketing tools to utilize, and grow their business by attracting more loyal customers.

IS: What do you like most about being a marketer?

NA: Let's face it: marketers don't exactly have sterling reputations. In fact, we're about a notch above used car salesmen on the food chain of trustability. But I truly love this work, and am passionate about sharing my expertise with my fellow entrepreneurs. Whether I'm teaching a workshop, giving a speaking presentation, or working one-on-one with a client, my favorite part is when I see my audience experiencing an "Aha!" moment.

They start getting excited and inspired and realize that branding isn't some mysterious concept that belongs to the Nikes and the Apples of the world, and that any small business can build a powerful and meaningful brand that resonates with their audience.

One of my specialties is simplifying the concept of branding and making the process of marketing fun. For me, there's no greater thrill than see people "get it" for the first time. After all, you have to be passionate about what you're doing, and when my passion for this subject resonates and inspires my clients to embrace concepts that were nebulous to them, it reinforces the belief I have in my purpose.

IS: How do you like running your own business?

NA: Personally, I don't fish, but I've heard a saying used by old-timer fishermen that goes, "The worst day fishin' is better than the best day workin'!" That's exactly how I feel about self-employment: all the stress, the problem-solving, the income tax headaches, the setbacks and the occasional client miscommunications are far better than the mind-numbing, soul-sucking, clock-punching tedium I've experienced working certain jobs as an employee.

IS: If you could change one thing about your business's day-to-day routine, what would it be?

NA: Well, the beauty of self-employment—and the consulting field in particular—is that you can create your own routine, and every day is different. If I want to go swimming with my girlfriend on Tuesday afternoon, hit the mall in Redding on a Friday morning and spend all day Sunday building a website, I can. In fact, that's exactly what I did last week!

IS: What do you consider your biggest weakness?

NA: I'm currently capacity-limited because I'm doing all the work myself (for my clients as well as my own company). While I do have a network of talented strategic partners, most of the client budgets I've been working with so far have not been large enough to allow for additional contractors to get involved.

[Author's Note: One of the biggest lessons I learned from BAM! was the importance of assembling a diverse and talented team. Biz owners, especially solopreneurs, tend to have a lone wolf, I-can-do-it-all mentality but it's best to focus on your primary strengths and surround yourself with others who compliment those strengths. Before I join or start any companies in the future, I will make certain that all the essential team members are in place.]

IS: How are you improving on that weakness?

NA: Seeking clients with bigger budgets! Also, I'm strengthening my relationships with my strategic partners, so when the larger projects do roll in, my extended team is ready to go.

IS: What is your biggest strength?

NA: I truly desire to help improve the conditions of each and every client. If I don't think I can do so, or if I don't feel the client is truly willing to so, I will not accept the assignment. I can occasionally be bold, direct and curt with my clients—BAM!—but that's because I truly want the best for them and their business.

IS: If you were a customer, what do you wish you knew about your trade? Any inside secrets to share?

NA: I would want to know the secret ingredient to a successful marketing campaign. Therefore, I'm going to give away that secret ingredient right here: successful marketing is the process of using the Right Tools to reach the Right Audience with the Right Message that speaks to your company's unique brand promise.

First, you must determine your brand promise: how do you want to position your company in the minds of your prospects? What one thing do you want to be known for? What do you do better than your competition? What is the greatest benefit of doing business with your company?

Then, create a meaningful marketing message that speaks to this promise. Next define your ideal audience: who are they? Where are they? How can you reach them? How does your offering improve their lives?

Finally, determine the tools to reach your audience: are they online, reading blogs, using social media? If so, you should be too, and if not, you shouldn't waste your time there. Do they read magazines, listen to radio, watch TV? How do they shop—online or in person?

By answering these questions, your company can create successful marketing initiatives that resonate with your intended market.

IS: What advice do you have for businesses looking to hire a marketing service provider?

★ HEAVYWEIGHT MARKETING ★

NA: The mistake I see most business owners making is not giving enough thought to their marketing message. All the marketing tools in the world are not going to help if you don't offer a compelling message that differentiates your company and resonates with your target audience.

Therefore, when hiring a marketing agency or consultant, make sure they can help you create the most meaningful content you can before determining which tools to implement. If their main focus is on setting up the tools and not on your unique message, you should probably keep looking.

Another bit of advice is: be ready to do the work! Shopping around is fine, but when you find the right vendor, make sure you're ready for action. In some cases, your marketing agency or consultant may be helping you with implementation, but usually, it's up to the client to have someone within their organization responsible for maintaining marketing content and activities. Remember, marketing is not an as-needed undertaking, it's an ongoing process that needs to be built into the foundation of your company.

IS: **What important information should buyers have thought through before seeking a marketing agency?**

NA: Business owners need to have a budget designated for their marketing strategies and resources within the company to maintain their marketing initiatives. They also need to reach an agreement within their own organization that they are ready and willing to do the work necessary to implement their strategy.

Having a desire to create a stronger brand or improve the success of your marketing is a great first step, but the aforementioned things need to be in place in order to turn your desire into action.

I've found prospects who express an interest and a need for my services, only to drag their feet on the scheduling of their sessions because they don't have all these other elements in order. When you step in the ring with any marketing agency, you need to be ready to rumble!

IS: Tell us about a recent job you did that you are particularly proud of.

NA: When I performed an initial brand audit for a contemporary art gallery in Northern California, I noticed they had a static HTML website that was not attractive or user-friendly and did not represent their online brand very well. I suggested moving them to an interactive WordPress platform, which was an expensive upgrade, and the idea wasn't received very well. I realized I had to earn their trust before they were ready to buy off on such a large project.

Instead, I focused on implementing a new email marketing program and a YouTube presence to better engage their audience, grow their membership and increase awareness. Within six months, both of those initiatives had proved successful, so I pitched my proposal for a website overhaul. They signed off, I went to work, and we launched their new site nine months after my first proposal was turned down.

The initial feedback from the staff, the Board of Directors, and the intended audience was outstanding. For the next three years I produced and maintained an active blog with rich media, resulting in a beautiful, user-friendly, well-trafficked site that represented the organization very well. Eventually, I handed the task off to a very capable employee who was very excited to take the reins. There's nothing like turning a group of skeptics into a satisfied client.

★ HEAVYWEIGHT MARKETING ★

IS: Do you do any sort of continuing education to stay up on the latest developments in your field?

NA: Absolutely! Of course, the best education is being active in the field. In addition to that, I'm a voracious reader of business blogs, books, e-books, articles, newspapers, trade journals and magazines. I'm thrilled that there are so many intelligent people out there sharing their knowledge.

I love visiting new and used book stores and I'm always reading at least one or two books on branding, marketing, selling, small business, social media, blogging, etc. As for magazines, I'm a huge fan of *Fast Company, Entrepreneur,* and *Inc.*

I don't own a TV, so Twitter is my main news source. I follow many people in the industry and read myriad marketing-related blog posts on a daily basis. Social media can be a tremendous time-waster, so I make sure the time I spend there is about education rather than mindless entertainment.

I've also taken several marketing workshops in the past few years, which I enjoy. However, since the amount of educational info available on the web is staggering, I'm mostly taking full advantage of that as often as possible. While the basic principles of marketing don't change much, the tools and methods to implement them do. Keeping up with these changes is a responsibility I take seriously, and I recommend every entrepreneur do the same—regardless of what field they are in.

BECOME A "HEAVYWEIGHT MARKETING" BRAND AMBASSADOR

Thank you for purchasing *Heavyweight Marketing*. Hopefully, this book inspired you to get in the ring, train like a champion, and build a small business brand that will knock out your customers—and your competitors! If you enjoyed the book and found it useful, helpful or beneficial to your business, please consider doing the following:

- Leave a review on Amazon.com.
- Share the book with any peers, friends or colleagues who would also find it useful.
- Mention *Heavyweight Marketing* on social media.
- Include @nikolas_allen in your tweets so I get notified.
- Use hashtags when discussing the book on social platforms (#HMBook #heavyweightmarketing #championbrand #nikolasallen, or make up your own).
- Write a blog post about your experience with the book (include link to book's website).
- Send me a testimonial about how the book benefited you using your fave method below.

To continue the conversation, connect with me online:

Twitter:	@nikolas_allen
Instagram:	@nikolas_allen
LinkedIn:	www.linkedin.com/in/nikolasallen
Websites:	www.heavyweightmarketingbook.com
	www.nikolasallen.com
Email:	bamsbc@gmail.com

MARKETING RESOURCES

The resources listed below correspond to some of the categories I mentioned throughout the book. This list will give you plenty of places to start in the categories you are researching. I have used some of these services but not all, so it will be up to you to visit the sites to see which ones resonate with you. There are many options available, but you only need to find a handful of reliable sources that you can continue to use as needed. The categories and company names below are listed in alphabetical order.

Blog Comment Platforms
Disqus .... disqus.com
Gravatar .... en.gravatar.com
LiveFyre .... web.livefyre.com

Book Publishing
CreateSpace .... createspace.com

Business Associations
America's SBDC.. www.asbdc-us.org
U.S. Chamber of Commerce .... www.uschamber.com
U.S. Small Business Association .... www.sba.gov

Digital Marketing Platforms
Curalate... curalate.com
Infusionsoft .... infusionsoft.com
Offerpop .... offerpop.com

★ HEAVYWEIGHT MARKETING ★

Domain Names
Enom .... enom.com
Go Daddy .... godaddy.com
Net Firms .... netfirms.com

Email Marketing Platforms
Aweber .... aweber.com
Constant Contact .... constantcontact.com
Exact Target .... exacttarget.com
iContact .... icontact.com
Mail Chimp .... mailchimp.com

Fonts
1001 Fonts 1001fonts.com
DaFont .... dafont.com
Font Squirrel .... fontsquirrel.com

Hosting Companies
Go Daddy .... godaddy.com
Host Gator .... hostgator.com
Host Monster .... hostmonster.com
Host Papa .... hostpapa.com

Logo Design
99 Designs 99designs.com
Fuel My Brand .... fuelmybrand.com
Logo Design Team .... logodesignteam.com
Logo Snap .... logosnap.com

Loyalty Programs
Belly .... bellycard.com
Perka .... perka.com

Mailing List Opt-In Forms
Pippity .... pippity.com
Pop-Up Domination .... popupdomination.com

Marketing Resources

Mobile Payment Platforms
Flint .... flint.com
PayPal .... paypal.com
Square .... squareup.com

Naming
Business Name Generator .... businessnamegenerator.com
Name Thingy .... namethingy.com
Naming .... naming.net
Panabee .... panabee.com
Thesaurus .... thesaurus.com

Online Marketplaces
Merchant Circle .... merchantcircle.com
Thumbtack .... thumbtack.com

Online Print Shops
1-800Postcards 1800postcards.com
Got Print .... gotprint.com
Moo .... moo.com
PsPrint .... psprint.com
Vista Print .... vistaprint.com

Online, Social and Mobile Commerce
8th Bridge 8thbridge.com
BookBaby .... bookbaby.com
Clickbank .... clickbank.com
Heartbeat .... heartbeat.com
PayPal .... paypal.com
Shopify .... shopify.com
Square .... squareup.com
Swipely .... swipely.com
WooCommerce .... woothemes.com/woocommerce/

★ HEAVYWEIGHT MARKETING ★

Podcasting
Apple iTunes .... www.apple.com/itunes/podcasts/

Press Release Services
24-7 Press Release... 24-7pressrelease.com
PR Buzz .... prbuzz.com
PR Log .... prlog.com
PR Web .... prweb.com

Promotional Items
Branded Gear .... brandedgear.com
Branders .... branders.com
Café Press... cafepress.com
Halo Branded Solutions... halo.com
Zazzle .... zazzle.com

Q & A Sites
AllExperts... allexperts.com
Quora .... quora.com
Yahoo Answers .... answers.yahoo.com

QR Code Generators
Go QR .... goqr.me
Kaywa .... qrcode.kaywa.com
The QR Code Generator.................... the-qrcode-generator.com

QR Code Readers
Available for download from your preferred app store.

Small Business Saturday Tools from American Express
Amex SBS .... www.americanexpress.com/us/small-business/shop-small/
On Facebook .... www.facebook.com/SmallBusinessSaturday

Marketing Resources

Social Media Management
Buffer .... bufferapp.com
Everypost .... everypost.com
Hootsuite .... hootsuite.com
Sendible .... sendible.com
Socialflow .... socialflow.com
Socialoomph .... socialoomph.com

Social Media Platforms
Facebook .... facebook.com
Foursquare .... foursquare.com
Google+ .... plus.google.com
Instagram .... instagram.com
LinkedIn .... linkedin.com
Medium .... medium.com
Pinterest .... pinterest.com
Twitter .... twitter.com
Snapchat .... snapchat.com
Tumblr .... tumblr.com
Vine .... vine.co
Yelp .... yelp.com
YouTube .... youtube.com

Social Sharing
Share This (social sharing buttons) ..... sharethis.com

Speaking Associations
National Speakers Association .... nsaspeaker.org
Toastmasters .... toastmasters.org

Text Message (SMS) Marketing Services
TextMarks .... textmarks.com
WootText .... woottext.com/whitelabel/

★ HEAVYWEIGHT MARKETING ★

WordPress (Content Management Systems – CMS)
Self-hosted sites and blogs......................................wordpress.org
WordPress-hosted sites and blogs.......................wordpress.com
WordPress Plug-Ins................................wordpress.org/plug-ins

WordPress Themes
Elegant Themes..elegantthemes.com
Ink Themes...inkthemes.com
Organic Themes..organicthemes.com
Studio Press..studiopress.com
Theme Forest..themeforest.com
Themes Kingdom .... themeskingdom.com
Wordpress...wordpress.org/themes

NOTES

Round 1: Build Marketing Muscle

Chapter 1. The Law of Effective Frequency
1. http://en.wikipedia.org/wiki/Effective_frequency
2. Thomas Smith, *Successful Advertising*, 7th edn, 1885.

Chapter 2. Three Primal Rules of Marketing
1. http://online.wsj.com/news/articles/SB10001424052702304367204579266201175528672
2. http://www.huffingtonpost.com/2013/08/28/naked-juice-class-action-lawsuit_n_3830437.html

Chapter 10. Gain Marketing Mileage from Business Milestones
1. http://www.nydailynews.com/news/national/oreo-sees-support-backlash-boycott-gay-pride-rainbow-cookie-article-1.1103369

Chapter 11. Thirteen Ways to Go BIG on Small Business Saturday and Beyond
1. http://www.nfib.com/article/aso-64404/

Chapter 12. Hook Seasonal Customers with Year-Round Marketing Trident
1. https://news.yahoo.com/snapchat-admits-photos-dont-disappear-124756882.html

Round 2: Tackle Your Tools

Chapter 21. Eight Insider Tips for Cracking the QR Code
1. http://www.vocus.com/blog/50-mobile-search-stats-and-why-you-should-care/

★ **HEAVYWEIGHT MARKETING** ★

Chapter 24. Were Social Media Ever Intended for Business?
1. Foster, Tom. "Along Came Lolly." *Inc. Magazine*, June 2014: p. 30. Print.

Chapter 27. Pinterest Is Hot, but Can It Benefit Your Business?
1. http://nymag.com/daily/intelligencer/2013/10/time-to-start-taking-pinterest-seriously.html
2. http://socialfresh.com/how-to-get-more-pinterest-followers-infographic/
3. http://digiday.com/brands/15-stats-retailers-should-know-about-pinterest/

Chapter 28. Is Google+ a Social Network or Data-Mining Experiment?
1. http://en.wikipedia.org/wiki/Google+
2. http://valleywag.gawker.com/google-admits-google-was-just-a-ploy-to-track-your-beh-1524403565
3. http://www.adweek.com/news/technology/google-plus-just-popular-twitter-us-study-says-156645
4. http://www.stonetemple.com/new-google-plus-views-count-important-metric-or-vanity-of-vanities/
5. http://www.forbes.com/sites/kashmirhill/2011/08/29/googles-eric-schmidt-says-plus-is-an-identity-service-not-a-social-network/

Chapter 29. Dispelling the Myth of YouTube
1. https://www.youtube.com/yt/press/statistics.html

Chapter 30. An Instagram Is Worth a Thousand Words
1. http://blogs.wsj.com/cmo/2014/04/29/instagram-is-great-for-marketers-but-probably-not-for-long/
2. http://socialfresh.com/instagram-drives-2-5mm-brand-interactions-during-new-york-fashion-week/
3. http://www.businessinsider.com/instagram-demographics-2013-12

Notes

4. Gary Vaynerchuk (2013), *Jab, Jab, Jab, Right Hook*, HarperCollins, p. 138.
5. http://blog.business.instagram.com/post/76235731349/tools-and-tips-to-help-marketers-inspire-and
6. http://blogs.wsj.com/cmo/2014/04/29/instagram-is-great-for-marketers-but-probably-not-for-long/

Chapter 32. Facebook Is Dead, Long Live Facebook
1. http://social.ogilvy.com/facebook-zero-considering-life-after-the-demise-of-organic-reach/
2. http://www.theatlantic.com/politics/archive/2014/01/what-happens-when-the-president-sits-down-next-to-you-at-a-cafe/283074/
3. http://youtu.be/oVfHeWTKjag — This video makes a compelling argument for Facebook's ad fraud problem. Definitely worth viewing.
4. https://www.jonloomer.com/2014/02/11/facebook-fraud-response/

Round 3: Buff Your Brand

Chapter 33. Why Branding Matters for Small Business
1. http://www.businessinsider.com/coolest-small-businesses-in-twin-cities-2014-5

Chapter 36. Getting Your Employees on the Brandwagon
1. http://www.forbes.com/sites/carminegallo/2012/12/11/how-wegmans-apple-store-and-the-ritz-carlton-wins-loyal-customers/
2. http://venturebeat.com/2014/02/11/paypal-chief-reams-employees-use-our-app-or-quit/

Chapter 37. Your Business Needs to Tell a Better Brand Story
1. http://usatoday30.usatoday.com/money/industries/food/story/2012-04-29/kashi-natural-claims/54616576/1

★ **HEAVYWEIGHT MARKETING** ★

2. http://www.nytimes.com/2006/01/27/books/27oprah.html?pagewanted=all
3. http://www.huffingtonpost.com/2012/05/03/scott-thompson-resume-yahoo_n_1475700.html
4. http://dealbook.nytimes.com/2012/05/13/yahoo-fires-thompson-and-nears-deal-with-loeb/

Chapter 45. Why "Jack of All Trades" Is a Poor Branding Strategy
1. "How to Juice a Saturated Market." *Fast Company*, May 2014: p. 23. Print.
2. Just kidding…I think.

INDEX

advertising, 9–12
  and fraud, 207–10
  and hype, 27–29
  and mixed messages, 31–33, 323–30
  print, 97, 103–9
affiliate programs, 70–72
Agent in a Kilt, 219
Airbnb, 251–52
Alford, Andrew (designer), 318
All That & More, 230
Alpine Originals, 230, 250
American Express, 51–52, 54
Amy's Soups, 284–85, 289, 291, 292
Art of Soup, The (Campbell's promotion), 46–48
audience, 40, 55, 174, 186–87, 234–35
authenticity, 14–15
BAM! Small Biz Consulting, 3–4, 227, 277–78, 335–42
benefits to customers, 13–14, 35–38, 288–92, 309–16
Birds Eye frozen foods, 187
Black Friday, 51
blogs, 131–34, 253–54, 295–98
books and e-books, 300, 307–8
brand names, 223–32
brand story, 245–57
branding, 133, 215–43
Chozu (bathhouse), 267
communication with customers, 73–76, 309–16
competition, 41–43, 83, 236–37
consistency, 9–12, 83–84, 98–99, 221, 259–64
consumer profiles, 37, 234–35, 313
Couch Critics (video store), 259–60
CreateSpace (self-publishing platform), 301
Cronos, Arthur, 120–24
customer service, 217–19, 239–40, 271–72
Cutts, Matt (Google), 296–97
Cyber Monday, 51
discount pricing, 273–81
Dutch Bros. (coffee chain), 271–72

e-commerce, 60–61, 300
Eat24 (food delivery company), 202–4
educating customers, 52–53, 56, 278, 295, 309–16
efficiency, 268–69, 310
email marketing and newsletters, 61–62, 111–18, 300–1
   AWeber, 113
   Constant Contact, 111–12
   Mail Chimp, 112–13
entrepreneurship, 19–22, 78, 233–38
expertise, 219–20, 278, 295–308
Facebook, see under social media
Fadell, Tony (Nest), 287, 290
fear-based marketing, 77–80
follow-up, 56, 91, 315
Ford Motor Company, 201–2
Frusciante, John, 293
Galactic Pizza, 219
Gallery, The, 224–26
General Motors, 201
Godin, Seth, 14
Google, 133, 229, 296–97, 328–29; see also social media: Google+
Grilla Bites (restaurant), 268
hashtags, 54, 146–47, 149–54, 182
Horowitz, Bradley (Google+), 167
HostMonster, 71
imitation (vs innovation), 287–88
Inn at Oyster Point, 317–21
innovation, 283–94, 317–21
Instagram, see under social media
InstagramGal, The, see Sue B. Zimmerman
instore promotion, 52–54
JCPenney, 135, 275
Joe's Coffee Shack, 41, 43
Johnson, Ron (JCPenney), 275
Krispy Kreme donuts, 326–27
Law of Effective Frequency, The, 9–12
Lennan's Junktion (antique store), 74–75
LinkedIn, see under social media
Loomer, Jon (Facebook marketer), 209
Lowe's Home Improvement, 255
mailing lists, 53–54, 89, 133; see also email marketing and newsletters
Maloney, Danny (Pinterest analyst), 158
Marcus, David (Paypal), 243

Index

marketing budget, 280, 340
marketing message, 9, 14, 25, 27–40, 220–21, 249, 252, 280, 288, 327, 328, 339, 340; see also purpose statement
marketing mix, 39–40, 97–101
marketing trident, 59–65
mascots, 249–50
McCormick, Brandon (Facebook), 203
McCullough, David, Jr. (commencement speaker), 265
milestones, as marketing opportunities, 45–49
   Campbell's Soup, 46–48
   Oreo cookies, 45–46
Muller, Derek (debunks Facebook ad scams), 208–9
multilevel marketing, 71–72
National Small Business Week, 57
Nest (thermostat), 286–87, 289, 290, 292
1/10th Rule, The, 135
online profile management
   Disqus, 297
   LiveFyre, 297
   Gravatar, 298
Outdoor Headquarters, The, 327–28
packaging, 256–57
payment processing software
   PayPal, 243, 253
   Square, 251
photos and photo-sharing, 143, 155–161, 179–89
Pinterest, see under social media
Pivot Power, 285–86, 289, 291–92
planning, 81–82, 279–80
podcasts, 306
positioning statements, 233–38
PR disasters and backlash
   Chobani yogurt, 15
   Dannon yogurt, 150
   James Frey, 252
   Kashi, 252
   McDonald's, 152
   Naked Juice, 15
   NYPD, 152–53
   Oreo cookies, 46
   Paula Deen, 152
   Scott Thompson (former Yahoo CEO), 253
press releases, 87, 255–56

Pressed Juicery, 326
pricing, 274–81, 309–11
Primal Rules of Marketing, 13–17
promotions, 127–28
Protect (smoke alarm), 287
public speaking, 88–89, 303–4
purpose statements, 23–25
Q & A sites
   LinkedIn Groups, 301–2
   Quora, 302
QR codes, 119–24
Quirky (crowdsourced development company), 285, 292
Rachkowski, Amy (herbalist), 217
Radio Shack, 228
Ramshaw's ACE Hardware, 239–41, 327
referral programs, 70–72
resources, 345–50
Ritz-Carlton, The, 242
Rule of Seven, The, 9, 98
Schultz, Howard (Starbucks), 267
seminars, 304–5
SEO (Search Engine Optimization), 157, 170–71
Skrillex, 293
Slanket, 283
Small Business Saturday, 51–57
Small Business Week, 57
Smith, Thomas, 10
SMS marketing, see text marketing
Snuggie, 283
social media, 16–17, 45–47, 62–65, 135–40, 254–55, 281, 299
   Facebook, 62, 135, 146, 150–51, 163, 179, 180, 199–210, 298
   Foursquare, 64
   Google+, 63, 151, 163–72
   Instagram, 62–63, 151, 179–97
   LinkedIn, 63, 135, 301–2
   Pinterest, 62, 155–61
   Snapchat, 64
   Twitter, 54, 62, 141–48, 149, 151, 163, 298
   Yelp, 63–64
   YouTube, 55, 63, 163, 173–77, 305
social media management, 138–39
Sony, 329
Soul Connections (New Age retailer), 261–62

Index

spam, 129, 296–97
specialization, 323–330
Sprinkles (dessert shop), 326
Starbucks, 41, 43, 247, 263, 267
strategic partnership, 67–72
    between Doritos and Taco Bell, 68
Stratten, Scott (marketing guru), 119
SueB.Do (boutique), 191–97
Sunday Funday (text marketing campaign), 125–26
teaching, 305
television appearances, 306–7
text marketing, 125–30
three-adjective descriptions, 108–9
Toys "R" Us, 228
Twitter, see under social media
Uber (ridesharing app), 251–52
underpricing, 274–77
uniqueness, see innovation
value, see benefits to customers
Vaynerchuk, Gary, 182
Vickerey (online clothing retailer), 269
videos, 55, 86, 88, 90, 255, 305; see also social media: YouTube
Virgin Group, 266–67, 328–29
Warhol, Andy, 46–48
websites, 60–61, 105, 121–23, 133, 245, 250, 254, 309–10, 311–12, 341
Weiss, Alan (consultant), 278
Wise Mountain Botanicals, 217
Women in Business Network, 85–92
workshops, 304–5
YouTube, see under social media
Zien, Jake (Pivot Power), 285–86
Zimmerman, Sue B. (The Instagram Gal), 185, 191–97

★ ABOUT THE AUTHOR ★

Heavyweight Marketing Champion Nikolas Allen has enjoyed a 20-year career in advertising that has instilled a deep passion for branding, marketing and the entrepreneurial spirit. In 2010, he launched BAM! Small Biz Consulting to help small business owners reach a wider audience through effective online and offline marketing strategies. He is currently director of marketing at an employee-owned renewable energy company in Mt. Shasta, California.

An accomplished musician, contemporary Pop artist and pop-culture junkie, Allen spent three years as marketing director for a non-profit art gallery and served on the Board of Directors for the Siskiyou Arts Museum. He is also author of the art marketing book *Death to the Starving Artist*.

Nikolas has lived in Greece, Africa, Minnesota, Louisiana, Texas, and New Mexico. He currently resides at the foot of a magical, mystical volcano in the far reaches of northern California, where the air is clean, the water is pure and the economy is slowly improving.

To contact the author, visit: HeavyweightMarketingBook.com
To view more of Nikolas Allen's work, visit: NikolasAllen.com

ALSO BY NIKOLAS ALLEN

Death to the Starving Artist—Art Marketing Strategies for a Killer Creative Career

Author Nikolas Allen merges his passion for art and marketing in his debut book, *Death to the Starving Artist*. Allen outlines a comprehensive marketing model for ambitious artists who are ready to turn their art hobby into an art career. He guides readers through a proprietary model of using the Right Tools to reach the Right Audience with the Right Message in an effort to educate, encourage and inspire ambitious artists with ideas, insights, and resources that will empower them to succeed in their creative field.

What artists are saying about the book:

"Death to the Starving Artist is saturated with Nikolas Allen's quirky personality. He may very well be the Daniel Grant of my generation. Daniel Grant...with an edge."
—Brian Sherwin, Editor of *The Art Edge*

"Death to the Starving Artist has changed and saved my art career! The [accompanying] workbook is a godsend! It has helped me to fine tune my career and to keep me on track." —Todd Bane, Artist

Learn more at DeathToTheStarvingArtist.com

Okay, we're done here, now get to work!

www.ingramcontent.com/pod-product-compliance
Lightning Source LLC
Chambersburg PA
CBHW051623170526
45167CB00001B/37

MARKETING // BRANDING // BUSINESS

Scan to view book trailer video from author Nikolas Allen

ATTENTION ENTREPRENEURS AND SMALL BUSINESS OWNERS:

Is your business a 98-lb. weakling? Do competitors kick sand in your face? Then muscle up your marketing and transform your brand into a champion!

Step in the ring with *Heavyweight Marketing* and learn how to punch your way out of the crowded, cookie-cutter landscape of typical small business marketing. The potent, practical strategies outlined within will help you build a distinctive brand bold enough to knock out your customers—and your competitors!

Follow the author's real-world client examples as you learn to:

- ★ Define and articulate your unique brand value
- ★ Create meaningful marketing messages
- ★ Identify and engage your ideal audience
- ★ Determine and deploy your optimal tools and tactics
- ★ Produce dynamic marketing strategies that pack a punch

Filled with rich stories, examples, anecdotes and case studies directly from his recent 3-year stint running marketing consulting company, BAM! Small Biz Consulting, Allen's brisk writing style is chock full of keen insights and irreverent opinions making this modern marketing manual both essential—and fun—to read.

> *"The concepts are presented in such a fresh, entertaining way. Nikolas Allen inspired us to take a deeper look at how we represent ourselves. I loved it!"* –Marguerite Lorimer, EarthAlive Communications

U.S. $16.

www.heavyweightmarketingbook.com ★ www.nikolasallen.com

ISBN 9781502931825